Food and Energy Resources

FOOD SCIENCE AND TECHNOLOGY

A SERIES OF MONOGRAPHS

Series Editors

A complete list of the books in this series appears at the end of the volume.

3

Food and Energy Resources

Edited by

DAVID PIMENTEL

Department of Entomology
Cornell University
Ithaca, New York

CARL W. HALL

College of Engineering
Washington State University
Pullman, Washington

1984

ACADEMIC PRESS, INC.

(Harcourt Brace Jovanovich, Publishers)
Orlando   San Diego   San Francisco   New York   London
Toronto   Montreal   Sydney   Tokyo   São Paulo

ACADEMIC PRESS, INC.
Orlando, Florida 32887

United Kingdom Edition published by
ACADEMIC PRESS, INC. (LONDON) LTD.
24/28 Oval Road, London NW1 7DX

Library of Congress Cataloging in Publication Data
Main entry under title:

Food and energy resources.

(Food science and technology)
Includes index.
1. Food industry and trade--Energy consumption.
2. Agriculture and energy. I. Pimentel, David, Date.
II. Hall, Carl W. III. Series.
TP370.5.F65 1984 333.79 83–22322
ISBN 0–12–556560–7 (alk. paper)

PRINTED IN THE UNITED STATES OF AMERICA

84 85 86 87   9 8 7 6 5 4 3 2 1

Contents

3 The Role of Energy in World Agriculture and Food Availability

CARL W. HALL

4 Food for People

MARCIA H. PIMENTEL

5 Energy Use in Crop Systems in Northeastern China

WEN DAZHONG AND DAVID PIMENTEL

6 Energy and Food Relationships in Developing Countries: A Perspective from the Social Sciences

GEORGE H. AXINN AND NANCY W. AXINN

7 Ethics, Economics, Energy, and Food Conversion Systems

GLENN L. JOHNSON

8 Solar Energy Applications in Agriculture

GIGI M. BERARDI

9 Biomass Energy and Food—Conflicts?

WILLIAM J. HUDSON

10 Potentials in Producing Alcohol from Corn Grain and Residue in Relation to Prices, Land Use, and Conservation

EARL O. HEADY AND DOUGLAS A. CHRISTENSEN

Contributors

Numbers in parentheses indicate the pages on which the authors' contributions begin.

George H. Axinn* (121), Department of Agricultural Economics, Michigan State University, East Lansing, Michigan 48824

Nancy W. Axinn* (121), Bean/Cowpea Collaborative Research Support Program, Michigan State University, East Lansing, Michigan 48824

Gigi M. Berardi (181), Department of Environmental Science, Allegheny College, Meadville, Pennsylvania 16335

Douglas A. Christensen† (237), The Center for Agricultural and Rural Development, Iowa State University, Ames, Iowa 50011

Wen Dazhong‡ (91), Department of Entomology, Cornell University, Ithaca, New York 14853

Carl W. Hall§ (25, 43), College of Engineering, Washington State University, Pullman, Washington 99164

Earl O. Heady (237), The Center for Agricultural and Rural Development, Iowa State University, Ames, Iowa 50011

William J. Hudson (207), Market Research, The Andersons, Maumee, Ohio 43537

Glenn L. Johnson (147), Department of Agricultural Economics, Michigan State University, East Lansing, Michigan 48824

David Pimentel (1, 91), Department of Entomology, Cornell University, Ithaca, New York 14853

Marcia H. Pimentel (65), Division of Nutritional Sciences, Colleges of Human Ecology and Agriculture and Life Sciences, Cornell University, Ithaca, New York 14853

*Present address: Food and Agriculture Organization of the United Nations, G.P.O. Box 25, Kathmandu, Nepal
†Present address: SCS National Technical Center, P.O. Box 6567, Fort Worth, Texas 76115
‡Present address: Institute of Forest and Soil Science, Chinese Academy of Science, P.O. Box 417, Shenyang, China
§Present address: Directorate for Engineering, National Science Foundation, Washington, D.C. 20550

Preface

Food and energy resources are basic to the survival and well-being of humanity. The abundance of both is affected by the magnitude of the human population and standard of living desired.

Although food is the energy needed for the maintenance of body processes, not all energy is food. Solar energy powers the growth of plants, and crustal action slowly forms fossil fuels. In the past, conversion of energy from its available form to useful products has been left to these natural processes.

Now with heavy demands on our fossil fuel supplies, particularly rapid depletion of oil, there is renewed interest in finding substitute fuels. One possibility would be to use solar-powered, biological resources for fuel. If use were instituted on a large scale, additional stress would be put upon these biological resources, because they are now heavily used throughout the world for food, fiber, and shelter. Hence, a concern arises regarding the feasibility as well as the ethics of diverting plant foods such as grains for fuel.

The rapidly expanding human population needs more nutritious food. Our ability to produce more food depends on sufficient arable land, water, and various forms of energy. Supplies of these basic agricultural resources are under pressure from the human population, because, as it grows, more land is required for forests, houses, and roads as well as for agriculture. At the same time, demands on energy supplies increase for various activities that include production of food crops. To some extent, energy in the form of fertilizers or irrigation water can be substituted for more land, or land can be substituted for energy inputs in crop production. These trade-offs are complex and illustrate not only the close interrelationships among the various factors but also the interdependencies of these relationships.

Contributors from several disciplines have drawn on their experiences to try to put in perspective the influence that energy, land, and water resources have on food production. Clearly, future supplies of energy resources will have a major impact on the ability of humans to provide themselves with food. A better understanding of these issues will help society make sound choices and enable government leaders to develop and organize the necessary programs for the effective use of energy and food resources.

We hope that this book will provide engineers, economists, agriculturists, geographers, ecologists, nutritionists, sociologists, and natural resource specialists a perspective that will allow us to work jointly on the problem of providing food for people while protecting our natural resources. Our objective is to give the reader a clearer understanding of the food and energy resource issues and to serve as a background for making difficult public policy decisions for the future.

This book represents the cooperative efforts of the authors and many other people. With sincere appreciation we wish to acknowledge the assistance of Ms. Nancy Sorrells and Ms. Rebecca Voog in assembling the numerous chapters and the editorial assistance of the staff at Academic Press.

David Pimentel
Carl W. Hall

Food and Energy Resources

Chapter 1

Energy Flow in the Food System

DAVID PIMENTEL

Department of Entomology
Cornell University
Ithaca, New York

I. INTRODUCTION

The ecological system of which man is a part is fundamentally a network of energy and mineral flows. Solar energy as well as plants that capture solar energy for use by the biological system and by man are essential to humans and to the ecosystem as a whole. At the same time, elements and minerals such as carbon, hydrogen, oxygen, nitrogen, phosphorous, potassium, and calcium provide the essential chemical structure of the diverse biological system of animals and plants. Basic to the survival of humans, other organisms, and plants are adequate supplies of food and water; these are both directly and indirectly related to the flow of energy and minerals through the ecosystem. To this end, the ecological system has evolved elaborate ways to conserve and recycle mineral resources.

For many centuries man obtained his food like other animals, that is, as a hunter–gatherer. During this early period he was completely dependent on solar

1

Copyright © 1984 by Academic Press, Inc.
All rights of reproduction in any form reserved.
ISBN 0-12-556560-7

energy. Nearly 500,000 years elapsed before man discovered fire and used wood as an energy source. Slowly he progressed to harnessing draft animals, water, and wind for power to augment his own energy. Then he developed engine power fueled by wood, coal, petroleum, and nuclear energy. For only about 300 years has man employed fossil energy to modify or manipulate land, water, plants, and animals to provide himself with food, clothing, and supplies for shelter. Discovering, controlling, and using energy has enabled humans to progress from a primitive life to a settled civilized state. Man alone of all animals can think creatively and use science and technology, and he has been able to use solar and fossil energy, plus other environmental resources, to provide food and other vital needs.

II. SOLAR ENERGY

Man's survival, and that of all the natural biota associated with him in his ecosystem, depends on adequate supplies of energy in the form of food. Indeed, the foundation of all life systems rests on the unique capacity of plants to convert or "fix" solar energy into stored chemical energy. This captured energy is then used directly by man and diverse animal and microbial species or indirectly, when man's food is from animals that have fed directly on plants.

The solar energy reaching a hectare of land each year averages about 14×10^9 kcal. During an average 4-month summer growing season in the temperate regions, nearly 7×10^9 kcal of solar energy reach each hectare. Then, under favorable conditions of moisture and soil nutrients, the plants convert the solar energy into food and fiber energy. What happens to a corn crop, one of the most productive food and feed crops per unit area of land, illustrates this phenomenon (Pimentel, 1980). In one season, high-yielding corn, grown on the fertile soils of Iowa, yields about 7000 kg/ha of corn grain plus another 7000 kg/ha of biomass as stover. Converted to heat energy, this totals 69×10^6 kcal and represents about 0.5% of the solar energy reaching a hectare during the year or 1% of that reaching the hectare during the growing season.

For other crops the conversion efficiency is much less than for corn. For example, potatoes, with a yield of 40,000 kg/ha, have a dry weight of about 8000 kg/ha. Based on total biomass produced per hectare of 12,000 kg and an energy value of 50×10^6 kcal, potatoes have a 0.4% efficiency of conversion. A wheat crop, yielding 2700 kg/ha of grain, produces a biomass total of 6750 kg/ha, which has an energy value of 28×10^6 kcal. The conversion efficiency of sunlight into biomass in the wheat system is only 0.2%.

Although all these conversion efficiencies are low relative to the total amount of solar energy reaching a hectare of land, they are still two to five times greater than those of natural vegetation. In the United States this is estimated to be only about 0.1% efficient (Pimentel *et al.*, 1978).

Each year, the total light energy fixed by all the green plants on earth is about 400×10^{15} kcal and is divided equally between the ocean and the terrestrial ecosystems (Pimentel *et al.*, 1978). Overall, then, the amount of energy captured by all plants amounts to less than 0.1% of the total light energy reaching the earth (Odum, 1971). Even so, because terrestrial ecosystems cover only about one-third of the earth, terrestrial plants are three times more effective in capturing sunlight energy and producing biomass than are those in the ocean ecosystem.

The success of any agricultural system in production of an adequate food supply is based on the amount of solar energy fixed by the plants as they are grown on fertile land, with adequate amounts of moisture and with the input of additional energy from man, tools, machines, and such fuels as wood, coal, gas, and oil.

III. ENERGY FLOW IN HUNTER–GATHERER SOCIETIES

Before agricultural systems were developed, humans obtained most of their food by gathering seeds, nuts, berries, and other plant materials. Certainly, hunting mammals and birds and capturing fish also provided some food resources, but because plants are generally abundant and easily harvested, it is logical to assume they were the mainstay of human diets.

As hunter–gatherers, a family system or tribal unit of 30–40 residents could effectively range over 300–400 km^2 (or 1 person/1000 ha) to find food (Lee, 1969). Further, Lee estimates it is energetically profitable to walk nearly 20 km to obtain food from a good source.

The !Kung bushmen, who presently inhabit the Dobe area of Botswana, Africa, illustrate the energy economy of a hunter–gatherer society (Lee, 1969; Lee and DeVore, 1976). The habitat in which the !Kung bushmen live is arid and has an annual rainfall of only 15–25 cm. During extremely dry periods the bushmen locate their camps near permanent watering holes and as close as possible to a food source.

How much food energy do the bushmen expend to obtain nuts? Using the data of Lee (1969), we calculated that about one-half of the energy inputs (1400 kcal) were expended just for travel and for collecting the nuts (Table I). However, another nearly 1300 kcal of energy input was also necessary for sleep and other activities related to the normal maintenance of the individual worker.

The total input to harvest an average of 12.5 kg (1.75 kg shelled) of nuts was about 2700 kcal (Table I). The food energy value of the nuts was calculated to be about 10,500 kcal. The kilocalorie return in food energy per kilocalorie of input invested in human effort was about 4:1. This can be considered a good return for the energy expended. Some surplus food is essential because the gatherer must

TABLE I

Input/Output Analysis of !Kung Bushmen Gathering Mongongo Nuts at a Distance of 4.8 km from Camp[a,b]

	kcal
Inputs	
Travel to location of nuts (4.8 km = 1.2 hr)	270
Collecting nuts (3 hr)	675
Return trip to camp (4.8 km carrying 12.5 kg nuts = 1.2 hr)	462
Subtotal	1407
Sleep (10.5 hr)	473
Other activities (8 hr)	800
Total	2680
Outputs	
Nuts shelled, 1.75 kg	10,500
Output/input ratio	3.9

[a]Calculation based on Lee (1969).
[b]From Pimentel and Pimentel (1979).

support children and the elderly who are unable to travel and support themselves.

IV. HUMAN-POWERED CROP PRODUCTION

When humans became less nomadic and established more stationary societies, agricultural practices also changed. "Swidden" or cut and burn agriculture is an example of early crop production that primarily uses manpower for production. For this only an ax and a hoe as tools plus a large amount of manpower are required. For example, Lewis (1951), investigating swidden corn culture in Mexico reported that a total of 1144 hours of labor was required to raise a hectare of corn (Table II). Other than the manpower, the only inputs were the ax, hoe, and corn seeds. The yield of 1944 kg/ha of corn provided about 6.9 million kcal. Thus, the output per input ratio is 10.7:1 or two and one-half times greater than that obtained by the !Kung bushmen gatherers (Tables I and II). More important is the fact that the food supply is stable because greater control of the environment is possible with organized crop production than with dependence on the wild for food.

V. DRAFT ANIMAL-POWERED CROP PRODUCTION

Although man and his use of tools can carry out most tasks more efficiently than either draft animals or tractors, both animal and tractor power can significantly reduce the large manpower input. Work by humans, horses, or tractors,

TABLE II
Energy Inputs in Corn (Maize) Production in Mexico Using only Manpower[a]

	Quantity/ha	kcal/ha
Inputs		
Labor	1,144 hr[b]	589,160
Ax and hoe	16,570 kcal[c]	16,570
Seeds	10.4 kg[c]	36,608
Total		642,338
Outputs		
Corn yield	1,944 kg[b]	6,901,200
kcal output/kcal input		10.74
Protein yield	175 kg	

[a]From Pimentel and Pimentel (1979).
[b]Lewis (1951).
[c]Estimated.

measured in terms of foot-pounds and requiring the expenditure of energy, is carried out at different rates. The term horsepower-hour (hp·hr) is the time–rate at which work is done or the capacity to do 33,000 foot-pounds of work per minute for 1 hr. One manpower-hour (mp·hr) equals about 0.10 hp·hr; thus a man would have to work 10 hr to equal 1 hp·hr. This can be illustrated by data on corn production in Mexico using ox power (Lewis, 1951). Employing ox power, about 200 hr of draft animal power was needed to till and cultivate plus about 380 hr of manpower (Table III).

TABLE III
Energy Inputs in Corn (Maize) Production in Mexico Using Oxen[a]

	Quantity/ha	kcal/ha
Inputs		
Labor	383 hr[b]	197,245
Ox	198 hr[b]	495,000[d]
Machinery	41,400 kcal[c]	41,400
Seeds	10.4 kg[c]	36,608
Total		770,253
Outputs		
Corn yield	941 kg	3,340,550
kcal output/kcal input		4.34
Protein yield	85 kg	

[a]From Pimentel and Pimentel (1979).
[b]Lewis (1951).
[c]Estimated.
[d]Assumed.

Based on the fact that producing corn by hand in Mexico requires about 1140 hr/ha, the 200 hr of ox power reduced the manpower input by about 760 hr (Tables II and III). Thus, under these farming conditions, 1 hr of ox power replaced nearly 4 hr of manpower.

An ox normally produces 0.5–0.75 hp equivalents. One horsepower-hour of work, as mentioned, is equal to about 10 mp·hr of work. Thus, 1 ox power-hour is equal to 5–7.5 mp·hr of work. Based on the Mexican data, 1 ox power-hour of work replaced about 4 mp·hr or slightly lower than the theoretical 5–7.5 mp·hr capacity of ox power.

An ox consumes about 20,000 kcal/day in feed (Pimentel, 1974), whereas a man doing heavy farm work consumes 4120 kcal/day. Therefore, the man/ox combination requires slightly more energy input than the man alone system. However, the ox can be fed mostly on forage, whereas man requires grain and similar high-quality food materials.

Over time, humans developed many tools and also learned to use animals to decrease manpower expenditures. An example is the man/ox combination, which expends about 770,250 kcal total and yields an output of 3.3 million kcal (Table III). Thus, the output/input ratio is about 4:1. This low ratio is due to reduced corn yield, which is less than half the yield obtained by manpower alone in the swidden system (Tables II and III). These low corn yields can be attributed to poor soil that had been cropped for many years, resulting in depletion of some of the soil nutrients. If manure or other organic matter had been added to the soil each season, the corn yields might have equaled those of the swidden technology.

One way to analyze the energy flow in modern corn production is by substituting horse power for diesel fuel and the tractor. In this example, the power attributed to the tractor was totally removed from modern corn production and 120 hr of horsepower plus 150 hr of manpower were substituted (Table IV). Another input is the estimated 136 kg of corn and 136 kg of hay required to feed a 682-kg (1500-lb) horse for the portion of the year it was used to cultivate 1 ha of corn (Morrison, 1956). Although the corn would come directly out of the corn produced, the hay would have to be grown on an additional 0.2 ha of land. Thus, based on the current high yields of corn and hay, a total of 1.2 ha of land area would be required to support a horse-powered system. However, this does not include the replacement cost of the horse that would occur in time. To produce and feed the replacement would require an additional 0.2 ha of land.

For the tractor-powered corn system, the labor input was only 12 hr compared with the 120 hr of manpower calculated for the horse-powered system (Tables IV and V). Thus the labor for the horse-powered system is 10 times that required by the tractor-powered system. Also, the total energy input for the horse-powered system is greater than the tractor system (Tables IV and V), making it slightly more energy intensive than the tractor-powered system. However, the energy ratio for a horse-powered system is 3.4:1 or slightly less than the 3.5:1 for the

TABLE IV
Energy Inputs per Hectare for Corn Production in the United States Employing Horse Power

	Quantity/ha	kcal/ha
Inputs		
Labor	120 hr	70,000
Machinery	15 kg	27,000
Horse		
Corn	136 kg	477,300
Hay	136 kg	409,000
LP gas	80 l	616,400
Electricity	33.4 kwh	95,500
Nitrogen	151 kg	2,220,000
Phosphorus	72 kg	216,000
Potassium	84 kg	134,000
Lime	426 kg	134,400
Seeds	18 kg	445,800
Insecticides	1.4 kg	119,950
Herbicides	7.8 kg	777,500
Drying	7000 kg	1,437,800
Transportation	150 kg	38,550
Total		7,219,200
Outputs		
Total yield	7000	24,500,000
kcal output/kcal input		3.4

tractor-powered system. Clearly it is not economically feasible at present to use that much manpower to produce corn.

VI. MECHANIZED CROP PRODUCTION

In industrialized nations like the United States, fossil energy has become as vital a resource for crop production as land and water resources. The dominant uses of energy in U.S. agricultural production are as fuel to run farm machinery and as raw material to produce fertilizers and pesticides (Table V). Pesticides are made from petroleum while nitrogen fertilizer is made from natural gas.

Again using the corn crop as an example, approximately 600 liters of oil equivalents are required to cultivate 1 ha of corn. This amounts to an expenditure of about 1 kcal of fossil energy per 3.5 kcal of corn produced (Table V). Most grains in the United States yield from 1–5 kcal/kcal of fossil energy expended (Table VI).

Producing other types of food products, however, is not as energy efficient as grain production (Table VI). For example, yields of apple and orange production range from 0.9–1.7 kcal/kcal input of fossil energy; vegetable yields range from

TABLE V

Energy Inputs per Hectare for Corn Production in the United States[a]

Item	Quantity/ha	kcal/ha
Inputs		
Labor	12 hr	7000
Machinery	55 kg	990,000
Gasoline	26 l	264,000
Diesel	77 l	881,500
LP gas	80 l	616,400
Electricity	33.4 kwh	95,500
Nitrogen	151 kg	2,220,000
Phosphorus	72 kg	216,000
Potassium	84 kg	134,000
Lime	426 kg	134,400
Seeds	18 kg	445,500
Insecticides	1.4 kg	119,950
Herbicides	7 kg	777,500
Drying	7000 kg	
Transportation	200 kg	51,200
Total		6,958,250
Outputs		
Total yield	7,000 kg	24,500,000
kcal output/kcal input		3.5

[a] Adapted from Pimentel and Burgess (1980).

0.2–1.4 kcal/kcal input of fossil energy. It is somewhat unfair to measure fruit and vegetable output in terms of food energy because most of these crops are not produced for food energy but for the many essential vitamins and minerals they supply.

Forages are another important plant crop because they are essential foods for cattle and sheep. In general, forage production systems are not intensively managed because forage crops on a per land area basis have a relatively low monetary return.

Corn silage, alfalfa, and tame hay are some of the most valuable forages produced in the United States (U.S. Department of Agriculture, 1981). Corn silage consists of mature corn plants that are cut green and then chopped and stored in silos. During storage, the chopped corn ferments and in this way preserves the corn for subsequent feeding to livestock. Corn silage production systems are fairly similar to corn production systems (Tables V and VI). The average yield, including corn grain plus the other biomass, is 9400 kg (dry) or total 29 million kcal/ha. Thus the output/input ratio for corn silage is 5.6:1 or significantly greater than the 3.5:1 output/input ratio for corn grain.

TABLE VI

Energy Inputs and Returns for Various Food and Feed Crops Produced per Hectare in the United States[a]

Crop	Crop yield (kg)	Yield in protein (kg)	Crop yield in food energy (10^6 kcal)	Fossil energy input for production (10^6 kcal)	kcal food/feed output/kcal fossil energy input	Labor input (manhours)
Corn (United States)	7,000	630	24.5	6.9	3.5	12
Wheat (North Dakota)	2,022	283	6.7	2.5	2.7	6
Oats (Minnesota)	2,869	423	10.9	2.1	5.1	3
Rice (Arkansas)	4,742	272	14.0	12.5	1.1	30
Sorghum (Kansas)	1,840	202	6.0	1.5	4.0	5
Soybean (Illinois)	2,600	885	10.5	2.3	4.5	8
Beans, dry (Michigan)	1,176	285	4.1	3.1	1.3	19
Peanuts (Georgia)	3,720	320	15.3	10.9	1.4	19
Apples (East)	41,546	83	23.3	26.2	0.9	176
Oranges (Florida)	40,370	404	19.8	11.8	1.7	210
Potato (New York)	34,468	539	21.1	15.5	1.4	35
Lettuce (California)	31,595	284	4.1	19.7	0.2	171
Tomato (California)	49,620	496	9.9	16.6	0.6	165
Cabbage (New York)	53,000	1,060	12.7	16.8	0.8	289
Alfalfa (Minnesota)	11,800(dry)	1,845	47.2	3.6	13.1	12
Tame hay (New York)	2,539(dry)	160	5.5	0.6	8.6	7
Corn silage (Northeast United States)	9,400(dry)	753	29.1	5.2	5.6	15

[a] Adapted from Pimentel and Pimentel (1979) and Pimentel (1980).

One major problem associated with silage production is that the removal of all the corn biomass leaves the soil exposed to rainfall and soil erosion. Also, the necessary organic matter in the soil is substantially reduced. Both substantially reduce productivity of the soil and, if not compensated for by increasing fertility inputs, can eventually result in low crop yield (Pimentel *et al.*, 1981).

Alfalfa, like corn silage, is both a productive and a nutritious forage. In contrast to corn silage production, however, little or no nitrogen is required for its production because alfalfa is a legume and has the capacity to "fix" or capture nitrogen from the air. The total energy input for alfalfa production is calculated to be 3 million kcal/ha. With a yield of about 11,800 kg or 47 million kcal, the output/input ratio is 13:1 or considerably more energy efficient than corn silage (Table VI).

The major forage feed for cattle, sheep, and other ruminants is tame hay, which consists of several kinds of grass species. Sometimes the hay is harvested at peak conditions and stored for use later; sometimes animals are allowed to graze this forage and do the harvesting. The total energy input for tame hay production in New York is calculated to be 0.6 million kcal (Table VI) for a yield of 2539 kg/ha or an output/input ratio of 8.6:1. This is less than for alfalfa but more than that for corn silage.

VII. ALTERNATIVES FOR REDUCING ENERGY INPUTS IN CROP PRODUCTION

Energy from fossil fuels flowing into agricultural crop production systems that are typical of industrialized nations can be reduced by altering some agricultural practices and substituting practices that require less fossil fuel energy. Most of the viable alternative practices are more in harmony with the natural ecosystem and lessen the manipulation of the ecosystem. These alternatives aim to decrease use of fossil-base fertilizers, pesticides, and large machinery and improve the management of soil and water resources.

A. Soil Nutrients and Alternative Fertilizers

Whenever crops are harvested, significant quantities of nutrients that once were in the soil are removed because they have been incorporated into the plant material as it grew. These must be replaced if a high yield is to be achieved in subsequent years. For example, when 7000 kg of corn is harvested an estimated 40 kg of nitrogen, 5 kg of phosphorus, and 6 kg of potassium are removed from each hectare of land (Table V). Often, a more significant loss occurs when corn fields are plowed right after the harvest and the soil is exposed to severe erosion by wind and rain. This loss is estimated to be about 10 times that attributed to the corn harvest and if fertilizers are not used, subsequent yields will decline. Thus, a sensible alternative to present cultural practices is to find ways to reduce soil erosion so use of costly, fossil-based fertilizer will be reduced.

In this analysis of possible ways to conserve and replenish soil nutrients for corn production, the focus will be primarily on nitrogen because this is the most energy intensive of the nutrients to produce. About 14,700 kcal of fossil fuel are expended to produce 1 kg of nitrate fertilizer compared with 3000 kcal/kg for phosphorus and 1600 kcal/kg for potassium (Lockeretz, 1980). The process of manufacturing fertilizer is energy intensive.

As a substitute for some or all commercial fertilizer, livestock manure can be used. Manure not only is a source of nutrients that crops need, but its addition to soil helps to reduce soil erosion and improves soil structure (Neal, 1939; Zwerman et al., 1970). In the United States, current manure production is estimated to be 1.1 billion tonnes per year, with about 420 million tonnes produced in feedlots and other confined rearing situations (Miller and McCormac, 1978; Van Dyne and Gilbertson, 1978). Although more than 70% of this collected manure is applied to land, it provides agriculture with only about 8% of the needed nitrogen, 20% of needed phosphorus, and 20% of needed potassium.

The amount of nitrogen from manure applied to U.S. lands could be doubled if proper management practices were employed in handling livestock manure (Muck, 1982). When manure is left standing in the barn and/or placed on the surface of agricultural land, most of the ammonium nitrogen is lost. To prevent this loss would require that manure be collected promptly and stored in large tanks or immediately turned under the soil when application is made to the land (Muck, 1982).

Although livestock manure can be effectively applied to land to reduce use of commercial fertilizers, its enormous volume and weight relative to amounts of nutrients contained makes the handling of manure labor intensive compared with commercial fertilizers. For example, to obtain sufficient nitrogen from livestock manure for a corn crop, about 25 tonnes (wet) of manure must be applied per hectare (1 tonne of cattle manure contains only 5.6 kg of nitrogen, 1.5 kg of phosphorus, and 3 kg of potassium) (Pimentel et al., 1973). To do this, an additional labor input of 6.4 hr is required for loading, transport, and application of the 25 tonnes of manure.

Thus while the nutrients are "free," a fuel input is required for the loading, transport, and application. This energy investment is calculated to be about 30,000 kcal of fuel per tonne of manure, collected and spread by tractor when the manure is located about 1.5 km from the cropland (Linton, 1968; Pimentel et al., 1983).

Thus, the 25 tonnes of manure applied to the land would require a fuel input of 750,000 kcal. If the same amount of nutrients contained in 25 tonnes of manure were obtained from commercial fertilizer, the fuel input would be 2.3

million kcal. Using manure therefore provides more than a threefold energy saving over commercial fertilizer. Obviously, as distance between field and manure source increases, so does energy expenditure. This is the major problem associated with making efficient use of manure from feedlots, which are usually far from agricultural land.

Before commercial fertilizers were so universally used in corn production, corn often was planted in rotation with a legume crop such as sweet clover (Pimentel, 1981a). By planting sweet clover in the fall after corn is harvested and plowing it under 1 year later, nearly 170 kg of nitrogen is added per hectare (Willard, 1927; Scott, 1982). However, because 2 ha of land must be cultivated to raise 1 ha of corn, widespread use of this practice is somewhat limited.

When legume rotations are not feasible, legumes can be planted between corn rows in August and then the plants, considered "green manure," are plowed under in early spring when the field is being prepared for reseeding. Winter vetch and other legumes, for example, planted in this manner yield about 150 kg/ha of nitrogen (Mitchell and Teel, 1977; Scott, 1982). Also, the use of a cover crop protects the soil from wind and water erosion during the winter and has the additional advantage of adding organic matter to the soil. One disadvantage is that the green manure must be plowed under during the spring when the farmer is pressed for time to plant the major crop.

B. Substitute Cultural Practices

Relying on a no-till or minimum-till system would reduce the tractor fuel inputs normally required to plow and disc soil by conventional tillage. About 60 liters of diesel fuel are used to till 1 ha of soil with a 50-hp tractor, compared with about 15 liters for no-till planting. Thus, in a season, the saving could be 45 liters or 513,630 kcal of fossil fuel per hectare for tractor fuel if a no-till system were adopted.

On the other hand, with a no-till system, herbicide and insecticide use must be increased over conventional tillage to control weeds and deal with the often increased insect and slug problems that occur (U.S. Department of Agriculture, 1975). Sometimes with no-till, pesticide use is doubled, thereby making the total energy inputs greater than conventional tillage. Another energy input associated with no-till is the cost of the larger amount of corn seed (about 13% more than conventional tillage) that is required to offset poorer germination in the no-till environment (Phillips *et al.*, 1980).

One way to minimize weed growth in small no-till plots is to apply organic matter (leaves and similar organic matter) at a depth of about 5 cm. This organic matter will control weeds and at the same time provide ample soil nutrients. To facilitate planting, a 15-cm opening can be made in the organic matter and the seeds inserted into the uncovered soil. Once the young plants are up about 10 cm, the organic matter can be pushed back around the base of the plants. Obviously, this technique substantially increases manpower inputs.

Whether energy-inputs are greater or about the same in total for no-till compared with conventional tillage will depend on the various practices used, tractor size, type of soil, abundance of pests, and environmental factors. No-till, however, has advantages over conventional tillage because it reduces manpower inputs, decreases soil erosion, and helps conserve soil moisture. This technology offers several advantages in reducing energy inputs, especially in small-scale crop production.

C. Alternate Pest Control

Each year, about 500,000 tonnes of pesticides are applied to U.S. cropland (U.S. Department of Agriculture, 1981). The total amount of fossil energy invested for production, formulation, packaging, and transport of these pesticides is about 43×10^{12} kcal. On a per kilogram basis, the average energy input for herbicide is about 100,000 kcal; insecticide, 87,000 kcal; and fungicide, 65,000 kcal (Pimentel, 1980). For just production, energy inputs may range from about 15 to as much as 110,000 kcal/kg pesticide.

A wide variety of alternative pest controls can be used as substitutes for pesticides (Pimentel *et al.*, 1982). One of these is biological control, or the use of parasites and predators to control insects and weeds. In some cases, the natural enemy is imported from another area of the earth to control a pest. If successful, as was the case when the vedalia beetle was introduced into California for control of cottony-cushion scale on citrus, then no further use of insecticides was required for this particular pest. Several wasp parasites that attack caterpillar and aphid pests have also been introduced for control on fruit and field crops (De-Bach, 1964).

Several different microorganisms, including viruses, bacteria, fungi, and protozoans, have been utilized effectively for insect pest control. One of the most commonly used is a bacterium, *Bacillus thuringiensis*, which has proven highly effective against a wide array of caterpillar pests.

In nature also, most pests are attacked by a wide array of parasites and predators that share their ecosystem. Sometimes heavy pesticide use has eliminated or decreased the effectiveness of natural controls. The technology, integrated pest management (IPM), aims at making maximum use of natural enemies (Pimentel, 1981b). In IPM programs both pest and natural enemy populations are monitored and pesticides are applied only when the pest population will escape natural enemy control and when economic damage will take place in the crop. Not only is care used as to when a pesticide is applied in IPM but also only pesticides are used that have a major impact on the pest and minor input on natural enemies. The use of natural enemies and other biological controls is ideal from an energy standpoint. Because parasites and predators obtain their food–fuel directly from the pests, they are solar powered.

Yet another successful way to control pests without pesticides is breeding food and fiber crops with resistance against plant pathogens, pest insects, and weed damage (Pimentel et al., 1973; Pimentel et al., 1982). Most crops now planted in the United States have had some resistance to plant pathogens bred into them. This is documented by the fact that only about 2% of U.S. agricultural acreage is treated with fungicides for plant pathogen control (Eichers, 1981). Some major pests controlled by host plant resistance include cabbage yellows and the Hessian fly.

In addition to the alternatives mentioned, various agronomic or cultural practices may be modified to enhance pest control (Pimentel et al., 1982). For instance, when corn is planted after a legume or small grain, the injurious corn rootworm complex is controlled (Pimentel et al., 1982). Crop rotations have also been employed for control of many other insects, plant pathogens, and weeds.

Other cultural practices for pest control include timing of planting to elude pests, tilling of the soil to destroy weed and insect pests, irrigation water applications to control growth sequences of crop and pests, plus the judicious use of organic and plastic mulches (Pimentel et al., 1982). All of these techniques have energy and environmental costs, but for certain pests of a particular crop and region they may be highly beneficial in terms of both energy and the environment.

D. Solar Crop Drying

Corn, like many other grain crops, is usually harvested as is grain, i.e., directly in the field. This corn contains about 27% moisture and must be dried to about 13% moisture before being placed in storage. To reduce the moisture level from 27 to 13% in 1 kg of corn, an input of 205 kcal fossil energy must be expended.

Solar energy (wind and sunlight) can be used to dry corn by placing it in screened corncribs exposed to air. The solar system requires less than one-third as much energy as that dried with fossil energy (Hudson, Chapter 9, this volume). Another advantage of harvesting corn on the cob is the availability of the cobs after the corn grain is removed so they either can be ground and fed to cattle or burned to provide a fuel source.

E. Irrigation Water

Water, both the total quantity available and its availability at the time needed, is undoubtedly the most seriously limiting factor in crop production throughout the world. Without water, crops will not grow even in the most fertile land. Little thought has been given to use and conservation of this most vital resource.

In some arid regions of the world, water is being pumped from great depths and then distributed over the land. Irrigation is an extremely energy-intensive operation. For example, to produce 1 ha of irrigated corn, 12,000,000 kcal are expended, or three times that expended for rainfed corn, which includes energy only for fertilizers, pesticides, etc. (Pimentel and Burgess, 1980). Looking to the future and considering the decline of supplies of cheap fossil fuel, hard decisions will have to be made as to if and when land will be irrigated.

While it is not the aim of this chapter to detail the problem, attention must be called to the more basic problem of water supply, which collects from precipitation and is available in the aquifers (large natural, underground storage areas). Concern is growing in many quarters about the overuse or "mining" of these vital reserves. Surely conservation of water deserves high-priority attention from all sectors of society.

Numerous techniques are available for conserving water and, not surprisingly, most of these are the same as those for preventing soil erosion. The following techniques both reduce soil erosion and conserve water: (1) using organic mulches as in no-till crop culture; (2) terracing of crops; (3) planting strip crops; (4) planting crops on the contour. All help retain the water on the growing crops where it is needed and slow runoff.

VIII. LIVESTOCK PRODUCTION

Animals used for human food are fed grains, forages, and grasses. Although forage and grasses are unsuitable for human consumption because they cannot be digested, grains surely are excellent foods. In this country about 90% of all grain produced each year (135 million tonnes) is fed to livestock, which eventually provide meat, milk, and eggs preferred by American consumers (Pimentel et al., 1980).

Energetically, anywhere from 7 to 88 kcal of fossil energy are required to produce 1 kcal of animal protein (Table VII). This contrasts with the production of protein in soybeans and corn grain that range from only 0.7 to 3 kcal of fossil energy input to produce 1 kcal of plant protein (Table VI).

The major reason that animal protein products are significantly more energy expensive than plant protein food is that first the forage and grain feeds have to be grown and then consumed by the animal to produce the desired animal food. In addition, forage and grain have to be fed to the breeding herd at added energy costs. For example, to produce one feeder beef calf a total of 2.3 animals have to be fed (1.3 are breeding cattle). Thus, the inputs for beef production are 25 kcal of fossil energy per 1 kcal of protein (Table VII). However, broiler (chicken) production is two and one-half times more energy efficient despite the fact that they consume only feed grains while beef consume grain and forage (Table VII). Not only are broilers more efficient in converting grain into animal protein than

TABLE VII
Energy Inputs and Returns per Hectare for Various Livestock Production Systems in the United States[a]

Livestock	Animal product yield (kg)	Yield in protein (kg)	Protein as kcal (10³)	Fossil energy input for production (10⁶ kcal)	kcal fossil energy input/ kcal protein output	Labor input (manhours)
Broilers	2000	186	744	7.3	9.8	7
Eggs	910	104	416	7.4	17.8	19
Pork	490	35	140	6.0	42.9	11
Sheep (grass-fed)	7	0.2	0.8	0.07	87.5	0.2
Dairy	3270	114	457	5.4	11.8	51
Beef	60	6	24	0.6	25.0	2
Dairy (grass-fed)	3260	114	457	3.3	7.2	50
Beef (grass-fed)	54	5	20	0.5	25.0	2
Catfish	2783	384	1536	52.5	34.2	55

[a]Adapted from Pimentel et al. (1980).

beef cattle (Pimentel *et al.*, 1980), but also only 1.005 animals have to be fed to produce one broiler (0.005 are breeding chickens).

In the United States, over 420 million ha of land are used just to grow forage and grains for livestock. Of this, 380 million ha are in improved pastures and extensively managed forest ranges, and the remainder is in grain production. It is interesting to speculate what could happen if the United States were to switch to a grass-fed livestock system and eliminate the use (and associated energy expenditures) of grains and forage. Estimates are that about 2.8 million tonnes of animal protein could be produced annually or slightly more than half that of the 5.4 million tonnes currently produced (Pimentel *et al.*, 1980). The 2.8 million tonnes of animal protein (meat, eggs, and milk) would provide 40 g protein per day per person. On average, each person in the United States consumes about 32 g of plant protein per day (Pimentel *et al.*, 1980). Thus, the 40 g of animal protein per day from a grass-fed system added to the 32 g of plant protein would total 72 g of protein per person per day. This is greater than the recommended daily allowance (RDA) of about 46–54 g per person per day (National Academy of Sciences, 1980).

We pointed out that animal protein products require significantly larger inputs of energy than plant protein production (Tables VI and VII). Some would argue in favor of using grains directly as food so more people would have food. One estimate is that if the 135 million tonnes of grain annually cycled through U.S. livestock were fed to humans, 400 million people could be sustained for 1 year on a vegetarian diet providing about 80 g of plant protein per person per day (Pimentel *et al.*, 1980).

Again it should be emphasized that livestock-based foods like plant foods contribute not only calories but also important vitamins and minerals to the human food supply. While they contain fairly high levels of saturated fats and cholesterol, their protein contribution is substantial and of high quality.

Livestock production has a major advantage in the food production system in that livestock can be utilized to make marginal land productive. Although no human food crops can be profitably produced on marginal land, it is possible to produce forage for livestock. This pasture and rangeland can be utilized effectively to produce valuable livestock protein (Pimentel *et al.*, 1980) and hopefully in the future, this type of animal production system will be augmented.

IX. ALTERNATIVE DIETS

Indeed, cycling plant protein through animals to produce animal protein is costly in both land and energy and is an inefficient way to produce protein. Perhaps in the future a drastic change in production patterns to curtail animal production will not be necessary. But if land and energy resources become scarce, and some modification of present protein production is needed, then it should be considered.

A comparison of the energy requirements to produce a high plant protein diet versus a high animal protein diet provides helpful insight into some of the differences. High plant protein diets or vegetarian diets are usually of two types: the lacto–ovo diet that includes eggs, milk, and milk products and the complete vegetarian diet that includes only plant proteins.

The following example illustrates some of the differences these dietary regimens have in fossil fuel requirements (Fig. 1). For these calculations, data from the United States are used and an average daily calorie food intake of 3300 kcal is held constant for the three diets. The amount of protein is over 100 g per day in the high animal protein or nonvegetarian diet and is still high or 80 g in the all-vegetarian diet.

Based on these sample calculations, the complete vegetarian diet is more economical in terms of fossil energy than either of the other two types of diets. Nearly twice as much fossil energy is expended to produce the food in a lacto–ovo vegetarian diet than is expended for the complete vegetarian diet (Fig. 1). For the nonvegetarian diet, the fossil energy input is more than threefold that of the complete vegetarian diet.

Energy expenditure is not the only factor to be evaluated when dietary choices are made. Personal choices are often based on social and cultural attitudes as well as taste, texture, color, and other palatability characteristics of food. Of major consideration are the nutritional differences between the pure vegetarian diet and diets that include animal products. First, because vitamin B^{12} (an essential nutrient) is lacking in pure vegetarian diets, it must be taken as a dietary

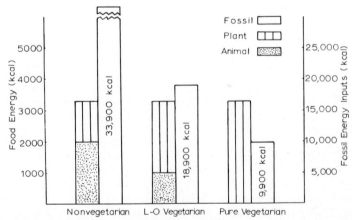

Fig. 1. Daily food energy intake of pure vegetarians, l–o (lacto–ovo) vegetarians, and nonvegetarians and the calculated fossil energy inputs to produce these diets under U.S. conditions. (From Pimentel and Pimentel, 1979.)

supplement. Further, the quality of protein consumed may not be adequate in the complete vegetarian diet because it depends on the combination of plant protein consumed. When the essential amino acids of different plant foods are matched or "complemented," then protein quality of a vegetarian diet can be made adequate. A diet of all plant foods is usually of greater volume and bulk, often making it difficult for young children and women to consume the quantities necessary to meet all nutritional needs. In addition, infants, rapidly growing adolescents, pregnant and lactating women, and other nutritionally vulnerable groups consuming pure vegetarian diets may need nutritional supplements of vitamins A and D and iodine.

Although these examples are based on limited data, they suggest that significant reductions in energy as well as land and water resource use are possible by modifying diets and eating patterns. Further reductions in quantity of energy and other resources are possible by reducing the total caloric intake of the population from the current 3500 kcal to less than 2500 kcal, depending on age and activity of the individual.

X. FOOD PROCESSING AND PACKAGING

Food products reach the marketplace in different ways. Some are sold fresh, while others are processed and packaged prior to sale. Because harvest yields of most food fruit and vegetables exceed the current demand of the market, processing preserves the excess and makes it available throughout the year, rather than just at harvest time.

In the United States the fossil energy inputs for preserving and processing foods and then placing them in a suitable package are substantial. For example, producing sweet corn on the farm uses only about 10% of the total energy used to produce, process, market, and cook a 1-kg can of sweet corn (Fig. 2). Most of the 6560 kcal that are expended in processing are used in making the steel can. Specifically, the heat processing (canning) of the corn requires only 575 kcal, while the production of the can requires about 2210 kcal.

Foods are also frozen to preserve them for future use. The fossil energy inputs for freezing are significantly greater than those for canning, about 7980 kcal/kg for frozen food compared with only 6560 kcal/kg for canned (Fig. 2 and 3). This is because processing by canning requires only heating and packaging while freezing may require brief heating (blanching), then cooking, packaging, and freezing.

Furthermore, once processed, canned foods can be stored at room temperature (actually slightly cooler is recommended), whereas frozen food must be kept in freezers at temperatures of −18°C or lower. Maintaining such a low temperature requires about 265 kcal/kg per month of storage (U.S. Bureau of Census,

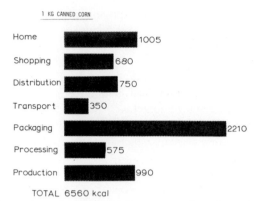

Fig. 2. Energy inputs for a 1-kg can of sweet corn. (From Pimentel, 1981c.)

1975). Since the recommended storage time for frozen foods is about 6 months, this energy cost must be added to the freezing cost, making the total energy input for frozen food much greater than that for canning (Fig. 2 and 3). However, the moisture-resistant plastic and paper containers for frozen foods require less energy to manufacture than the metal cans or glass jars used for canned food. Another important factor to consider is that the nutritive value and palatability of frozen foods, especially vegetables, is superior to that of canned foods.

Drying is another way of preserving foods. It is energy intensive when done in fossil-fueled ovens, but when dried by the sun the external energy cost is eliminated. Solar drying of foods, placed in simple racks, in suitably dry climates is one of the least costly processes for preserving fruits, vegetables, and meats. Salting is a long-used method of processing vegetables and meats for safe storage. Salting is also one of the least energy-intensive methods of processing foods, requiring only 23 kcal/kg of meat processed (Pimentel and Pimentel, 1979). It

Fig. 3. Energy inputs for a 1-kg frozen package of sweet corn. (From Pimentel, 1981c.)

has some disadvantages, especially related to palatability and ultimate salt content of the rehydrated food. For some individuals, the high residual sodium content of foods may be a concern.

Two of the most energy-intensive methods of processing foods are freeze-drying and smoking. Freeze-drying requires about 3540 kcal/kg of food processed and smoking requires about 4500 kcal of wood per kilogram of food smoked (Casper, 1977; Pimentel and Pimentel, 1979).

Food processing techniques employed in the future will have to be based more on energy efficiency than on mere convenience or maintenance of desired palatability characteristics of the food. The safe preservation of bountiful harvests for future use will continue to be the aim of food processing.

Because canning is less energy intensive than either freezing or freeze-drying fruits, vegetables, and meats, it may become more advantageous as energy costs rise. Although freeze-drying is one of the most energy-intensive methods of food preservation, it does have the advantage that without water the food is light in weight, can be transported cheaply, and requires little space for storage (Pimentel and Pimentel, 1979). Thus, if foods have to be transported long distances it may prove more energy efficient in the long run. In addition, freeze-dried foods can be stored without refrigeration and are similar to canned foods in this respect.

Food packaging is a facet of the food system where substantial energy savings are possible. For example, one can seriously question the efficiency of placing two crackers in a plastic pouch when more energy is expended in producing the package than the crackers. Another example is a diet soft drink, which has only 1 kcal itself but is packaged in an aluminum can that required 1600 kcal to produce. In addition, another 600 kcal of energy are expended to process the 12-oz soft drink, making a total input of 2200 kcal to produce a soft drink containing only 1 kcal. A quick survey of U.S. supermarkets reveals many examples where the energy content of packaging is higher than the energy value of the food.

Although convenient for the consumer, the individual wrapping of fruits and vegetables with plastic and individual serving boxes of cereal are other energy-costly technologies that could be eliminated with little adverse effect on food quality or supply. In addition to energy costs, this excessive packaging contributes to waste disposal problems and environmental pollution.

XI. FOOD TRANSPORT

Transport of food products in the United States is estimated to be about 60% by truck and about 40% by rail (U.S. Department of Commerce, 1963). Based on energy requirements for truck and rail transport (Pimentel and Pimentel, 1979), the energy required to move 1 kg of food product is calculated to be approximately 0.5 kcal/km. Assuming 640 km (400 miles) is the average distance that goods are moved (U.S. Department of Commerce, 1963), then the energy input is about 350 kcal/kg.

Frequently, however, much greater energy inputs are required for transporting foods from production areas to far distant marketplaces. Consider the journey frequently taken by a 0.5-kg head of lettuce that has a food energy value of only about 50 kcal. When this head of lettuce is transported by truck from California to New York, a distance of 4827 km, the energy expended is about 1800 kcal of fossil energy. This means that just for transport, about 36 kcal of fossil energy are expended per kilocalorie of food energy in the lettuce.

In searching for ways to decrease fossil energy in the distribution component of the food supply system, all methods need to be reevaluated. Railroads are five times more energy efficient than trucks on a per kilogram per kilometer basis (Pimentel and Pimentel, 1979), making them more suited to long hauls to major distribution centers. Yet trucks, because of their greater mobility, seem well suited to distribution to smaller market centers. Water transport is more efficient than railway, but obviously it cannot be employed as widely as trains. There are areas, however, where the use of water transport could be augmented or reinstated and save significant amounts of energy. Thus there are alternatives to be studied and distribution systems reevaluated to see which are the most energy efficient for the particular job that needs to be done.

XII. PREPARING FOOD FOR CONSUMPTION

For over the 500,000 years that humans were on earth, they must have eaten their food raw, for the use of fire dates back only 500,000 years. The palatability, especially taste and texture, of many foods is improved with cooking. Some foods, like cereals, are more easily digested after cooking.

Heat processing makes some foods safer to eat. For example, soybeans contain a protease enzyme that inhibits the production of trypsin enzyme involved in digesting protein while cassava contains the poison cyanide (Pimentel *et al.*, 1982). Both the enzyme and the cyanide toxin can be destroyed by sufficient heating or cooking.

Proper heat processing destroys many bacteria and parasites that have the potential to cause human illness. Thus, heating to 100°C and boiling for 1 min will inactivate *Salmonella*, a common bacterium on meat, especially poultry. Heating pork products to an internal temperature of 80°C ensures the destruction of trichina worms and also improves the flavor of the meat.

In the United States, an estimated 8025 kcal of fossil energy are used per person per day just for home refrigeration and cooking of foods by gas or electricity (U.S. Bureau of Census, 1975). Added to this are the nearly 5000 kcal required for the paper and plastic products used in serving and/or their washing.

Since the per capita consumption of food is 3500 kcal/day, this amounts to about 4 kcal of energy expended to prepare and serve each kilocalorie of food eaten.

Cooking over an open wood fire requires even more energy than either gas or electricity and is only 8–10% efficient in transferring heat to food (Stanford, 1977). In contrast, the electric stove is 20% efficient in transferring energy to food when the production of electricity itself is taken into account (Pimentel and Pimentel, 1979). Of the three, gas stoves, which are 33% efficient in the transfer of heat energy to food, are the most efficient. Thus, the kind of fuel and equipment will influence the amount of energy needed to heat process the same amount of food.

Because large amounts of energy are expended in all countries for cooking foods, more attention should be given to common household cooking methods and the types of equipment that conserve energy. Much research needs to be done to develop equipment that efficiently transfers heat from fuel to food. Once this is done, individuals will have to be educated to use both the fuels and the equipment. Even now with present equipment, individuals often do not understand the principles of efficient heat transfer, and educational programs in this area would prevent waste of high-cost fuels.

REFERENCES

Casper, M. E., ed. (1977). "Energy Saving Techniques for the Food Industry." Noyes Data Corp., Park Ridge, New Jersey.
DeBach, P. H., ed. (1964). "Biological Control of Insect Pests and Weeds." Van Nostrand-Reinhold, Princeton, New Jersey.
Eichers, T. R. (1981). Use of pesticides by farmers. In "Handbook of Pest Management in Agriculture" (D. Pimentel, ed.), Vol. 2, pp. 3–25. CRC Press, Boca Raton, Florida.
Lee, R. B. (1969). !Kung bushman subsistence: An input–output analysis. In "Environmental and Cultural Behavior: Ecological Studies in Cultural Anthropology" (A. P. Vayda, ed.), pp. 47–79. Natural History Press, Garden City, New York.
Lee, R. B., and DeVore, I., eds. (1976). "Kalahari Hunter–Gatherers." Harvard Univ. Press, Cambridge, Massachusetts.
Lewis, O. (1951). "Life in a Mexican Village: Tepoztlan Restudied." Univ. of Illinois Press, Urbana.
Linton, R. E. (1968). The economics of poultry manure disposal. Cornell Ext. Bull. 1195, 1–23.
Lockeretz, W. (1980). Energy inputs for nitrogen, phosphorus, and potash fertilizers. In "Handbook of Energy Utilization in Agriculture" (D. Pimentel, ed.), pp. 23–24. CRC Press, Boca Raton, Florida.
Miller, R. H., and McCormac, D. E. (1978). "Improving Soils with Organic Wastes." U.S. Dept. Agric. Task Force, Washington, D.C.
Mitchell, W. H., and Teel, M. R. (1977). Winter annual cover crops for no-tillage corn production. Agron. J. 69, 569–573.
Morrison, F. B. (1956). "Feeds and Feeding." Morrison Publ. Co., Ithaca, New York.
National Academy of Sciences (1980). "Recommended Dietary Allowances," 9th ed. Natl. Res. Coun., Natl. Acad. Sci., Washington, D.C.
Neal, O. R. (1939). Some concurrent and residual effects of organic matter additions on surface runoff. Soil Sci. Soc. Am. Proc. 4, 420–425.

Odum, E. P. (1971). "Fundamentals of Ecology." Saunders, Philadelphia, Pennsylvania.

Phillips, R. E., Blevins, R. L., Thomas, G. W., Frye, W. W., and Phillips, S. H. (1980). No-tillage agriculture. *Science* 208, 1108–1113.

Pimentel, D. (1974). Energy use in world food production. *Environ. Biol. Rep.* 74-1, Cornell University, Ithaca, New York.

Pimentel, D., ed. (1980). "Handbook of Energy Utilization in Agriculture." CRC Press, Boca Raton, Florida.

Pimentel, D. (1981a). The food-land-fuel squeeze. *Chem. Technol.* **11**, 214–215.

Pimentel, D., ed. (1981b). "Handbook of Pest Management in Agriculture," Vols. 1–3. CRC Press, Boca Raton, Florida.

Pimentel, D. (1981c). Food, energy, and the environment. *Proc. N.S. Inst. Sci.* **31**, 85–100.

Pimentel, D., and Burgess, M. (1980). Energy inputs in corn production. *In* "Handbook of Energy Utilization in Agriculture" (D. Pimentel, ed.), pp. 67–84. CRC Press, Boca Raton, Florida.

Pimentel, D., and Pimentel, M. (1979). "Food, Energy and Society." Resource and Environmental Sciences Series. Arnold, London.

Pimentel, D., Hurd, L. E., Bellotti, A. C., Forster, M. J., Oka, I. N., Sholes, O. D., and Whitman, R. J. (1973). Food production and the energy crisis. *Science* **182**, 443–449.

Pimentel, D., Nafus, D., Vergara, W., Papaj, D., Jaconetta, L., Wulfe, M., Olsvig, L., Frech, K., Loye, M., and Mendoza, E. (1978). Biological solar energy conversion and U.S. energy policy. *BioScience* **28**, 376–382.

Pimentel, D., Oltenacu, P. A., Nesheim, M. C., Krummel, J., Allen, M. S., and Chick, S. (1980). Grass-fed livestock potential: Energy and land constraints. *Science* **207**, 843–848.

Pimentel, D., Moran, M. A., Fast, S., Weber, G., Bukantis, R., Balliett, L., Boveng, P., Cleveland, C., Hindman, S., and Young, M. (1981). Biomass energy from crop and forest residues. *Science* **212**, 1110–1115.

Pimentel, D., Glenister, C., Fast, S., and Gallahan, D. (1982). "Environmental Risks Associated with the Use of Biological and Cultural Pest Controls." Final Report to the National Science Foundation, Report No. PB-83-168-716. Nat. Tech. Inf. Serv., Springfield, Virginia.

Pimentel, D., Fast, S., and Berardi, G. (1983). Energy efficiency of farming systems. *Agric. Ecosyst. Environ.* **9**, 359–372.

Stanford, G. (1977). "Energy Conservation." Agro-City, Inc., Cedar Hill, Texas. (Mimeo.)

U.S. Bureau of the Census (1975). "Statistical Abstract of the United States 1975," 96th ed. U.S. Bur. Census, U.S. Dept. Comm., U.S. Govt. Printing Office, Washington, D.C.

U.S. Department of Agriculture (1975). "Minimum Tillage: A Preliminary Technology Assessment." Office of Planning and Evaluation, U.S. Dept. Agric., Washington, D.C.

U.S. Department of Agriculture (1981). "Agricultural Statistics 1981." U.S. Govt. Printing Office, Washington, D.C.

U.S. Department of Commerce (1963). "Census of Transportation, Vol. III: Commodity Transportation Survey, Parts 1 and 2." U. S. Dept. Comm., Washington, D.C.

Van Dyne, D. L., and Gilbertson, C. B. (1978). "Estimating U.S. Livestock and Poultry Manure and Nutrient Production." U.S. Dept. Agric.-ESCS Publ. No. ESCS-12, U.S. Dept. Agric., Washington, D.C.

Willard, C. J. (1927). An experimental study of sweet clover. *Ohio, Agric. Exp. Stn. Res. Bull.* **405**, 1–84.

Zwerman, P. J., Drielsma, A. B., Jones, G. D., Klausner, S. D., and Ellis, D. (1970). Rates of water infiltration resulting from applications of dairy manure. *Proc. Cornell Agric. Waste Manage. Conf., 2nd, 1970*, pp. 263–270.

Chapter 2

Energy Sources and Conversions Relating to Food

CARL W. HALL*

College of Engineering
Washington State University
Pullman, Washington

> *So runn'st thou after that which flies from thee,*
> *whilst I thy babe chase thee afar behind.*
>
> Shakespeare, Sonnet 143

I. INTRODUCTION

The "ancient" energy source trapped when the earth was formed provides a reservoir of internal energy, whereas the burning of gases in the sun provides a continual source of external energy. Both are important energy resources for sustaining life on this planet, but the latter has received the most attention

*Present address: Directorate for Engineering, National Science Foundation, Washington, D.C. 20550.

25

because of its intensity, cyclic effects as a result of the rotation of the earth, direct impact on the biological systems of the earth, and visibility. The energy from the sun is the driving force behind the formation of fossil fuels and in the growth and evolution of our biological systems.

Several paths exist for flow of solar energy (Fig. 1). The path that the energy takes as it enters the earth's atmosphere until it is utilized and rejected determines, to a large extent, the availability of food and other energy and material resources for various needs, such as fuel. Food must be the top priority in the utilization of solar energy. Through planning and careful management, several human needs can be met, so that the obvious conflict between using materials for food or for fuel can be minimized and food will remain readily available for the population of the earth. A wealthy society might be able to afford the use of potential food for fuel, whereas in a poor society such use would impose a high cost, and possibly starvation. In this chapter we present and compare alternatives for the use of the external solar energy available throughout the world (Buvet *et al.*, 1976; Leach, 1975; Pimentel *et al.*, 1978).

II. ENERGY SOURCES

A. Internal Sources

The energy trapped under the crust when the earth was formed by the condensation of a large, hot ball of burning gases (much like the sun) is gradually being transferred to the surface in the form of heat. The rate of heat transfer internally through the earth to the surface is only about 1/10,000 of that transmitted externally by the sun to the earth and is not sufficient to sustain present life. That internal energy source, called geothermal heat, is generally considered

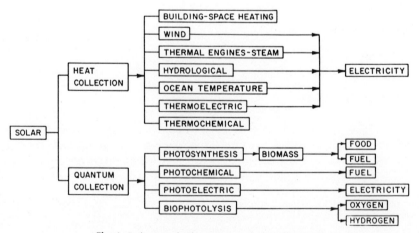

Fig. 1. Pathways of solar energy to fuel (Hall, 1981a).

to be renewable, based on the assumption that radioactive materials beneath the earth's surface continue to produce heat in a manner similar to that of an "internal sun" in the earth. Of course, our knowledge of the internal temperature of the earth is based primarily on indirect measurements, because the deepest probes into the earth have thus far penetrated only about 40,000 ft. Recent findings also suggest that large quantities of methane, which would be known as abiogenic methane, may have been produced and trapped in the crust as the earth was formed. The presence of carbon and hydrogen and the appropriate temperature of the environment at the time of the formation of the earth support this theory. Should it be found that considerable abiogenic methane does exist, major changes in our perceptions of the availability and utilization of energy will develop.

B. External Sources

The sun provides the major source of energy for sustaining life on this planet. It also provides a continuous source of energy not only for the earth but also for the solar system. About one-half of a billionth of the sun's energy falls on the earth. The earth's atmosphere receives 1.94 cal/cm^2 min (429.1 Btu/ft^2 hr) on the average, which is known as the solar constant. If this energy all reached the surface of the earth, it would be sufficient to boil one-half pound of water over each square foot of the earth's surface each hour.

The energy that enters the earth's atmosphere may be turned away as a result of particulates in the air, absorbed, reflected by the earth, trapped around the earth, or reach the earth's surface and be used by soil, plants, animals, and people. Obviously, a very delicate system must exist, in which there is an appropriate relationship between the inflow and outflow of energy, if reasonable temperatures are to be maintained over the face of the earth. Any actions taken that increase or decrease the flow of solar energy could affect this delicate balance and cause the demise of some or all of the biological systems. Actions that change the heat transmission of the air, such as introducing more dust into the atmosphere (e.g., by cultivation of land, changing the chemical content of the air, and increasing the burning of fuels) could have negative effects. Any or all of these could then affect food and energy relationships. Likewise, changing the absorbing or reflecting characteristics of the earth's surface, (e.g., by removing or changing plants, or cultivating the land) could change the earth's temperature.

III. CHANGES OVER THE EARTH

Considerable changes have occurred over the surface of the earth and in the atmosphere surrounding the earth, principally since the beginning of the industrial age. Crops now use about 1.5 billion ha of land that was originally in grass and forests: this represents about 11% of the land surface (Chrispeels and Sadava, 1977). About twice that amount of land surface is estimated as being potentially available cropland. The extent to which additional land could be cultivated depends on many factors such as water, climate, elevation, or costs, but one should also consider the secondary effects such as the potential impacts on the surface and environment of the earth, as mentioned previously (National Academy of Sciences, 1977). Only recently has attention been given to the determination of the kinds and quantities of particulates and chemicals, as well as compounds such as carbon dioxide and sulfur dioxide, etc., in the atmosphere as related to various agricultural and industrial practices. It is difficult to obtain representative data and to apply these data beyond a local area to a regional, national, or worldwide basis. Perhaps the best documentation exists with respect to the effective level of carbon dioxide in the atmosphere. During the past 30 years, the carbon dioxide level has increased from 310 to 325 parts per million, and it is believed that this increase in carbon dioxide will increase the temperature and alter the rainfall patterns surrounding the earth (Pales and Keeling, 1965) (Fig. 2). However, other factors might be changing to balance this potential change. It not only takes a long time to obtain the data and information needed, but also would probably take a long time to effect a change in the environment, if a change in our practices is required. A truly important consideration in these matters is therefore the time scale.

IV. PHOTOSYNTHESIS

The sun provides the energy that is the driving force in photosynthesis, the basic process by which green plants, in the presence of water and carbon dioxide, produce oxygen and carbohydrates and, in some cases, hydrocarbons. The exact mechanisms involved in photosynthesis have been explained by Calvin and his associates and have been identified as the Calvin Cycle, which is basically the energy relationships in the utilization of carbon. Although the theoretical effi-

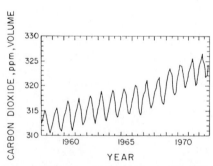

Fig. 2. Carbon dioxide concentration change, 1958–1972 (Pales and Keeling, 1965).

ciency of conversion of energy through photosynthesis is 12%, in practice the daily peak efficiency of conversion is 1–2%, with some systems reaching 5% (Heichel, 1974). A group of plants known as C_4 plants are especially efficient converters of solar energy, particulary at high temperatures and in intense light. Examples are sorghum, sugarcane, and corn, all of which are food crops. Direct conversion of solar energy to electricity with solar cells can be as high as 25%, but present systems operate at less than 10%.

The carbon cycle (Fig. 3) and the carbon dioxide cycle or flow (Fig. 4) describe the exchanges that take place during the photosynthetic process. Carbon is the principal actor in the process so that the carbon cycle is sometimes called the energy cycle.

The carbon cycle describes the formation and utilization of fossil fuels. Carbon is the critical element, from beginning to end, for supplying most of the energy resources from which fuels are derived. The quantity of carbon in the world, the base resource from which we have to operate in this cycle, is estimated at somewhat less than 21 million billion tons. About 10 thousand billion tons are in fossil fuels. A lesser amount of about 1000 billion tons is in biological materials. The amount of carbon in the world remains rather constant. The major problem is that fossil fuels are being mined more rapidly than they are being replaced by natural means, so that underground carbon is moving to the environment. Also, there is competition between the use of these fossil fuel resources for producing food and for nonfood purposes, principally fuel. As the cost of the fossil resources increases, it also causes an increase in cost of the food produced by use those fossil resources.

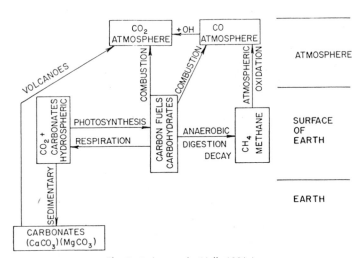

Fig. 3. Carbon cycle (Hall, 1981a).

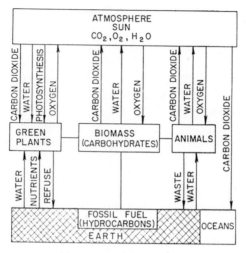

CARBON DIOXIDE FLOW

Fig. 4. Carbon dioxide flow.

V. CARBON DIOXIDE

The utilization of hydrocarbon minerals, hydrocarbons, carbohydrates, and the products from these, which involve combustion, give off heat, carbon dioxide, and water (Fig. 3 and 4). Carbon dioxide is a significant factor in the flow of carbon involving fuels from fossil and plant resources. In the combustion process, the ratio of carbon dioxide given off for the same amount of heat produced for different fuels, beginning with natural gas as a base, is as follows: gas (1.0), oil (1.25), wood (1.5), and coal (1.75).

The present rate of increase of carbon dioxide in the atmosphere is nearly double the average increase over the previous 50 years, which reflects the effect of increased combustion. Growing more plants, whether for food or for fuel, will utilize carbon dioxide from the atmosphere and oceans. In addition, some plants respond by increased growth in a carbon dioxide-enhanced environment, providing a self-correcting feature in the atmosphere.

We are confronted with a reduction of readily available carbon in hydrocarbon fuels, particularly gas and oil, and a potential crisis of an overabundance of carbon dioxide in the atmosphere. Also, burning of more coal will place additional particulates in the atmosphere. It is easy to understand why so much emphasis is being placed on an energy approach that would use the carbon dioxide from the atmosphere and abundant solar energy to produce carbon in plants for almost immediate use.

VI. HYDROCARBON AND CARBOHYDRATE PRODUCTION

The hydrocarbon fuels are generally referred to as nonrenewable resources. If the time scale for production could be shortened greatly from several million years for coal or from a million years for oil and gas, fossil fuel resources could be considered as renewable. The remains of plants and animals, primarily carbohydrates, that have occupied the biosphere are converted to hydrocarbons in the earth's crust. Time, temperature, and pressure are the principal natural conditions involved in the conversion.

A short cut in the carbon cycle of the formation of hydrocarbons in the earth is to use carbohydrates more directly as a source of fuel. These carbohydrates may be used directly in combustion or as an energy source to produce other fuels, such as gases and liquids. The gaseous fuels could be principally methane, which is natural gas. Liquid fuels from carbohydrates can be used for fuel oil and gasoline. These are nearly equivalent to hydrocarbon-based fuels, although they provide less energy per gallon (e.g., methanol, 1/3; ethanol, 2/3). The hydrocarbons can be converted to alcohols, which can be used as a fuel. Alcohols can be used directly as a fuel or can be mixed with hydrocarbon fuels. Under appropriate conditions of pressure and temperature, the addition of a gas such as oxygen, and possibly the use of catalysts, carbohydrates can be converted to hydrocarbons. During the conversion there is a consumption of energy that results in there being less energy available in the fuel, but in the hope that a fuel of higher availability could be produced. Major processes for the conversion of biomass for fuels are given in Fig. 5.

The use of carbohydrates as fuel will often compete with the use of carbohydrates as food. To minimize this problem, crops that do not compete with food crops for land and crops that are not food crops should be given the greatest

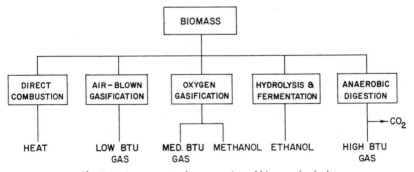

Fig. 5. Major processes for conversion of biomass for fuel.

consideration as sources of fuel. Perhaps emphasis should be placed on using those parts of plants for fuel that are not returned to the land or that are not edible.

Although most of the materials produced by plants are primarily carbohydrates or lignocellulose, many plants produce hydrocarbons. Plants with high hydrocarbon content could be converted almost directly to fuel and with a higher conversion efficiency than that possible when using plants rich in carbohydrates. In practice, however, the production of these plants is quite low. Hydrocarbon-producing plants are not generally, if ever, used as food. Thus, except for competition for land on which to grow these hydrocarbon producers, there would be no conflict involved in replacing food plants used as food with those used as energy sources. Agriculture and forestry account for 80% of the usable land area in the United States.

Hydrocarbon-Producing Plants

The plant best known for producing hydrocarbon is the rubber tree, which produces the hydrocarbon in the form of a latex. The milkweed is a similar hydrocarbon-producing plant. The guayule shrub, another rubber source, is also a hydrocarbon producer. Altogether, about 200 plants have been identified as having the potential for producing hydrocarbons. These plants should receive more attention. The conversion process from hydrocarbon to fuel is considerably more efficient than conversion from carbohydrate to fuel. Some of the hydrocarbon-rich liquids obtained from plants can be used directly in appropriately adjusted internal combustion or diesel engines.

VII. BIOMASS

All forms of materials derived from plants and animals grown on land or in or on the water and substances derived from biological growth such as animal, plant, and human wastes and residues, which consist primarily of carbon, hydrogen, and oxygen (carbohydrates), and to a lesser extent carbon and hydrogen (hydrocarbons), are known as biomass. Of particular interest here are the biomass products for food and fuel grown on the land. Solid biomass carbohydrates can be categorized as starches and sugars and lignocellulose materials. The former, although combustible, can also be used to produce ethanol by fermentation or methane by digestion. The lignocellulose materials include plant products, such as straw, cotton, wood, and those used to produce cloth, from which methanol is most easily produced. However, these can also be broken down chemically to produce sugar, which can be fermented to produce ethanol. Initially, lignocellulose materials will be used primarily as a solid fuel for combustion. More competitive uses exist for sugar and starches, primarily for food and feed. Some lignocellulose can be used for feed for ruminant animals, such as cattle.

Biomass provides a means of storing solar energy that otherwise is available on an instantaneous basis only. Through perennial plants, solar energy accumulated over years can be stored until it is to be used. However, production on the land on which such plants are grown then declines. If biomass in the form of carbohydrates, which could otherwise be used as food, is to be used for fuel, it might be desirable to require that the material be held for use as food for 1 year to ensure that food supplies are not unduly degraded by a less important use or demand.

Biomass (plants) is characterized by the following:

1. *Higher cost of collecting, assembling, and transporting materials.* Unless biomass to be used for fuel can be collected as a part of the cost, gathering adds to the cost. The gathered material must then be transported to the location of use. Sawdust, straw, and fodder may have to be compressed to be used as a fuel.

2. *High moisture content, often 50–85%.* Before burning as fuel, wet products need to be dried. Some of the energy from the biomass is used for drying wet products that are to be burned. Noncommercial energy, such as the sun, should be used for drying. Normally, it does not pay to dry biomass that is to be burned to a point below 30% moisture content. Fermentation processes require high moisture mixtures and are relatively inefficient.

3. *Lower energy density.* Fossil fuels yield from 11,000 to 20,000 Btu/lb, whereas the yield for biomass solids ranges from 4000 to 8000 Btu/lb.

4. *Lower carbon content.* The energy content is related to the carbon content. Fossil fuels contain 70–90% carbon, whereas biomass solid fuels have 30–60% carbon. Hydrocarbon plants produce liquids with a wide range of carbon content, which is greatly influenced by moisture content.

5. *Erosion.* Removal of biomass such as straw and other vegetation exposes the land to soil erosion and rapid water runoff. The result is precious land and environmental degradation; this may result in land that is unproductive in the future.

Unless certain codes, restrictions, guidelines, or laws are established, the principal factors involved in the development and use of biomass as fuel will be the cost of producing energy from it and the environmental degradation that results from its removal from the soil. The major defect in using present day economics as the driving force for use of biomass as fuel is that the system for production and utilization of biomass cannot respond rapidly enough to the fluctuations in the marketplace. Rapid changes in the marketplace could unduly affect the cost or quantity of biomass used for food. Improved land management practices can help to reduce environmental problems, but the presence of biomass is essential on most land areas to prevent environmental degradation.

A. Hierarchy of Biomass Uses

Fossil energy resources are used primarily for fuels (about 90%), with the remainder being used for producing chemical and industrial products. There are many competing uses of biomass (Fig. 6). Food, feed, fiber, feedstock, fertilizer, and fuel identity the major uses for biomass. If a pound of biomass were first used for food and put through each step, the utilization of the resource would be extremely high. Going directly from a potential food resource to fuel without any intervening steps is less productive and perhaps more wasteful than if a step-by-step route could be followed (Hall, 1980). The entropy (loss of availability) is the same whether biomass is converted directly to fuel or converted in several steps from food to fertilizer to fuel.

B. Biomass Production

The annual worldwide production of biomass is estimated to be about 100×10^9 tons of dry matter (Pimentel et $al.$, 1978) and will provide about 800 quads of energy on land and 800 quads from water. The annual production of biomass in the United States on land is 3.2×10^9 tons (Pimentel et $al.$, 1978) and will provide about 50 quads of energy. The annual production of solid organic wastes in the United States is 2.0×10^9 tons of dry matter. The heat content of all the biomass produced in the United States is equivalent to about 70% of the energy used there. The likelihood of meeting a major portion of our energy needs with biomass in the near future is unlikely.

Considerable energy, often taken from natural gas, is required to manufacture fertilizer. The amount of energy needed to produce 1 kg of nitrogen is 14.7×10^3 kcal; of phosphorus, 3×10^3 kcal; and of potassium, 1.6×10^3 kcal. Assuming that an application of 100 kg of nitrogen per acre is needed to increase production from 60 to 100 bushels of corn per acre means that a ratio of input energy to net energy produced is 1:1.7, which comes close to an uneconomical procedure considering the higher cost of nitrogen compared with the value of the

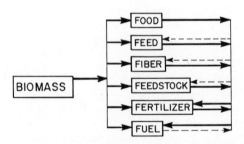

Fig. 6. The hierarchy of food to fuel, the six Fs (Hall, 1981a).

product (Leach, 1975). In areas of intensive crop production in the United States, the point of diminishing returns is being approached in the use of fertilizer for increasing crop production. Thus, it appears unrealistic to use a primary plant food as a fuel in our economy.

C. Classification of Biomass

Because there is a need for food on a worldwide basis, even though there are a few pockets of surplus, and in the long range there is the potential problem of not being able to properly feed the world population, it would seem appropriate that only nonfood products should be considered as a steady source for fuel. Thus, plants grown only for fuel should be hydrocarbon-producing plants: the lignocellulose plants, trees, etc. Plants should be grown that will not require high amounts of manufactured fertilizers, excessive irrigation, or unusually heavy applications of chemicals for weed control. For food-producing plants, those parts of the plants not used for food or feed, not needed for replacement in the crop cycle, and not essential to prevent soil erosion and rapid water runoff or to maintain environmental quality might be used for energy. This is a relatively small amount of biomass.

Waste is the general name given to the materials and products or to the remains that are left following a process or operation. Of particular interest are the organic wastes from biological processes and the solid wastes from commercial and industrial processes. The solid wastes of most importance for energy production are those that are combustible, as distinguished from metals, alloys, and other noncombustibles included in solid waste. Those wastes collected in a city, which include a wide variety of items, are known as municipal solid wastes (MSW). One useful waste may be found in the whey by-products from cheesemaking, which may be dried and used as food or feed.

Biological waste is made up of garbage and sewage. These biological or organic wastes may be treate by enzymatic fermentation to convert the material into alcohol, if treated by anaerobic digestion they produce methane gas. In addition to the production of methane, the solids remaining from the fermentation or the digestion processes can be used for fertilizer.

Biomass may be grown specifically as a *product* for fuel, such as sugar cane to produce ethanol, wood to produce combustion, and carbohydrate or hydrocarbon liquids to produce engine fuels. Likewise, biomass may be produced for a combination of purposes so that *coproducts* such as food, feed, or fiber may be produced while another component is produced for fuel, such as plant oil squeezed from seeds, with the fresh product remaining to be used for animal feed. A grain crop such as corn, wheat, or sorghum could be grown specifically as both a grain for food and a plant material for burning, or it could be grown for animal feed or fertilizer. *By-products*, the materials remaining after the principal product desired is removed, can also be used as a source of fuel. The by-product could be bagasse from sugarcane processing, pulp from sugar beet processing, or distiller's dried grain from fermentation of grain for alcohol. These by-products can be used for animal feed, fuel, or perhaps fertilizer.

Wastes include a wide variety of products that might also be identified as residues, refuse, and trash. Generally, wastes are materials disposed because they do not meet quality standards; such substandard materials might result from damage caused by contamination; insects; improper shape, size, or color; or deterioration during handling and storage. Materials given off by animals and people as wastes, such as urine and organic waste, can be used as fertilizer or can be decomposed to produce methane. Human wastes are often included as a part of the product treated by a municipal waste treatment plant. Sludge is a product of waste treatment and can be used for fuel or fertilizer.

Residues are the left-overs from plant materials produced for another purpose and that are available for use as feed or to produce energy; examples are fruit or vegetable pulp that remains after juice is squeezed, pits removed from fruits for canning, or parts of plants originally meant to be used for feed but not eaten by the animals because of coarseness, poor taste, or poor quality.

Refuse includes wastes, rubbish, garbage, and debris of plant or animal materials discarded from the principal product that have not entered into processing activities. Generally, but not always, refuse is that material removed ahead of a processing operation, whereas residues are those materials not used following the processing operation. Thus, straw, fodder, or cotton stems removed before the operation might be called refuse by some but called residues by others.

Heavy metals in sludge and chemicals in waste water, sludge, and plant materials may militate against using these materials for feed or fertilizer. Chemicals in materials to be burned may have deleterious effects on the environment.

Trash is made up of the foreign materials removed from the biomass that are not usually a part of or associated with the primary product, such as stones, glass, and soil in harvested crops; but this can include other extraneous matter such as sticks, weeds, and foreign plants, which can be used for fuel.

Whether a particular biomass material will be used for a specific purpose depends largely on the cost, including assembling, handling, and transporting costs.

Biomass that can be used for fuel will often occur initially as those materials already assembled, such as cobs, husks, and vegetation matter, and taken to the food or feed processing plant as a part of the processing operation. Likewise, bark and slabs from logs that are assembled as a part of the lumber-making operation are charged to that process instead of to the process of handling the material for fuel production purposes. Thus, the cost of collecting and assembling these materials is charged to a previous operation, making the cost for the fuel less.

Methane produced from wastes already present at a waste treatment plant or a landfill or manure produced by animals in concentrated feedlots will be available before that produced from material that would have had to be assembled from a field or forest for that process. High moisture content materials (above 60–70%) can often be used for anaerobic digestion to produce methane. If these high moisture materials are to be burned they would normally be dried to about 30 to 50%, although high moisture combustors are available. Generally, it is not economical to dry below 50%, and it desirable to dry without using fossil fuel, which suggests that sun drying should precede the operation if possible.

Many potentials exist for utilizing waste products. Although these products at one time were considered waste, many can now be considered as usable materials. Solid wastes might now be looked on as wasted solids that can be used productively rather than accumulating and possibly causing problems of sanitation, environmental degradation, and poor appearance. When consideration is given to using these waste materials and products, first consideration should be given to using them as feed, second as fiber, third as feedstock, fourth as fertilizer, and only as a last resort as fuel.

VIII. COMBUSTION CHARACTERISTICS

There is now a move to use more biomass materials, primarily waste products, refuse, or residues, such as municipal solid wastes and wood, for heat. The heat is used for space heating and boilers. Generally, the heat content of a biomass product is about one-half that of an equivalent weight of fossil fuel on a dry basis.

Initially, biomass will be looked on primarily as a source of thermal energy, but as technology and demand develop, methods of converting the material to more readily available liquid and gaseous fuels will become more prominent.

As a rule, the combustion of wood and other biomass produces more hydrocarbons in the form of a gas or vapor in the environment. Three times as much carbon monoxide is produced from wood burning than is produced from fossil fuel, and more chlorine compounds are produced. Fewer oxides of nitrogen are produced because biomass contains less nitrogen and burns at a lower temperature than do fossil fuels. The sulfur content of wood is much lower, and therefore wood produces one-eighth the amount of sulfur dioxide compared with that produced by coal. These are important factors that affect the heat transmission properties of the environment and affect the amount of solar energy reaching the earth. The burning of biomass produces more carbon dioxide than that given off by burning gas and oil but less than that given by coal during the production of the same amount of heat (Hall, 1981b).

IX. THE METHANOL APPROACH

Considerable emphasis will be placed on replacing the use of oil for the production of gasoline with some other liquid product. In particular, ethanol and methanol have received considerable attention as engine fuels (Stokes and Waterland, 1981) (Fig. 7). Ethanol is made through a fermentation process from carbohydrates, primarily from those that provide principal food sources. Methanol is produced from cellulosic materials such as wood, but most commercial methanol is now produced from natural gas. Methanol may be produced from coal in the future, in much the same way as from biomass, which will save natural gas for other uses.

To meet future United States energy fuel needs, both gaseous and liquid fuels must receive considerable attention. The system to be developed should be based on the national and the international energy networks now in place. Thus, the one million miles of pipeline for natural gas and the existing gasoline and fuel-oil networks will be utilized. This suggests that methane, the principal component of natural gas, will be produced from biomass. Methane can be obtained by digestion of carbohydrates or from lignocellulose materials (following hydrolysis) with residues remaining for other purposes, principally animal feed.

X. NATIONAL AND INTERNATIONAL NETWORKS

To minimize the negative impact of using biomass for fuel, fuels produced must eventually be in a form that can be handled in the present energy/fuel networks: electricity, natural gas, transportation fuel (liquid), and heating fuel (heavy liquid). Until the biomass fuels are converted to a form that can be handled by one of the networks, the biomass will meet local needs; its principal use will be for heating. If an adequate amount is available at a uniform quality, the biomass will be used to produce electricity via a boiler or gas turbine. If alcohol is used as an engine fuel, it will find its way to the market along with gasoline. Methane gas produced from biomass can meet some local (nearby)

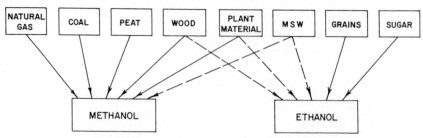

Fig. 7. Routes to methanol and ethanol from biomass.

heating purposes, but it will have to meet the same energy density and quality standards as for natural gas to permit its use with presently available burners, as well as its use with other standard equipment, and to enter the national pipeline network.

XI. CONVERSION EFFICIENCY

There is a tendency to use the efficiency of conversion as the basis for comparing the various pathways available for converting solar energy to fuel. Efficiency can be quite misleading and is only one factor. For instance, the conversion of solar energy into biomass is only 0.1–0.2% efficient and direct conversion of solar energy to electricity may be almost 20% efficient. Yet the costs of the latter may be much greater. Efficiency provides a reasonable but not complete means of comparing different processes for converting the biomass to a particular fuel.

Biomass is one of several methods of collecting and storing solar energy. The efficiency of conversion is about 1 W stored for each 1000 W entering the atmosphere, and if converted to electricity, this would become 0.3 W. The efficiency of direct conversion to electricity, by photovoltaics, is much higher (7 W per 100 W entering) but considerably more expensive and lacks the advantage of energy storage. Various methods of converting solar energy to gas and electricity are shown in Fig. 8. Systems for converting biomass to electricity and gas are given in Figs. 9 and 10.

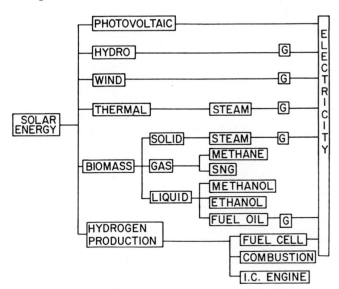

Fig. 8. Solar energy to electricity (Hall, 1981a).

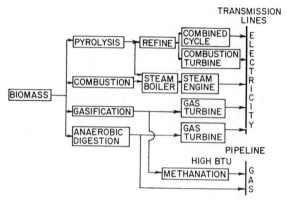

Fig. 9. Biomass for electricity and gas utility production (Hall, 1981a).

XII. ENTROPY AND NEGENTROPY

The natural flow is for energy to decrease in availability, which means an increase in entropy. Energy input to a system is required to block this increase in entropy. For the earth, energy enters the atmosphere from the sun. However, much of this energy is reflected back into the solar system. That energy absorbed

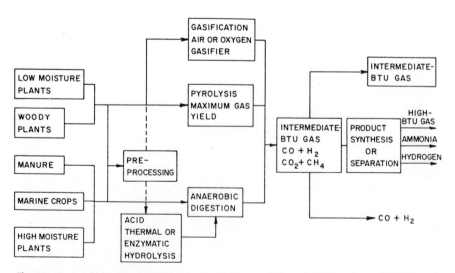

Fig. 10. Biomass conversion to gas (From Schooley et al., 1978. Used with permission of SRI International, Menlo Park, California.)

and used by plants builds an energy reservoir that is called by some negentropy. The plant system and the animal systems that depend on the plants provide the only means on earth for increasing the mass that sustains the hierarchy of biomass uses (Fig. 6). If the plant systems were to decrease, the earth would begin to die and would become like our present deserts.

XIII. SECONDARY EFFECTS

Some secondary effects in the energy–food picture should be considered. Burning more fuel to obtain energy, whether by using fossil or biomass fuels, will put more carbon dioxide in the atmosphere. If the only effect of increased combustion were the addition of carbon dioxide to the atmosphere, the temperature surrounding the atmosphere would increase. However, the additional particulates, especially from burning biomass such as wood, tend to counterbalance the potential increase in temperature from the CO_2 produced by burning and the particulates increase the reflection of solar energy from the earth. If the temperature of the atmosphere surrounding the earth were to increase, even in only certain localities, those areas could shift from food-crop-producing areas and yields could be affected, among other things.

XIV. SUMMARY

The carbon cycle and the carbon dioxide cycle describe the exchanges that take place in the photosynthesis process; this results in biological products, which are used for food (carbohydrates) and formation of fossil fuel (primarily hydrocarbons). Carbon is a principal actor in this process so that the carbon cycle is sometimes called the energy cycle. There is considerable competition for the use of the fossil resources for production of food or for nonfood purposes, principally fuel. There is also competition for using plant resources for food and fuel.

Plants and their products, biomass, provide a means of storing solar energy that otherwise is available principally on an instantaneous basis. Biomass energy can be used for a wide variety of purposes, ranging from a higher to a lower use— food, feed, fiber, feedstock, fertilizer, and fuel. Only a few of the plants provide acceptable food resources. The most effective and efficient way of using biomass for fuel in our economy has not been resolved. Direct burning, methanol, and ethanol production presently provide the most acceptable conversion routes to fuel.

In the future there will be increased emphasis on the production of biomass and greater use of biomass resources and a greater competition for fossil resources for producing fuel and food.

REFERENCES

Buvet, R., Allen, M. J., and Massue, J. P., eds. (1976). "Living Systems as Energy Converters."
    North-Holland Publ., Amsterdam.
Chrispeels, M. J., and Sadava, D. (1977). "Plants, Food, and People." Freeman, San Francisco,
    California.
Hall, C. W. (1980). The role of energy in world agriculture. *Int. Meet. CENECA, 1980*, pp. 1–22.
Hall, C. W. (1981a). "Biomass as an Alternative Fuel." Gov. Inst. Inc., Rockville, Maryland.
Hall, C. W. (1981b). Fossil and biomass compared for fuels. *Western States Sect. Combust. Inst.*,
    Pap. No. WSS/CI-81-4.
Heichel, G. H. (1974). Energy needs and food yields. *Technol. Rev.* **76,** 19–25.
Leach, G. (1975). "Energy and Food Production." IPC Sci. Tech. Press, Guildford, England.
National Academy of Sciences. (1977). "World Food and Nutrition Study." Natl. Res. Counc.,
    Natl. Acad. Sci., Washington, D.C.
Pales, J. C., and Keeling, C. D. (1965). The concentration of atmospheric carbon in Hawaii. *J.
    Geophys. Res.* **70**(24), 6053–6076.
Pimentel, D. (1979). "Food, Energy and Society." Arnold, London.
Pimentel, D. (1980). "Food, Energy, and the Future of Society." Colorado Assoc. Press, Boulder,
    Colorado.
Pimentel, D., Nafus D., Vergara, W., Papaj, D., Jaconetta, L., Wulfe, M., Olsrig, L., Frech, K.,
    Loye, M., and Mendoza, E. (1978). Biological solar energy conversion and U.S. energy policy.
    BioScience **28,** 376–382.
Schooley, F. A., *et al.* (1978). Mission analysis for the Federal Fuels for Biomass Program. *Fuel
    Biomass Symp., 1978*, pp. 1–27.
Stokes, C. A., and Waterland, D. (1981). Alcohols: The old new fuels. *Technol. Rev.* **83,** 68–79.

Chapter 3

The Role of Energy in World Agriculture and Food Availability*

CARL W. HALL†

College of Engineering
Washington State University
Pullman, Washington

I. INTRODUCTION

Energy is the driving force for all of our earthly systems. Nearly all of the energy for running our economy is derived from the sun, either directly, in the form of light and heat, or indirectly, from plants and animals. The remains of plants and animals have accumulated over millions of years to form fossil fuels or precursors to fossil fuels.

Solar energy is the principal driving force in the production of plants; these plants are the source of most of our food, which is one of the basic needs of man. We started using fossil fuels heavily in agriculture about 50 years ago, but even today U.S. agriculture is 90% dependent on solar energy (Pimentel *et al.*, 1973). With the industrialization of farm and factory production, fossil fuels, the stored solar energy of the past, became more important.

As more countries moved to industrialization there was a greater demand for

---

*Based on a talk first presented by the author at CENECA International Symposium on Energy, Paris, France, February 27–29, 1980.

†Present address: Directorate for Engineering, National Science Foundation, Washington, D.C. 20550.

FOOD AND ENERGY RESOURCES

fossil fuels, particularly oil, which has led to the present situation of high demand for these limited resources. It would be impossible in this short chapter to summarize the energy relationship, that is, the inflow and outflow of the various kinds of energy used in all the countries of the world. The supply and use of various types of energy must be considered in the context of the country and its development while, at the same time, considering the international environment. On a local or single country basis, the stage of development establishes the conditions for the demands on various types of energy. Most countries do not want to be overly dependent on another country for vital energy resources.

With a few exceptions, the discussion in this chapter will contrast developed economies, developing economies (Fig. 1), and world energy supply and demand rather than compare specific countries. Generally, raw materials flow from developing to developed economies and manufactured products flow from developed to developing economies. An exception might be the flow of cereal grains from developed to developing economies, but these are produced under industrialized conditions. The countries that do not have the raw materials, often called the Fourth World, have the greatest challenge.

II. OBJECTIVES

In order to keep our perspective when comparing or analyzing energy, we need to define the objectives of agriculture, which are

1. to collect and store solar energy as food energy in plants,
2. to utilize plant products and convert them into feed for animals and food for people, and
3. to distribute food to the consumer.

Various resources are needed to produce the food: people, both as intelligent beings and as providers of manpower; land, as the resource to be nourished with water and nutrients; and external or commercial energy in addition to solar

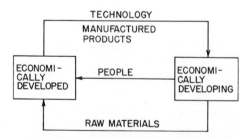

Fig. 1. Primary flow of raw materials, technology, and people.

energy. Of course, climate, seeds, and protection of the growing plants are parts of the system we must consider.

III. PROCEDURE

The procedure for meeting the objectives that have evolved over time is as follows: Given land, water, appropriate plants, and solar energy, production is enhanced through the use of muscle power from humans and animals, fossil energy for power, fossil energy for nutrients in fertilizer, fossil energy for plant control and pest control with chemicals, as well as by the application of additional water, which requires energy both in preparing and operating the system. These same procedures will be followed to increase productivity of presently cultivated land and to develop new land for food production.

IV. PRODUCTION CHARACTERISTICS

There are several characteristics in the production of food, feed, and fiber that are different from the production of industrial goods. These characteristics are as follows: the products are usually of a seasonal nature; production is highly dependent on the weather (solar energy, rainfall, and temperature); various varieties of plants are available or can be developed for different geographical areas, environmental conditions, and uses; the plants are subject to damage by pests; and the product is of a biological nature which can be difficult to store. To modify these production characteristics requires an input of energy.

V. FOOD SYSTEMS

A simplified description of two major food systems, although several categories could be provided, can be given by calling one primitive and the other modern (or mechanical). As we move from the primitive system to the modern mechanical systems, increased external or commercial energy must be added to the system.

In primitive or traditional food production, people on the land produce and utilize their own food and fiber with little of their production leaving the farm. As modern industries developed, people moved from the farm to work in these industries (Fig. 2). The farm was left with fewer hands, who had to become more productive in order to meet not only the food and fiber needs of those living on the farm but also that of those working in industry, who usually lived in cities. Food and fiber flowed from the farm to the cities and industry; and, at the same

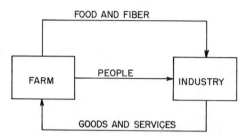

Fig. 2. Primary flow between farm and industry.

time, the farm became more dependent on goods and services from industry. A principal external need was energy, either directly, as a fuel, or indirectly, in the form of nutrients, environmental control, and water supply. In countries having rapid industrial development and low population per unit of land area, extension of mechanization, with high use of external energy, occurred.

Those countries with more mechanization are usually so identified by the fact that they use more horsepower per hectare than do less industrialized countries. However, other factors, such as mechanical aids for field production; water control; and materials handling, storing, and processing, become important for producing more and saving more of the product.

There is a feeling among some people that the agricultural sector can satisfactorily utilize the surplus, that is, the untrained and possibly some potentially untrainable people from other segments of the economy as industrialization occurs. Those holding this false belief do not consider the fact that talent, training, and education are required to operate a mechanized agricultural enterprise that parallel the complexity of industry. Thus, mechanization must be considered in the context of the economic development, educational level, and industrialization of the country and should parallel those technological developments occurring elsewhere in the economy. In the use of mechanization to support development in agriculture one often overlooks the importance of reducing drudgery; improving safety and human and animal health; meeting human desires; and providing satisfaction with the job. With the industrialization of agriculture, additional external energy is required when using present systems.

VI. ENERGY RELATIONSHIPS: DEVELOPED VERSUS DEVELOPING ECONOMIES

With the recent attention being paid to the use of commercial energy in production or industrialized agriculture, comparisons of systems are often made in terms of energy input versus energy output (Table I). For each unit of commercial or fossil fuel used in industrialized agriculture there is the potential to

TABLE I
Ratio of Energy Output/Input for Various Products[a]

Shifting crop system	65
Rice and beans, peasant farming	41
Corn, manual	30
Cereal grains, sugar beets	2.5–5
Potatoes	1.6
Fruits and vegetables	0.1–1.0
Milk	0.4–0.5
Grass-fed beef	0.3
Eggs, intensive	0.2
Poultry, meat animal production for meat	0.1

[a] Adapted from Pimentel, 1980.

produce from 0.5 to 3.0 units of food and feed energy (Heichel, 1974; Leach, 1975; Pimentel, 1980). The primary energy used per unit of food produced is 2 to 100 times greater in developed economies than that used in developing economies. The digestible energy produced per unit of commercial energy is 5 to 7 times greater under manual operations than that produced by using modern methods (Fig. 3).

From an energy perspective, one might conclude that we should return to primitive or manual farming, but note that the amount of food produced per man-hour may be 200 to 300 times greater when using industrialized production methods (Leach, 1975; Pimentel and Pimentel, 1979). Under a regime of shifting crop cultivation, there may be 65 times as much energy output as energy input; for cereal grains, sugar beets, etc., only 3 to 5 units of output per unit of

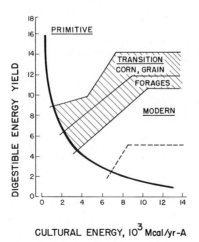

Fig. 3. The caloric gain, or ratio, of the yield of digestible energy to the investment of cultural energy.

input; and with food from animals, less than 1. In the shifting crop and manual operations, solar energy and human labor provide the input, with a very small amount of energy being provided by external or fossil fuels.

The daily utilization of energy per person increases rapidly from 2000 kcal consumption by primitive man to 230,000 kcal utilized by those in a technological society, which represents a 100-fold increase (United Nations, 1978) (Table II). The increase in energy consumption for food is not much greater in advanced economies. The major increase in the use of energy is in the industrial, commercial, and transportation sectors. The commercial energy used per worker-hour in the developed economies is about 30 times the amount used in developing economies. Likewise, the commercial energy per tonne of production is 5 to 6 times greater in the developed economies, food production in tonnes per hectare is twice as great, and in tonnes per worker is 6 times greater in developed economies than it is in developing economies (Table III).

The energy efficiency of subsistence crop production is high, but the output per worker-hour is 2 to 10 kcal. By contrast, the energy output for cereals in an industrial economy is 50 to 1500 kcal per worker-hour, or up to 150 times as much in industrial agriculture as in subsistence crop production.

As expected, the percentage of the total commercial energy that is used for agricultural production is greater in developed economies (6%) than in developing economies (4%) (Penner and Icerman, 1974; Pimentel and Pimentel, 1979). In the United States, for example, 6% of all energy, including the energy used to manufacture the machines for mechanization, is used for agricultural production or farming (Pimentel, 1980). The greatest amount of energy is used for fertilizers and the next is used for fuel to run tractors, engines, and machines. The amount of energy used for the total food system in a developed economy is twice that used for production.

For the grazing of land and growing of forage there is a high biomass energy output per unit of fossil energy output (Fig. 4). Usually, however, the products from these fields are not in a form suitable for human food, but can be used for

TABLE II
Daily Utilization of Energy (1000 kcal per Person)

	Food	Industry, agriculture	Commercial residential	Transportation	Total
Primitive man	2	—	—	—	2
Hunting man	3	—	2	—	5
Primitive agriculture	4	4	4	1	12
Advanced agriculture	3.5	7	12	1	26
Industrial	3.5	24	32	14	77
Technological	3.5	91	66	63	230

TABLE III
Commercial Energy[a]

	Hectare	Worker	Tonne of grain
Developed economies	4.3	15.6	1.8
Developing economies	0.6	0.5	0.3
World (average)	2.0	2.5	1.1

[a]Expressed in terms of 10 kcal per hectare, worker, or tonne of grain.

cattle feed. Developed economies use a high percentage of energy in the form of commercial energy, about 90% as contrasted to 50% for developing economies (National Academy of Sciences, 1977). Agriculture will follow the pattern of using more commercial energy in a country as industrialization develops.

Development is usually characterized by the following factors: the cultivation of more area per person, the use of more external energy, a trend to the planting of fewer kinds of crops per farm, the use of higher yielding plant varieties, the feeding of added nutrients to plants, the use of more commercially processed foods, and the change to a marketplace economy (National Academy of Sciences, 1977).

VII. EFFICIENCY OF SYSTEMS IN AGRICULTURAL PRODUCTION

Considerable confusion may occur when discussing energy relationships and efficiency, particularly in agriculture. Energy comparisons should be used with great care. A kilocalorie of energy exhausted from a heating unit such as a stove or dryer clearly does not have the same economic value as that of a kilocalorie of energy in food. If food is the need, the kilocalories of energy in oil will not be equivalent to the kilocalories of energy in food. Conversions must take place. For

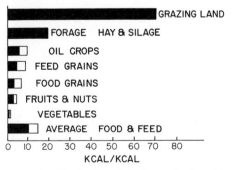

Fig. 4. Energy output per unit of fossil energy input for production of food, feed, and fiber.

every energy conversion, some of the energy is lost, usually in the form of heat, and efficiency decreases. We commonly define efficiency as output divided by input. The agricultural production system (farming) is the only system in which there is the potential of attaining 100% efficiency or higher in terms of fossil fuel input compared to food energy output, because solar energy is converted into food. In this case, solar energy is added to offset the energy lost in fossil energy conversion.

Another measure of the efficiency of a system is productivity, either in weight or energy produced in terms of land, labor, cost, or population. All of these can be valuable measures or indicators but must be used with judgment.

Also, the term production or yield can be used as a measure of a system. Production could be in terms of weight of material, energy produced, or digestible energy produced either in the form of carbohydrates, protein, and lignocellulose material, or in terms of crop quantity per year per hectare. Each of these, when used individually, is often inadequate to compare a country's past, present, and future energy–food relationships. For example, the most efficient system in terms of yield per kilocalorie of input usually has a low productivity per unit of manpower and is not the most productive in terms of the use of land area (Pimentel and Pimentel, 1979).

More intensive use of manpower with more workers per acre is not unreasonable, even though there is a general feeling that with development there should be fewer workers per acre. In Japan, for example, which is considered to have a developed economy, 700 hr of manpower per hectare may be used in producing rice, whereas in the United States the input is about 25 hr (Pimentel and Pimentel, 1979; Rutger and Grant, 1980).

Using external energy balances is not a proper method of measuring the quality of life or productivity in rural subsistence economics. In rural subsistence agriculture, the people provide the inputs and consume their own outputs. Materials are recycled within the unit, with solar energy as the primary outside, or external, energy source. Axinn and Axinn (Chapter 6, this volume) have determined that under such conditions in Nepal a recycling ratio of 62 to 73% of materials occurs on 1.5 to 3.0 hectare subsistence units.

As the economy develops and more energy (Table IV) is required for processing and transportation, more people are involved. In fact, in the United States the total number of people involved in the food system, including production, processing, and marketing personnel, is approximately the same as the number of people living on the land as farmers in the premechanization era.

VIII. COMMERCIAL ENERGY

There is general agreement that a relationship exists between the gross national product (GNP) and the commercial energy used per person. In general,

TABLE IV
Annual Energy Used in United States for Food System[a]

	10^{12}	kcal
Food production	1140	(35%)
Food processing and packaging	1140	(35%)
Food storage, transportation, preparation	950	(30%)
Total	3230	

[a]Adapted from Pimentel and Pimentel, 1979.

those countries with the highest consumption of commercial energy have a higher GNP than do those with lower commercial energy consumption. Generally, countries can be identified as developed and developing by comparing these figures. However, there is considerable variation in the relationship between the amount of energy used per person and the GNP. The quantity of energy consumption at which a country goes from developing to developed cannot be determined. It is also characteristic of people in a developing country, where a large percentage of the working population is involved in farming, to also spend a high proportion of their income for food. As an example, in India where 70 to 75% of the population is involved in farming, people spend about 60% of their income on food, leaving a lower percentage of the income for other uses (Fig. 5). In a developed economy the population usually spends less than 30% of its income on food, making the economy more responsive to the desires of the consumer that go beyond the necessity for food (USDA, 1981).

The consumption of food energy does not vary greatly from one country to another, being 3500 kcal or less per person each day in the developed countries and 2000 to 3000 kcal in the developing countries (Fig. 6). About 500 million of the estimated 4 billion people on earth are malnourished and live in tropical areas (National Academy of Sciences, 1977; FAO, 1974). The Fourth World, deficient in resources except for people, is a major problem area for nutrition.

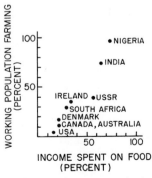

Fig. 5. Income spent on food.

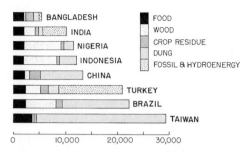

ENERGY CONSUMPTION, KCAL/DAY-PERSON

Fig. 6. Consumption of food and renewable fuels for eight countries.

North America and Western Europe average a consumption of 3500 kcal per person. Only in North America and Western Europe do people consume 75 to 105 gm of protein per day (Food and Agriculture Organization, 1974). The Fourth World, lacking in resources, generally does not generate enough exchange to purchase energy-based resources.

In many countries, wood is being used as a fuel for food preparation; which depletes natural resources and could lead to the formation of denuded land and serious soil erosion. As a country becomes developed, following the patterns of the past, there has been an increasing demand for fossil fuels, which demand now appears to be outpacing the ability of natural processes to replace the fossil fuels consumed. The increase in use of fossil fuels in the United States and many western countries is 5 to 20 times that for countries such as Bolivia or Kenya. One developed country shows a doubling of agricultural input on the farm from 1920 to 1970; at the same time there has been a 40-fold increase in energy input (Steinhart and Steinhart, 1974). Note, however, that beginning in about 1965 there has been a leveling off of output as the energy input was increased. A point of near diminishing returns has been reached with respect to the use of existing methods and plants. As the energy input increased over the same period the man-hours of work decreased greatly to approximately one-sixth of the previous amount (Fig. 7). The total effect has thus been positive in terms of output per unit input; that is, the output per man-hour has increased quite rapidly, while the number of the man-hours required to produce a given amount of work has decreased.

As the energy input to the food system is increased, the index of output increases rapidly at first and then levels off, after which there is a very slow increase in output with an increase of input (Fig. 8). Considerable increase in output of food per hectare can be obtained in developing countries where the energy input is now low (National Academy of Science, 1977). The greatest potential for increase, when one overlooks the availability and cost of energy for the next decade, will be found in the developing countries.

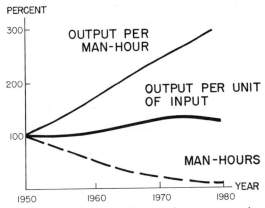

Fig. 7. Farm output per unit of input and output per man-hour.

The cropping systems used can have much to do with the amount of food energy produced as related to energy input. As an example, sugarcane, potatoes, and cereal grains have (in the order given) a higher energy to output ratio than do vegetables and fruits. In Fig. 3 the general area for plants used for food and fiber is shown by the hatched line and fruits and vegetables are represented by the dashed line. Note again that these relationships show that as the external or commercial energy is increased, the energy ratio is decreased. Even though fruits and vegetables might have a low energy ratio, these plants and the products obtained from them contain necessary nutritional components and would not be selected on the basis of energy alone. Further, if one relates the energy required in terms of protein, considerable fossil fuel energy is required per unit of protein, 50,000 to 100,000 kcal/kg protein, when produced from animals, which is about 100 times that needed for cereals (Pimentel *et al.*, 1975) (Fig. 9). Although a low energy ratio exists, ruminant animals provide a means of harvesting a diffuse and diverse forage crop and converting it to protein that can be digested by humans.

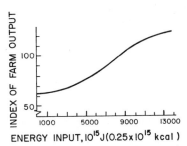

Fig. 8. Relationship of index of output to energy input to the total food system.

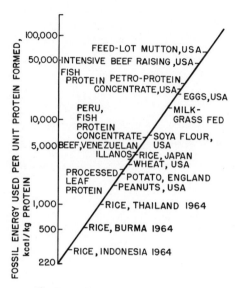

Fig. 9. Fossil energy per unit of protein.

How Energy Is Used

When we look at the world situation, we see that the major increase in energy use will be for fertilizer (Fig. 10). Much of this increase will occur in the developed countries. If food needs are to be met, there must be a greater use of fertilizer by the developing countries. In order of importance, the energy used for food, feed, and fiber production in a developed economy is fertilizer, fuel, machine manufacturing, irrigation, drying, and pesticides (Pimentel and Pimentel, 1979) (Table V). The production of 1 kg of nitrogen requires 14,700 kcal of energy (Lockeretz, 1980). The production of 1 kg of chemical pesticide or fungicide requires 75,000 kcal of energy for production, packaging, and transportation (Pimentel, 1980). The addition of these production inputs, when ap-

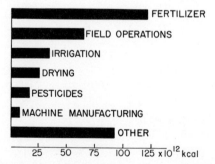

Fig. 10. Energy for food, feed, and fiber production.

TABLE V
Energy for Crop Production Inputs (Typical Values)[a]

	Kilocalories
1 kg equipment	21,000
1 kg nitrogen fertilizer	14,700
1 kg phosphorous fertilizer	3,000
1 kg potassium fertilizer	1,600
1 kg seed	25,000
1 kg herbicide	57,000
1 kg fungicide	22,000
1 kg insecticide	44,000
1 liter of fuel	10,000
1 kg irrigation water	2

[a]Adapted from Pimentel, 1980.

propriately managed, generally results in an increase in output. As a particular input is increased, a point is reached at which the ratio of output to input decreases, as shown by the amount of nitrogen used to produce corn. For nitrogen, the peak ratio occurs at about 130 kg/ha (120 lb/acre), which corresponds to the amount of nitrogen needed to yield about 7.5 tonnes/ha (Pimental et al., 1973). As varieties are improved, moisture more appropriately controlled, and other elements properly applied, the peak yield can be higher if a greater supply of an input such as nitrogen is provided. The ratio of output to input must be analyzed not only from an energy standpoint but also from that of the cost of supplying the input. The value of adding nitrogen, based on costs and returns, will be more persuasive than merely the consideration of the energy ratio. However, the general objective should be to reduce energy input without increasing the cost of production and while increasing yield, a difficult combination to obtain. The greatest plant response on a worldwide basis would be obtained from an increase in the input of nitrogen. In 1981, the U.S. retail cost of nitrogen was $0.31/lb; phosphorous, $0.41/lb; and potassium, $0.40/lb. There is little correlation between cost and energy inputs in the production of these plant nutrients. For example, the energy inputs for nitrogen, phosphorous, and potassium per kilogram are 14,700 kcal, 3000 kcal, and 16,000 kcal, respectively (Lockeretz, 1980).

An estimate of commercial energy for inputs of fertilizer, machinery, pesticides, and irrigation can be given for developed and developing economies. It is anticipated that the potential return from investing in fertilizer that is appropriately applied will be the most economic investment for increasing production, but not necessarily efficiency, over the next 10 years. The percentage of the increase in the total energy used for production will be the greatest in developing economies. However, the consumption of the developed economies will increase by a factor of 1.5 times that of the countries with developing economies over the 10-year period. In any case, the stage of development of a country, status of international trade, availability of resources, and cost of these resources are among the factors to be considered as one attempts to balance the cost of energy against the value of the food produced (Hudson, Chapter 9, this volume). The cost of controlling weeds with appropriate, safe, and expensive chemicals might be less than would be working the soil through mechanical cultivation, but it would probably be more expensive than it would be if the hoeing were done as a family affair, without use of external energy (Instituto Centroamericano de Investigacion y Tecnologia Industrial, 1977).

IX. LOOKING AHEAD: FUTURE ENERGY DEMANDS AND SOURCES

In the near future, the projected annual percentage increase in population is expected to be approximately twice as great in developing as in developed countries, resulting in a threefold increase in the world population over the next 10 years (Population Reference Bureau, 1982). The increase in population of the developing countries will put an additional demand on the food supply system of the world. Presently, of the more than 150 nations in the world there are only 10 nations that are not food exporters; the United States is the largest exporter of food (National Academy of Sciences, 1977).

The food needed to support the projected increase in population probably cannot be provided by the developed economies without a major financial sacrifice, and the developing countries may not have the financial resources to pay for the food, because countries in the Fourth World do not have the resources needed to generate sufficient foreign exchange to meet their food needs (National Academy of Sciences, 1977). However, since there would be a greater return per unit increase of energy input in many of the developing economies (because of the present low rate of productivity), perhaps institutions in developed countries will be persuaded to provide the investments required to increase production in developing countries.

An increase in food production could be obtained by irrigating land not now producing food, which is estimated at 140×10^6 ha (National Academy of Sciences, 1977). Also, some additional cropland could be made available through clearing and reclamation. However, in many areas the land is not suited geographically or climatically for removal of the natural vegetation, and doing so might result in damage to the soil. All of these proposed actions would require an input of energy, energy that few of the developing countries have at their disposal.

On the one hand, the increase in cropland area is encouraged. At the same time, particularly as industrialization occurs in a country, there may be a decrease in available cropland area, countering the objective of producing more food. This decrease in cropland area might be caused by urbanization; erosion of land; development of highways, roads, and transportation systems; and development of energy sources, including the building of transmission lines and pipelines (Pimentel et al., 1976).

A large input of energy from fossil fuels has been used to date to increase production in agriculture. As exemplified by developed economies, more energy is normally required for increasing the speed with which operations are performed, providing a greater variety of products, using additional processes to prepare a product for consumption, and extending the storage life of products.

Much can be done in a highly mechanized, developed country to reduce energy by decreasing the amount of fuel consumed to provide power in the field (Council for Agricultural Science and Technology, 1975). Fuel consumption can be reduced by avoiding operating equipment at excessive speeds; operating gasoline and diesel powered equipment at full load, with the speed matched to the load; utilizing diesel instead of gasoline powered engines (assuming that diesel fuel is available) to obtain better efficiency; using low energy tillage methods, such as plow-plant and no-till; using solar energy for drying products in the field and in storage; making efficient use of water, e.g., using spot or trickle irrigation; and using waste water and heat obtained as by-products from other industries such as power plants.

A major saving in energy could be obtained by preventing losses of products before and after they are harvested. About 35% is lost before harvesting and from 10 to 20% of food produced is lost after harvesting (Pimentel, 1978). As food products become more valuable, it becomes more economical to prevent losses. The amount lost, if associated with an appropriate educational program, will adjust itself, based on the demand and value of the product in the marketplace.

On a worldwide basis, but particularly in the developing economies, there will be an increase in energy used in the food system (National Academy of Sciences, 1977). The energy would be used to increase productivity of the land and the worker, consumption of animal products, processing of food products to serve consumers some distance from the producer, and transportation of feed and food.

The transportation energy will increase as additional inputs are provided to increase agricultural production. Transportation energy will be needed to move produce from production to processing centers. Additional energy for transportation will be needed to distribute the products of agricultural processing locally, nationally, and internationally. Savings in energy might occur by using the more efficient transportation systems. The shipping industry is the most energy efficient per tonne-kilometer and should be used where possible (USDA, 1981). Long-range planning, control of operations, and effective loading and unloading devices will develop. The energy used by animals to transport materials is about 10 times greater than that used by a truck (Makhijani and Poole, 1975). However, these figures provide a misleading comparison because the animals are fed on plant energy and the truck is normally fueled with fossil energy.

Additional external energy will be needed to feed the future population. Oil and natural gas have been the principal energy sources during the past 50 years. In effect, we have been eating oil through the production of food (Green, 1978). If we look ahead, we see that coal will provide the major fossil energy resource. But even the use of coal will be limited by the fact that burning more coal will put more carbon dioxide into the atmosphere, only some of which can be used by plants.

The agricultural sector, and society in general, will place greater emphasis on the use of biomass, a product of agriculture, to provide a small amount of energy (Energy Research Advisory Board, 1981). The biomass can be converted to food, feed, fiber, feedstock (chemical), fertilizer, and fuel (Hall, 1981). These six Fs have been listed in order, with the highest priority going to food. The material remaining after the food is used should go to the next highest possible use. Cycling of these products through a lower step provides for increased efficiency in the use of the energy, as represented by feeding waste back to animals. The wastes from animals, and people as well, could be used for producing solid, liquid, or gaseous fuels. As the cost of fossil fuels increase, some of the energy products from wastes become more competitive. By comparing the present costs of liquid and gaseous fuels to biomass fuels, we find that these fuels are not yet competitive in national or international energy networks. However, where products of agriculture are collected following a processing operation, such as cannery wastes, bark and slab material from lumber mills, and animal wastes in confined housing, the *potential* of these for energy use is high.

The most apparent practical use of solar energy will be to grow the plants that can be used as food or converted to energy for other uses. Another viable approach to use of solar energy is that of sunlight to dissociate water. With an appropriate catalyst it seems possible that water could be dissociated to hydrogen and oxygen directly by sunlight. The hydrogen would then be available for use as a substitute for fossil fuels and when burned would produce minimal pollution.

X. PRINCIPLES USED IN CONSIDERING ENERGY AND FOOD RELATIONSHIPS

Energy from an external source is required to initiate a process or to cause that process to continue, whether it be for a seed to germinate, a plant to grow, a product to be converted to food or feed, or a product to be moved from one place to another. An interesting relationship is involved between energy-producing materials and nonenergy-producing materials such as metals. Energy flows from a higher to a lower level of availability, a process resulting in an increase in entropy. Thus, although nonenergy-producing materials can be cycled and re-used numerous times with an input of energy, energy-producing materials cannot be reused in this way.

The most efficient food system in terms of output per unit of input is usually not the most productive system. The most efficient food system we know would not be adequate to feed today's population. Various inputs can be used to increase labor and land productivity, and thereby production, to provide adequate food for people and animals. Many trade-offs must be considered and evaluated in terms of resource inputs and their effects on production. In one situation fertilizer may provide a greater response, whereas in another case water might provide a greater response either per unit of energy input or on the basis of the cost of the input.

Food contains many vital components in addition to those that provide energy, and therefore it is a mistake to use only a simplistic comparison of energy-providing components. Energy is the principal driving force for producing other vital components such as vitamins and minerals. Also note, for example, that the energy in oil cannot be compared directly with the energy in food. If the need is for food, the energy in food is more valuable than the energy in oil. If the critical need is liquid fuel, then the energy in oil is more valuable than that in food. Should we want to convert food sources to fuel, or fuel to food, there will be considerable use of energy. In an analysis in which the focus is on calories, the fact that economics plays a principal role in decision making in the marketplace could be overlooked. Decision making in government at the national or international level, whether in developing or developed economies, can be approached on the basis of energy as well as that of economics. Understanding the energy flow in systems can aid in economic decision making.

Reducing Dependence on External Energy

The challenge is to maintain production of food while decreasing dependence on external or commercial energy. There are several possible methods: increase photosynthetic efficiency of plants, which now convert only about 1% of the solar energy received during the growing season (Stout *et al.*, 1979); use nitrogen-producing plants to reduce dependence on nitrogen-based fertilizers, for which two approaches are foreseen: (a) to alter nonleguminous plants so that they will produce nitrogen (e.g., make cereal plants act like legumes) and (b) to use nitrogen-producing plants in intercropping to provide nitrogen for other plants; use urban and industrial wastes to a greater extent to provide gaseous fuel, plant nutrients, and tilth; and, to an increasing extent, use of plant coproducts, by-products, wastes and residues of agricultural production and processing of fuel.

An intensive use of external energy in industrialized agricultural operations is that for drying. Equipment and procedures will be developed to carry out more of the drying process by using solar energy (Hudson, 1983). The cost of fossil fuel will be a driving force for greater efficiency. If the efficiency of an operation were to be increased by only 1% or so, that 1% would be important and significant when considered on a worldwide basis. To provide more food will require more land, more irrigation, and more fertilizer, all of which require additional energy.

XI. SUMMARY

It should be obvious that a close relationship exists between energy and food production, processing, packaging, transport, and preparation. The amount of energy expended in processing is equal to the amount of energy expended in producing food in the developed economies. Solar energy is the source of about 90% of the energy used in food production. Solar energy can be used more productively to grow food if its use is assisted by the use of improved tillage and cultivation methods and appropriate crop types. The assistance provided for tillage and cultivation is in the form of human and animal power in primitive and developing systems. In the developed agricultural systems, commercial energy sources (such as fuel, fertilizer, and chemicals) are used to a large extent to augment the effective use of solar energy. The efficiency of using energy decreases with increased energy input, but total production increases. The amount of food required by a country depends on the size of the population. As population increases, whether in a developing or developed country, there will be a need to increase food production while conserving land and water resources. As a country becomes more developed, it becomes more dependent on others and will have lower energy efficiency, higher productivity, increased trade, and a greater dependence on commercial energy. The food produced, although often evaluated in terms of energy, also supplies important constituents for a healthy population: vitamins, carbohydrates, sugar, fat, minerals, and minor elements. As far as the individual consumer is concerned, the economics of the marketplace rather than energy ratios will become the basis for more of the decision making. In the future, greater emphasis will be placed on using indirect solar energy sources, such as biomass, wind power, and photovoltaics, to meet the needs of agricultural and industrial production.

REFERENCES

Abelson, P. H. (1974). "Energy: Use, Conservation and Supply." Am. Assoc. Adv. Sci., Washington, D.C.

American Society of Agricultural Engineers. (1976). "Increasing Agricultural Productivity." Am. Soc. Agric. Eng., St. Joseph, Michigan.

Calvin, M. (1977). The sunny side of the future. *Chem. Technol.* 7, 352–363.

Central Treaty Organization (1968). Report. Working party on fertilizer. Islamabad, Pakistan, 1968.

Cervinko, V., *et al.* (1974). "Energy Requirements for Agriculture in California." California Dept. Agric. and Univ. of California at Davis, Sacramento, California.

Chancellor, W. J. (1977). "The Role of Fuel and Electrical Energy in Increasing Production from Traditionally Based Agriculture," An Occas. Publ. East-West Center, Honolulu, Hawaii.

Council for Agricultural Science and Technology (1975). "Potential for Energy Conservation in Agriculture Production," Rep. No. 40. Council Agric. Sci. and Tech. Ames, Iowa.

Darmstadter, J., Dunkerley, J., and Alterman, J. (1977). "How Industrial Societies Use Energy." Resources for the Future. Washington, D.C.

Dorf, R. C. (1978). "Energy, Resources, and Policy." Addison-Wesley, Reading, Massachusetts.

El Mallakh, R., and McGuire, C. (1974). "Energy and Development." Int. Res. Cent. Energy, Boulder, Colorado.

Energy Research Advisory Board (1981). "Biomass Energy." Report of the Energy Research Advisory Board Panel on Biomass. U.S. Dept. Energy, Washington, D.C.

Engineering Foundation and American Society of Agricultural Engineers. (1977). "Energy Policy for the U.S. Food System." Asilimar Conference Grounds, Pacific Grove, California.

Esmay, M. L., and Hall, C. W. (1973). "Agricultural Mechanization in Developing Countries." Shin-Norinsha Co., Ltd., Tokyo.

Faidley, L. W. (1977). Energy requirements and efficiency for crop production. *Pap.—Am. Soc. Agric. Eng.* 77-5528, 1–19.

Food and Agriculture Organization (1974). "Assessment of the World Food Situation." United Nations World Food Conference, November. Food and Agriculture Organization of the United Nations, Rome.

Food and Agriculture Organization. (1978). "Production Yearbook 1977." Food and Agriculture Organization of the United Nations, Rome.

Geissbuhler, H., ed. (1978). "World Food Production." Pergamon, Oxford.

Green, M. B. (1978). "Eating Oil." Westview, Boulder, Colorado.

Hall, C. W. (1981). "Biomass as an Alternate Fuel." Government Institute, Inc., Rockville, Maryland.

Heichel, G. H. (1974). Comparative efficiency of energy use in crop production. *Bull.— Conn. Agric. Exp. Stn., New Haven* 739, 1–26.

Instituto Centroamericano de Investigacion y Tecnologia Industrial (ICAITI) (1977). "An Environmental and Economic Study of the Consequences of Pesticide Use in Central American Cotton Production," Final Report. UN Environ. Prog.

Jewell, J. N. (1975). "Energy, Agriculture and Waste Management." Ann Arbor Science, Ann Arbor, Michigan.

Kinne, I. L., and McClure, T. A. (1977). Energy in the food system. *In* "Encyclopedia of Food, Agriculture and Nutrition" (D. N. Lapedes, ed.), pp. 17–21. McGraw-Hill, New York.

Kuether, D. O., and Duff, B. (1979). Energy requirements for alternative rice production systems in the tropics. *SAE Tech. Pap.* 790491, 1–20.

Lappe, F. M., and Collins, J. (1977). "Food First." Ballantine, New York.

Leach, G. (1975). "Energy and Food Production." Intl. Inst. Environ. Dev., Washington, D.C., and IPC Sci. Technol. Press, Guildford, England.

Lockeretz, W., ed. (1977). "Agriculture and Energy (Proceedings of a Workshop Held at Washington University, St. Louis, Missouri, June 1976)." Academic Press, New York.

Lockeretz, W. (1980). Energy inputs for nitrogen, phosphorous, and potash fertilizers. *In* "Handbook of Energy Utilization in Agriculture" (D. Pimentel, ed.), pp. 23–24. CRC Press, Boca Raton, Florida.

Makhijani, A., and Poole, A. (1975). "Energy and Agriculture in the Third World." Ballinger, Cambridge, Massachusetts.

National Academy of Sciences (1977). "World Food and Nutrition Study." Natl. Res. Counc., Natl. Acad. Sci., Washington, D.C.

Nelson, L. F., and Burrows, W. C. (1974). Putting the U.S. agricultural energy picture into focus. Pap.— Am. Soc. Agric. Eng. 74-1040, 1–14.

Penner, S. S., and Icerman, L. (1974). "Energy. Vol. 1: Demands, Resources, Impact, Technology, and Policy." Addison-Wesley, Reading, Massachusetts.

Pimentel, D., ed. (1978). "World Food, Pest Losses, and the Environment." Westview, Boulder, Colorado.

Pimentel, D. ed. (1980). "Handbook of Energy Utilization in Agriculture." CRC Press, Boca Raton, Florida.

Pimentel, D., and Pimentel, M. (1979). "Food, Energy and Society." Arnold, London.

Pimentel, D., Hurd, L. E., Bellotti, A. C., Forster, M. J., Oka, I. N., Sholes, O. D., and Whitman, R. J. (1973). Food production and the energy crisis. Science 182, 443–449.

Pimentel, D., Dritschilo, W., and Kutzman, J. (1975). Energy and land constraints in food-protein production. Science 190, 754–761.

Pimentel, D., Terhune, E. C., Dyson-Hudson, R., Rochereau, S., Samis, R., Smith, E., Denman, D., Reifschneider, D., and Shepard, M. (1976). Land degradation: Effects on food and energy resources. Science 194, 149–155.

Population Reference Bureau (1982). U.S. population: Where we are; where we're going. Popul. Bull. 37, 1–47.

Rutger, J. N., and Grant, W. R. (1980). Energy use in rice production. In "Handbook of Energy Utilization in Agriculture" (D. Pimentel, ed.), pp. 93–98. CRC Press, Boca Raton, Florida.

Saltzman, S. A., and Borgese, E. M., eds. (1973). "Energy Technology and Global Policy." Clio, Santa Barbara, California.

Scarpia, I. E., and Kiefer, H. S. (1978). Perspectives on world food production. In "Sourcebook on Food and Nutrition" (I. E. Scarpia and H. S. Kiefer, eds.), pp. 403–480. Marquis Academic Med., Chicago, Illinois.

Scientific American, eds. (1971). "Energy and power: Special issue." Sci. Am. 224, 36–224.

Slesser, M. (1978). "Energy in the Economy." St. Martin's, New York.

Smil, V. (1979). Energy flows in the developing world. Am. Sci. 67, 522–531.

Steinhart, J. S., and Steinhart, C. E. (1974). Energy use in the U.S. food system. Science 184, 307–316.

Stivers, O. O. (1974). Energy efficiency and its implications to agriculture. Pap.— Am. Soc. Agric. Eng. NA74-111, 1–6.

Stout, B. A., Meyers, C. A., Hurand, A., and Faidley, L. W. (1979). Energy for World Agriculture. FAO Agriculture Series No. 7, Food and Agriculture Organization of the United Nations, Rome, Italy.

Taiganides, E. P. (1977). "Animal Wastes." Applied Sciences Publ., Ltd., London.

United Nations (1978). "Statistical Yearbook." UN, New York.

United States Department of Agriculture (1976). "Energy and U.S. Agriculture: 1974 Data Base, Vol. 1." Econ. Res. Serv., U.S. Dept. Agric., Washington, D.C.

United States Department of Agriculture (1977). "Energy and U.S. Agriculture: 1974 Data Base, Vol. 2." Econ. Res. Serv., U.S. Dept. Agric., Washington, D.C.

United States Department of Agriculture (1981). "Agricultural Statistics 1981." U.S. Dept. Agric. U.S. Govt. Printing Office, Washington, D.C.

Waelti, H. (1974). Facts and figures on energy. *Energy/Land Conf.*, 1974 pp. 1–16.

Wilson, C. L. (1977). "Energy: Global Prospects, 1985–2000. (Workshop on Alternative Energy Strategies)." McGraw-Hill, New York.

Chapter 4

Food for People

MARCIA H. PIMENTEL

Division of Nutritional Sciences
Colleges of Human Ecology and Agriculture and Life Sciences
Cornell University
Ithaca, New York

For many centuries humans had little control over their environment and existed in what can be characterized as a hostile world. But slowly they progressed and found ways to manage the natural environment to their advantage. Each advance, from hunting and gathering of food to producing food by modern, fossil-driven agricultural systems, has increased control and resulted in a

65

FOOD AND ENERGY RESOURCES

more dependable food supply. This stability has supported the rapid rate of growth in human population that we are now witnessing.

As indicated in Fig. 1, for most of the time humans have been on earth, population numbers did not exceed 8 million or about the present population of the city of New York (Coale, 1974). During this time the annual growth rate, although positive, was extremely slow or about 0.001% (Keyfitz, 1976). Birth rates were high but only slightly greater than high death rates. At present, the rate of growth has escalated to about 2% per year.

In the 18th century, Malthus (1959), commenting on human population growth, postulated "first that food is necessary to the existence of man. Secondly, that the passion between the sexes is necessary and will remain nearly in its present state. . . Assuming then my postulata as granted, I say, that the power of population is definitely greater than the power of the earth to produce substance for men." Although his estimate of when humans would reach the carrying capacity of their resources has been extended because of new technologies like

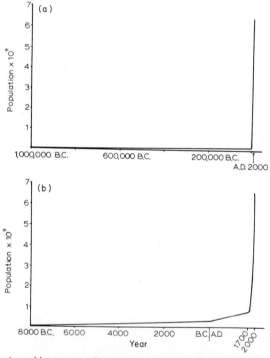

Fig. 1. (a) An overview of human population growth starting about 1 million years ago. Note the almost vertical rise in population in recent years. (b) The beginning of agriculture, about 10,000 years ago, and the initial increase in population growth. The second and most rapid rise in population started after the year 1900 when fossil energy was used for both agriculture and protecting humans from a wide array of diseases.

the discovery and use of fossil energy which he did not foresee, Malthus' prediction seems to be coming true.

All biological populations, including humans, are "imperialists" and tend to convert as much as possible of their environmental resources into themselves and their progeny (Russell, 1961). Indeed, studies of such diverse species as amoeba, fruit flies, and deer have demonstrated the tendency of animals to increase numbers to the limits of "carrying capacity" of resources unless prevented from doing so by diseases, predators, and/or other environmental forces (Allee *et al.*, 1949).

The world population now stands at an all-time high, and, further, is increasing at an unprecedented rate. As a result, world resources of arable land, water, and energy are also being used at an unprecedented rate. Because many of the stressed resources are nonrenewable, there is grave concern as to whether a dependable food supply, ample in quantity and nutritive quality, can continue to be produced to sustain the people of the earth.

I. SECURING FOOD

A. Hunter–Gatherers

For 99% of the time that humans have been on earth, they were hunter–gatherers, living like wild animals off the land (Deevey, 1960). Existence was precarious and survival was influenced by the ability to find food over large areas of land and by the many fluctuations in climate and moisture that normally occur. Many of the factors that influenced the abundance of a food supply were beyond human control. Hunter–gatherer adults had to supply their own needs as well as those of the young children and elderly adults. Thus, obtaining food, an essential resource for survival of the family group, was a vital activity and one that required a major investment of the human energy resource of primitive societies.

First consider the availability of food to the hunter–gatherer who must search the countryside for his food. Even under the most favorable environmental conditions, relatively little food suitable for human consumption exists per hectare of land. For example, in the temperate region of North America the total annual production of plant biomass (dry) averages about 2400 kg/ha (Pimentel and Pimentel, 1979). Most of this biomass is unsuitable for human food. The edible portion, consisting of grains, seeds and nuts, roots, fruits, and leaves comprises only about 0.2% of the total biomass, under the most optimal growing conditions.

Under favorable environmental conditions, 2400 kg of plant biomass can support an animal and microorganism biomass of about 200 kg/ha/year. Of this, the largest amount consists of microorganisms, while much smaller percentages are represented by birds, mammals, insects, and earthworms (Fig. 2). In summary, only a relatively small amount of the plant and animal biomass is suitable for human food.

Let us assume the hunter–gatherer needs 2500 kcal/day (912,500 kcal/year) to meet energy needs. If 1.2 kg of animal biomass and 6.3 kg of plant material is available as food per hectare, then the hunter–gatherer must search for and harvest food from about 40 ha (or 100 acres) to meet energy needs.

Based on this premise, the animal biomass will contribute about 136 kcal/day and 26 g protein, and the plant biomass will contribute about 2100 kcal and 34 g protein. Note that the contributions of fats, approximately 260 kcal from 28 g fat, were omitted as a part of the plant and animal biomass. Except for limited amounts of animal flesh and such plant foods as nuts and seeds, the fat content of the hunter–gatherer diet is estimated to be about 10% of total calories or substantially less than the 40% that fat contributes to the average U.S. diet (U.S. Senate, 1977).

Therefore a hunter–gatherer family of five, living in a favorable habitat, would need to have access to about 200 ha from which to gather their yearly food supply. These estimates are more optimistic than those suggested by Clark and Haswell (1970), who calculated that at least 150 ha of favorable habitat are needed per person, or 750 ha for a family of five. Further, they point out that for land located in marginal growing regions such as cold northwestern Canada, about 14,000 ha per person are needed to provide 2500 kcal/day per person.

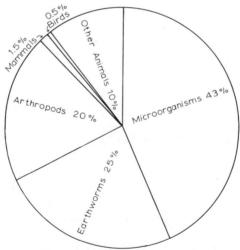

Fig. 2. The proportion of total biomass of 200 kg (dry) present in 1 ha that is made up of animals and microorganisms. From Pimentel and Pimentel (1979).

Based on the availability of 150 ha per person, the United States could support a theoretical maximum of 20 million people as hunter–gatherers. However, considering that at least half of the U.S. land area has a low productivity, a more realistic estimate is that the United States could support a maximum population of 10 million. On a world basis and using this ideal estimate, the maximum population that could be supported is about 100 million or one-fiftieth of the current world population.

In these discussions, average yields per hectare throughout the season were considered. Yet in temperate regions, many foods such as vegetables, fruits, and nuts are abundant in the fall or spring, depending on the hemisphere, but scarce at other times. Late winter months in the temperate regions were extremely difficult for hunter–gatherers even if they stored nonperishable foods such as grains, nuts, and seeds. As a result, food supplies fluctuated and their instability had a devastating impact on the survival of individuals in these primitive, nomadic societies.

Indeed, the impact of food shortages and death due to disease, predators, and exposure to extremes of heat or cold contributed to the short life span of 20–30 years and the slow annual population growth rate of about 0.001% (Keyfitz, 1976). The high mortality rate of the hunter–gatherer societies in a harsh environment helped keep the growth rate slow even though the birthrate was relatively high.

B. Early Agriculture

No doubt early agriculture evolved slowly from the nomadic societies of gatherers. When gatherers brought grains, fruits, and vegetables back to camp for consumption, seeds were dropped or discarded on the soil in the campsite and, subsequently, some grew. On return to the same campsite later, one can imagine the concentration of seed grains, vegetables, or fruits being discovered there. This probably encouraged some of the more venturesome people to associate seeds with plants and to begin to plant seeds in lands adjacent to the camp.

The relative ease of harvesting such crops compared to random gathering certainly would give encouragement for more planting. The trend to produce food is thought to have been slow at first, with only a small percentage of the food supplied from cultivated areas. But gradually by trial, error, and observation, the idea of culturing plants flourished.

One important step in speeding seed germination and growth was the deliberate removal of the existing natural vegetation, including shrubs and trees, which interfere and compete with crop growth. Burning was the easiest and most common way to clear land and not only helped destroy weeds but also added some nutrients to the soil.

Undoubtedly, little formal care was given to early plantings. After a few months or even a year, the early farmers might return to harvest their crop or what was left of it. As occurs today, insects, pathogens, birds, and mammals shared the harvest, and weed competition reduced yields.

Expanded crop plantings produced more of the food supply. With time, as societies became less nomadic because ample food supply was nearby, men and women no longer had to travel great distances to search for food. Then, too, living close to the plantings enabled groups to claim ownership and protect the plantings from birds, mammals, and other environmental pests as well as from other humans. With a more settled existence, animals could be captured and perhaps domesticated or at least herded and kept close by for food.

Field plots of the early agriculturalists were planted and cropped for 2 or 3 years, then abandoned because production declined as nutrients in the soil gradually became depleted and other problems such as pest outbreaks developed.

Interestingly, this cut/burn or swidden type of agriculture is practiced today in many parts of the world (Ruthenberg, 1971). Swidden agriculture requires that the land lie fallow for 10–20 years before being recleared and planted again. During the long fallow period, the soil gradually accumulates the nutrients needed for successful crop production.

Until recently, the generally held theory was that farming began about 10,000 years ago, probably in southwestern Asia. Recent excavations in Egypt's Western Desert along the Nile challenge these long-accepted assumptions about the origin of agriculture (Wendorf et al., 1982). Evidence gathered there indicates that 17,000–18,500 years ago the people not only raised crops of wheat, barley, lentils, chick peas, capers, and dates but also hunted and fished. Nonetheless, Wendorf concludes that these activities do not represent the origin of agriculture but rather that this farming was "one more resource in a broad-based way of life," which continued to include hunting, fishing, and gathering.

No doubt future archeological research will clarify the origins of agriculture. However, it is logical to assume that early agriculture helped stabilize food supplies and was an important factor in the growth of the human population (Fig. 1).

C. Fossil-Energy Agriculture

From the haphazard survival of nomads, agriculture changed to a more planned yet primitive crop culture. Gradually, tools and animal power were used to augment or replace man power. Viewed in retrospect, the development of agricultural technology is a continuum with few distinct markers to denote a new era.

The exception to this seems to be the use of abundant, inexpensive fossil fuels that occurred in the mid-1800s. As a result, fossil energy was used to manufacture fertilizers so that farmers no longer had to practice swidden agriculture and wait years for cropland to become fertile again. Fossil energy was used to make pesticides and to replace man and animal-powered machinery, as well as to pump irrigation water. In this same time span, plant breeders developed high-yielding crop varieties. Crop yields increased dramatically, especially in the industrial, highly mechanized countries of eastern Europe, Canada, and the United States.

All in all, ample food supplies are being produced in those areas of the world where, at present, fossil fuel supplies are adequate.

II. NUTRIENTS AND FOOD

The food crops produced by man contain an array of nutrients and these foods are the conveyors of nutrients to individuals. Major nutrients are classified as carbohydrates, fats, amino acids that are the building blocks of proteins, plus vitamins and minerals. These nutrients are needed, in varying amounts, by man for metabolism, growth, reproduction, and other vital activities of life. Therefore, the nutritional adequacy of a food supply is critical for the survival of man.

Although much is known about the biology, chemistry, absorption, and metabolism of specific essential nutrients, information about why individuals eat or do not eat certain foods is not so precise. Individuals make dietary choices from a variety of foods and are influenced by many factors in making choices. Sometimes availability of the food in the marketplace and the cost in dollars and cents constrain selection. For most population groups, customs, religion, and social practices also play an important role. For the individual, personal likes and dislikes and palatability characteristics of the particular foods, as well as social and emotional feelings associated with the food determine how food is selected. Food selections ultimately determine the nutritional status of the individual (Sanjur, 1982).

A. Nutrient Allowances and Standards

Various guides have been compiled by nutritionists to serve as standards for evaluating how well food intakes or food supplies meet nutritional needs of individuals. The guide established by the Food and Agricultural Organization (FAO) recommends a daily energy intake of 3000 kcal for a 65-kg moderately active male and 2200 kcal for a 55-kg moderately active female. The recommended protein intake, consisting of animal and plant materials, is 41/day per person (Food and Agriculture Organization, 1973a).

In the United States, the National Research Council established the Recommended Dietary Allowances (RDA), now in its ninth revised edition. The RDAs are "the levels of intake of essential nutrients considered on the basis of available scientific knowledge, to be adequate to meet the known nutritional needs of practically all healthy persons" (National Academy of Sciences, 1980). In the RDA, the recommended energy intake is specific for age, weight, height, and for light physical activity. Thus, for males 23–50 years of age, who weigh 70 kg and are 70 in. tall, the recommended intake is 2700 kcal and 56 g protein; for females in the same age bracket, but who weigh 55 kg and are 64 in. tall, the intake is 2000 kcal and 44 g protein/day (National Academy of Sciences, 1980). The RDA protein recommendations are corrected for the efficiency of protein utilization. Based on information collected in the Nationwide Food Consumption Survey (NFCS) of 1977–1978 24% of the 37,785 Americans sampled had energy intakes that met or exceeded their RDA while 88% had protein intakes that met or exceeded their RDA (Pao and Mickle, 1981).

B. Nutrient Intakes

Both the FAO guide and the RDA also list recommended intakes of essential minerals and vitamins. For this discussion, however, the focus will be on energy and protein intake.

In comparing human diets, distinct differences are immediately apparent between those typical of industrialized nations and those of developing nations. For example in the United States, about 3500 kcal and 103 gm of protein are consumed per person per day (U.S. Bureau of Census, 1981). In contrast, the majority of the world population consumes about 2100 kcal and 56 g protein per person per day (Roberts, 1976).

Further differences emerge when the type of protein consumed is analyzed. In the United States, over two-thirds of the protein is of animal origin (U.S. Department of Agriculture, 1981a). Although the per capita grain use is high in the United States, only about 10% is consumed directly as food. The remainder is cycled through the livestock system to provide the beef, pork, and poultry foods that Americans prefer (Pimentel et al., 1980). However, in developing nations, 80–85% of the protein consumed is of plant origin and the remainder is of animal origin (President's Science Advisory Committee, 1967). In China, the plant protein content of the diet is even higher, averaging 98%, with animal and fish making up the remainder (Barer-Stein, 1979).

C. Vegetarian Diets

Examples of typical vegetarian diets can be found in many parts of the world, particularly in developing countries. In a survey of 12 rural villages in India, the average daily consumption per family member was beteeen 210 and 330 g of dry rice and wheat, 140 ml of milk, and 40 g of dry pulses and beans (Tandon et al., 1972). This food intake provides about 1400 kcal and 48 g of protein per day.

In Central America, where corn is the staple food, laborers commonly consume about 500 g of dry corn and 100 g of dry black beans per day, which provide about 2120 kcal and 68 g of protein daily (E. Villigran, personal communication). In this diet, corn and beans "complement" each other in essential amino acid patterns and together improve the quality of the two incomplete proteins consumed.

When these consumption patterns are compared with nutritional guidelines, the U.S. average intake of protein is excessively high while both the two predominantly vegetarian diets discussed meet the FAO protein allowance. The calorie intakes for the vegetarian diets, however, seem low, especially for physically active, male adults.

Dietary patterns of a particular country or area of the world are not static and change over time. Changes that have occurred in the American diet since 1960 illustrate this and are reflected in the data in Table I. Although data are based on *food disappearance* rather than *consumption*, an accurate view of the food *avail-*

TABLE I
Civilian per Capita Consumption of Major Food Commodities (Retail Weight)[a,b]

	1960	1979[c]
Meats (retail)	134.1	147.1
Fish (edible weight)	10.3	13.2
Eggs (pounds)	42	35.8
Chicken/turkey	34.0	61.6
Cheese	8.3	17.6
Fluid milk (pounds)	321.0	283.2
Ice cream	18.3	17.5
Total fats and oils	45.3	57.7
Fruits (fresh)	90.0	81.3
Fruits (processed)	22.6	19.4
Fruits (frozen and juice)	9.2	12.3
Vegetables (fresh)	96.0	94.2
Vegetables (canned)	45.7	55.7
Vegetables (frozen, except potatoes)	6.9	11.5
Potatoes	87.9	75.0
Sweet potatoes	6.4	5.1
Wheat flour	118.0	120.0
Rice	6.1	9.2
Edible beans (dry)	7.3	6.4

[a]Quantity in pounds, retail weight. Data on calendar year basis except for dried fruits, fresh citrus fruits, and rice, which are on a crop-year basis.
[b]Data from U.S. Department of Agriculture, 1981a.
[c]Preliminary.

able per person is given (U.S. Department of Agriculture, 1981a). Obviously, consumption on a per person basis cannot be determined from this data.

In the 20-year time span from 1960 to 1980, meat, chicken, and cheese consumption substantially increased while egg and milk consumption declined. Fat consumption, based on disappearance figures, increased over 4.5 kg per capita. Changes occurred also in consumption of fruits and vegetables, due to improved transportation, storage, and preservation. Note that legumes, excellent sources of plant protein, consistently rank low in amounts consumed, and even decreased slightly by 1980.

D. Productivity and Income

The availability of food is influenced only in part by the productivity of the agricultural system in a country. Supply and demand, governmental policy, developments in processing that enable perishable foods to be preserved, improvements in distribution of foods from rural areas to urban centers, plus greater nutritional knowledge all have an impact. In countries where major food crops are exported, additional problems may develop in providing adequate food supplies for home consumption.

Also related to the structure of the diet is income, as illustrated by the analysis of Perisse *et al.* (1969). Their study included 85 countries in Europe, the Americas, Africa, Asia, and Oceania. In contrast to the increase in carbohydrate consumption as income declined, protein consumption, especially animal protein, was positively correlated with increases in income. Likewise, as income increased fat consumption increased, especially consumption of separated fats like oils, butter, and shortenings and edible animal fats associated with increased consumption of meat, milk, and fish.

III. MALNUTRITION

Malnutrition can be defined as faulty or inadequate nutrition, as undernutrition or overnutrition, or an imbalance of nutrients. Thus malnutrition occurs both where food is plentiful and where it is scarce. An example is the increase in obesity that has occurred in the United States where, for most poeple, the food supply is abundant. The obesity problem, in large measure, is the result of not balancing energy intake with decreasing energy requirements for an increasingly sedentary population (U.S. Senate, 1977).

Obesity as well as arteriosclerosis, hypertension, and certain cancers are prevalent here and have been associated with diets high in calories, high in fats, especially saturated fats, and high in cholesterol. Nutritionists seem to agree that diet is a major factor in the incidence of these chronic diseases but that many other factors, such as genetic predisposition, stress, and smoking also influence their incidence in the population.

A. Assessment of Nutritional Status

The full dimensions of the present world food situation are difficult to assess on an individual level because accurate data are scarce and because assessing nutritional status is not always complete or standardized in the scientific studies available. Ideally, assessment should include data on *clinical* or *visual* physical signs of a disease, e.g., *biochemical* analyses of tissue, blood, or urine (e.g., hemoglobin levels); *anthropometric measurements*, e.g., relationship of height and weight and skinfold thickness; and an evaluation of the *dietary intake*, preferably over a long period of time.

Table II summarizes the type of data needed for the assessment of nutritional status as set forth by the World Health Organization (1963). Even to the uninitiated, it is obvious that such complete assessments take competent scientists much time in the field and in the laboratory.

B. Major Nutritional Problems

On a worldwide basis, scarcity of calories and other essential nutrients is a major nutritional problem. Some reports indicate there is "famine in various developing nations, and death rates are reported rising in at least 12 and perhaps 20 nations, largely in Central Africa and Southern Asia" (National Academy of Sciences, 1975). Many other estimates support this view and suggest that up to one-fourth of the human population, or one-half billion people, are malnourished (U.S. Department of Agriculture, 1974; Food and Agriculture Organization, 1974). In some areas of the world there is simply not enough food to sustain normal human activity. In these areas the food intake, consisting primarily of grain, may be as meager as 0.5 kg/day per person (National Academy of Sciences, 1975).

The World Food Council, meeting recently in Mexico, concluded that imbalances in food supplies are causing increased hunger and severe malnutrition (New York Times, 1982). Further, they predicted the number of malnourished would increase from the present 400 million to 600 million by the year 2000 *unless* food supplies were shared.

Perhaps the world is better fed now than in previous times, as evidenced by the average increase in life expectancy of 15 years that has occurred in the last 30 years (Poleman, 1982). But better-fed does not necessarily mean well-nourished. The increase in life span may be due as much to the improvements of environ-

TABLE II
Data Needed for the Assessment of Nutritional Status[a]

Sources of information	Nature of information obtained	Nutritional implications
1. Agricultural data Food balance sheets	Gross estimates of agricultural production Agricultural methods Soil fertility Predominance of cash crops Overproduction of staples Food imports and exports	Approximate availability of food supplies to a population
2. Socioeconomic data Information on marketing, distribution, and storage	Purchasing power Distribution and storage of foodstuffs	Unequal distribution of available foods between the socioeconomic groups in community and within family
3. Food consumption patterns Cultural anthropological data	Lack of knowledge, erroneous beliefs and prejudices, indifference	
4. Dietary surveys	Food consumption	Low, excessive, or unbalanced nutrient intake
5. Special studies on foods	Biological value of diets Presence of interfering factors (e.g., goitrogens) Effects of food processing	Special problems related to nutrient utilization
6. Vital and health statistics	Morbidity and mortality data	Extent of risk to community Identification of high-risk groups
7. Anthropometric studies	Physical development	Effect of nutrition on physical development
8. Clinical nutritional surveys	Physical signs	Deviation from health due to malnutrition
9. Biochemical studies	Levels of nutrients, metabolites, and other components of body tissues and fluids	Nutrient supplies in body Impairment of biochemical function
10. Additional medical information	Prevalent disease patterns including infections and infestations	Interrelationships of state of nutrition and disease

[a]From World Health Organization, 1963, with permission.

mental sanitation and the development of drugs and other chemicals, like pesticides, that have improved health in many ways as it is to a more adequate food supply.

The extent of protein-energy malnutrition (PEM) characterized by marasmus and kwashiorkor among the infants in developing nations (Reddy, 1981) cannot be overlooked. Protein-energy malnutrition occurs when there is an inadequate energy intake. In such cases, the effectiveness of an apparently adequate protein intake decreases because protein is metabolized to make up the shortfall in energy. In addition to PEM, vitamin A deficiency (leading to blindness), iodine-deficiency goiter, and iron deficiency (causing anemia) are major nutritionally based problems throughout the world (Wilson et al., 1979). Although current life spans have increased over those of previous decades, it is generally accepted that malnutrition decreases the body's ability to resist disease (Wilson et al., 1979; Chandra, 1981) and that it also decreases the capacity to work (Keys et al., 1950). Perhaps the noted differences in the assessment of the extent of malnutrition rest on the quality of health and life used as yardsticks.

Caliendo (1979), reviewing the many worldwide assessments of malnutrition that have been made, concludes that although there is a lack of detailed information about the precise assessment of the extent of malnutrition, "it is clear that problems of nutritional deprivation touch the lives of a large proportion of the world's population."

Because such great differences exist between the amount and kinds of foods consumed in the industrialized and developing nations, one cannot help but be concerned whether future food needs can be met.

IV. CURRENT WORLD FOOD PRODUCTION

In the 1970s we have witnessed a plateauing and, in some instances, a decline in the worldwide production levels of grains and cereals and beef, as well as fishery products. Until then, yearly production levels showed substantial increases and it was difficult to imagine that there might be a time when production would not always increase.

A. Grain Production

Since 1970, the rate of increase in per capita grain production slowed, reached a high in 1978, and then started a slow decline (Table III). In part, the reduction in soil quality caused by increased rates of soil erosion was responsible for the decline (Brown and Shaw, 1982). At the same time, shortages of oil and other fossil energy reserves resulted in increased prices for fertilizers, pesticides, and other fossil-based inputs commonly used in agricultural production. This has meant that many farmers, especially those with small farms, could no longer afford the fertilizer and pesticide that formerly had assured a high yield.

B. Beef Production

Beef production also peaked in the mid-1970s (Table III). Undoubtedly, increased grain prices have been a factor in the subsequent slow decline because

TABLE III
World per Capita Production of Fish, Beef, and Grain[a]

Year	Fish (kg)	Beef (kg)	Grain (kg)
1950	8.4	—	251
1955	10.5	—	264
1960	13.2	9.3	285
1961	14.0	9.6	273
1962	14.9	9.8	288
1963	14.7	10.7	282
1964	16.1	10.1	292
1965	16.0	9.9	284
1966	16.8	10.2	304
1967	17.4	10.4	303
1968	18.0	10.7	313
1969	17.4	10.7	311
1970	<u>18.5</u>	10.6	309
1971	18.3	10.4	330
1972	16.8	10.6	314
1973	16.8	10.5	332
1974	17.7	11.0	317
1975	17.2	11.3	316
1976	17.7	<u>11.6</u>	337
1977	17.3	11.5	330
1978	17.3	11.4	<u>351</u>
1979	16.9	10.9	331
1980	16.1	10.5	324
1981 (prelim.)	—	10.4	331

[a]Source: Food and Agriculture Organization, U.S. Department of Agriculture and Energy, and U.N. Demographic Division. (After Brown and Shaw, 1982). Peak years are underlined.

in the United States much of the grain produced is used for animal production. In the future there may be less grain available for animal production because more will have to be consumed directly as human food to support the increased human population. Also, animal production may be reduced as valuable pasture and rangelands deteriorate because of overgrazing by large animal populations.

C. Fish Production

Fish production has steadily declined since 1970 because of overfishing or outstripping the fish resources of the ocean (Table III). Catches are reduced despite greater energy inputs associated with larger fishing vessels and new fish-finding devices (Rochereau and Pimentel, 1978).

D. Overall Food Availability

Even though the production of these major foods has declined, ample food now is being produced in the world so that each person could have a nutritious diet. This assumes that the food could be distributed in an equitable way. The remedy for more equitable distribution of food lies in the political sector. Many inequities exist between countries like the United States, which is in position to export excess grains, and countries like Argentina and Mexico, which are using their grains to produce meats for the U.S. consumer.

Nevertheless, in the future solutions will be more difficult. First, will nations that presently enjoy and expect high protein, high animal protein, and highly varied diets be willing to modify their intake so there will be more food to share with others? Second, and an equally important obstacle, is the fact that the underfed live in areas of the world where, even now, population is dense relative to the resources of land, water, and energy required to produce food. All projections of world population growth predict continued rapid population expansion in those same areas, thereby increasing the demand for food and increasing pressure on the resources needed for food production.

V. POPULATION EXPLOSION

As recently as 1650 the world population was only about 545 million (Deevey, 1960). But shortly after 1700, coinciding with the industrial revolution and the availability of cheap fossil fuels, the explosive increase in world population numbers started (Fig. 3). A similar pattern occurred in the United States, where the population was about 4 million in 1790 and expanded to 232 million by 1982 (Population Reference Bureau, 1982).

Certainly, the ability of man to secure a relatively abundant, stable, and nutritious food supply, thanks to improved agricultural and technological ideas, contributed to the rapid increase. But an equally important factor has been the improvement of disease control, which decreased the usual high death rate that previously had balanced high birth rates.

Because fossil fuels are the basis of fertilizers and pesticides (1 gallon of oil produces 1 lb of DDT), their availability was instrumental in decreasing disease and death. An example is the dramatic reduction in death rates that occurred in Mauritius following the eradication by DDT of malaria-carrying mosquitoes (Fig. 4). Death rates fell from 27 to 15 per 1000 over a period of 5 years. Because fertility (birth) rates did not decrease, an explosive increase in population resulted. Recent history documents similar changes in population growth in such countries as Guatemala and Mexico where medical technology and availability

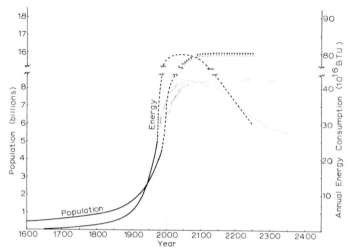

Fig. 3. Estimated world population numbers (_____) from 1600 to 1975 and projected numbers (- - - - -) (?????) to the year 2250. Estimated fossil fuel consumption (_____) from 1650 to 1975 and projected (- - - - -) to the year 2250. (Data from Environmental Fund, 1979; Linden, 1980.)

of medical supplies have significantly reduced death rates (Corsa and Oakley, 1971).

In the United States, based on the census bureau's median projection and assuming an annual immigration rate of 400,000 and a fertility rate of 2.1, estimates are that the population will expand from 230 million to 260 million in 20 years. By the year 2030, the U.S. population is expected to reach 300 million (Population Reference Bureau, 1982). Several population levels have been pro-

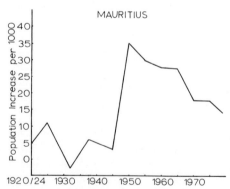

Fig. 4. Population growth rate on Mauritius from 1920 to 1980. Note from 1920 to 1945 the growth rate was about 5 per 1000 whereas after malaria control in 1945 the growth rate exploded to about 35 per 1000 and has since very slowly declined. (Data from Political and Economic Planning, 1955; United Nations, 1957–1971.) After 25 years, the rate of increase is still over three times the 1920–1945 level.

jected, depending both on fertility rate and net immigration rates (Fig. 5). Depending on these variables, U.S. population could begin to level off at about 260 million in the year 2000 or could increase to 300 million by 2000 and continue to escalate.

Added to the birth rate is the impact that immigration is now having and probably will continue to have in countries like the United States. At present the United States accepts more immigrants than any other country (Population Reference Bureau, 1982). Although the annual net immigration rate may stabilize at current levels, this cannot be assured. Indeed because nations are no longer isolated from one another, the pressure to accept refugees from areas of unrest may be even greater in the future than in the past decades.

A. Future Worldwide Trends

The world population now stands at almost 4.5 billion and is projected to expand to 6.19 billion in less than 20 years, provided the present rate of increase of 2.0% declines (United Nations, 1979).

But what will happen in countries like China, which now has a population of 1,008 billion and manages to support 22% of the world population on only 7% of the arable land (Wren, 1982)? If 70% of the married couples have only one child, the population is expected to reach 1.2 billion by the year 2000 (Wren, 1982). With more than half the Chinese population below the age of 21, one must be skeptical that the aims of the State Family Planning Commission can be

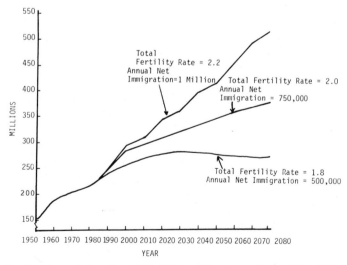

Fig. 5. U.S. population size, 1950–1980, and three scenarios for 1990–2080.

met. Similar problems of population growth exist in India, Indonesia, and in many South American and African countries.

B. Effects of Birth Rate

The actual birth rate that will occur in the United States and throughout the world in future decades will be a major factor in determining population growth. So far in history it has been easier to reduce death rates than to reduce birth rates. Birth rates are influenced not only by health and food supply but also by a complexity of social customs, religious beliefs, and personal desires. Because human emotions are so involved in decisions about reproduction, birth rates are difficult to modify.

VI. CONSTRAINTS ON AGRICULTURAL PRODUCTION

In simplest terms, more people will need food than ever before. Balanced against these human needs is the capacity of the earth to sustain a high population pressure. To gain some insight about the potential carrying capacity of the earth, estimates based on present knowledge were made of the constraints land, water, and fossil energy resources could impose on agricultural production.

A. Land Resources

Is there sufficient arable land for food production to feed a world population of 4.5 billion with a U.S. high-protein-calorie diet produced with U.S. agricultural technology? At present in the United States about 160 million ha are planted in crops (U.S. Department of Agriculture, 1981b). With about 230 million people in the United States, this averages about 0.69 ha planted in crops per capita. But because about 25% of U.S. crop yield is exported, the estimated arable land per person is reduced to about 0.52 ha (U.S. Department of Agriculture, 1981b; Pimentel et al., 1975).

World arable land resources are approximately 1.5 billion ha (Food and Agriculture Organization, 1973b), and with a world population of 4.5 billion, the per capita land available is only 0.33 ha. Therefore, in the world today, arable land supplies are not sufficient to feed the current world population a diet similar to that presently consumed in the United States, even assuming that the energy resources and other technology were also available.

Certainly not all humans desire a typical U.S. diet, nor is it nutritionally so perfect that we advocate its export. Nevertheless, this example highlights again the land-intensive nature of our agricultural system.

B. Energy Resources

In the previous analysis, resources of fossil energy were assumed to be unlimited. That is, only arable land was limited but fertilizers, fuels, and pesticides could be used to enhance the yields. Unfortunately, future projections must be based on a more limited and a higher costing fossil energy supply. The following illustrates this energy constraint. Seventeen percent of the total per capita energy used each year in the United States is expended for food (Pimentel, 1980). This means that about 1900 liters of gasoline equivalents will be used for food production, processing, distribution, and preparation per capita per year.

When this example is expanded to include the world population of 4.5 billion, the equivalent of 8550 billion liters of gasoline equivalents would be expended to feed them the high-protein-calorie diet of the United States for 1 year.

Based on this rate of use, how long would it take to deplete the known world petroleum reserves of 113,700 billion liters (Linden, 1980)? Assuming that 76% of the raw petroleum can be converted into fuel (Jiler, 1972), this would provide a usable reserve equal to 86,412 billion liters gasoline equivalency. Therefore, if petroleum were the only source of energy for food production, and if all petroleum reserves were used only to feed the current world population, the reserve would last less than 10 years.

These estimates indicate that the present world population already has exceeded the capacity of arable land and energy resources to provide a U.S. diet, produced with U.S. technology. Note that these estimates were based on known arable land and known petroleum resources. If *potential* arable land and *potential* petroleum reserves are included, the projection improves. Also, the current world population figures were used in this analysis. Estimates based on various combinations of population size, dietary standards, and production technology are possible and can be expected to give slightly different projections. This example, however, suffices to focus on two of the major factors, land and fossil fuel, that will limit food production in the future.

C. Forest Land

Land, in addition to being used for food production, also is needed for wood production. Forest products provide lumber for shelter, pulp for paper, and biomass for energy. Although not a major fuel source in the United States, wood is the primary one in developing nations.

Forest areas are used for recreation and are natural habitats for wildlife. Once deforested, these activities are no longer possible. Further, deforestation exposes soil to wind and water erosion, which depletes soil nutrients and pollutes streams with silt, eventually causing flooding.

Worldwide the rate of deforestation is increasing. Each year a forested area the size of Indiana (9.4 million ha) is cleared for farms and urban expansion (Webb and Jacobsen, 1982). As expanding populations need more food, forest land will be cleared for farms and pastureland. On the other hand, more forest products also will be needed.

Urban growth, with its associated increase in transportation, will continue to impinge on agricultural land. This causes a significant change as was demonstrated in the United States where, in a mere 30-year period, an area of fertile cropland the size of Nebraska (20.0 million ha) was "blacked-topped over" to make room for expanding urbanization and highways (Pimentel et al., 1976).

More people will generate needs for additional housing, factories, roads, and the loss of land will be accelerated. As in the past, much of the land used for development will be arable land that is needed for increased food production. Inevitably, land use will change as various sectors of society exert their pressures.

D. Water Resources

Next to sunlight, which powers photosynthesis, water vies with fertile land as the most vital resource for agricultural production (Pimentel et al., 1982). In the United States at present, to sustain the high standard of living, 7200 liters of water per capita are withdrawn daily from rivers, lakes, and underground aquifers (U.S. Water Resources Council, 1979). Some of the water that is withdrawn is consumed directly by individuals and industry, but most, about 83%, is used in agriculture (Pimentel et al., 1982).

A major share of that used for U.S. agriculture is for irrigation, especially in the western agricultural region. For example, to produce 1 kg of the following food and fiber products under irrigation requires: 1400 liters for corn; 1910 liters for sugar (beets); 4650 liters for rice; and 17,100 liters for cotton (Ritschard and Tsao, 1978).

With regard to land resources, suggestions have been made that the world's potential arable land might be doubled with irrigation and other significant alterations of the ecosystem (Kellogg, 1967). Any answer to this suggestion is complicated by the future availability of both water and energy. Only about 12% of the world's cultivated land is now irrigated (Food and Agriculture Organization, 1970). Unfortunately, irrigation and other major environmental manipulations require the expenditure of enormous amounts of energy. For example, about 6 million kcal of fossil energy are required to produce 1 ha of corn under rainfed conditions in the United States, while about 18 million kcal are necessary to produce irrigated corn (Pimentel and Burgess, 1980). Thus, irrigated corn production is three times as energy intensive as rainfed.

In recent decades the agricultural system of the United States has become increasingly water intensive and in some areas high crop yields are directly dependent on irrigation practices. Water shortages are fast becoming a major resource problem in this country (Pimentel et al., 1982). Overdraw problems in regions over the Ogallala Aquifer in the Great Plains, water deficits along the Colorado River, and water shortages in the San Joaquin Valley are symptomatic of the pressure for irrigation water. A study of 32 counties in the Texas Panhandle, where the Ogallala Aquifer is unusually shallow, estimated that by 1995 the combination of fuel increases and water depletion will eliminate irrigation and force a return to dryland farming (Brown, 1981). Indeed, the use of groundwater in parts of the West now exceeds the limits of natural water recharge and recycling. In adjoining states, water overdraft exceeded replenishment by about 25% while in the Texas–Gulf area, overdraft is as high as 77% (U.S. Water Resources Council, 1979). This signals serious problems for all who need water for agricultural production.

The problem of water supply and allocation is by no means limited to the United States. As many as 80 other countries, which account for nearly 40% of the world population, are now seriously beset by droughts (Kovda et al., 1978). Although at present the amount of water withdrawn per capita on a global basis is less than one-third of the amount withdrawn in the United States per capita, the growth in the world population can be expected to double water needs by the year 2000 (Council on Environmental Quality, 1980). At that time, world agricultural production will need an estimated 64% of all the water withdrawn from aquatic systems.

The conflicting needs for available water among agriculture, urban population growth, industry, and fossil-energy mining portends major changes in water use throughout the world. Among the four competing groups, evidence suggests that the proportion of water allotted to agriculture will decline because the economic yields from agriculture are far less than yields from industry and mining, If so, the potential shift in water use could seriously curtail agricultural productivity.

VII. FOOD NEEDS OF THE FUTURE

Overlook the major impact that dwindling supplies of land, water, and energy have on agricultural production and consider how much more food will have to be produced to meet the food needs of the ever-expanding human population. Food production in all countries, but especially in the developing nations, must increase at a greater rate than ever before. Especially targeted for major increases are the following eight food sources: rice, wheat, corn, sugar, cattle, sorghum, millet, and cassava (National Academy of Sciences, 1977). Currently these foods provide about 70–90% of the calories and 66–90% of the protein consumed in the developing nations, with grains providing as much as 70% of the total calories.

Recently the National Research Council (National Academy of Sciences, 1977) recommended that developing countries increase food production by 3–4% per year until the year 2000. Is this a realistic expectation when the annual increase in food production has been only 2.5% in the last 15 years (National Academy of Sciences, 1977)?

For the United States, USDA projects that domestic needs for food, feed, and fiber will increase 52% between the years 1977 and 2000 (Webb and Jacobsen, 1982). Also projected is a 52% rise in export of grains. A basic question to be answered is whether U.S. farmers can grow the quantities and kinds of foods that Americans prefer, while providing the surplus needed for the future exports.

Concerning the U.S. food exports, "the mid-range projection" of the National Agricultural Lands Study estimated that "the volume of export demand would nearly triple over the next two decades" (Doyle, 1982). More agricultural land will be required to satisfy the export need plus the nation's domestic food needs. The overall impact of increasing food exports will influence the kind of agriculture that flourishes in the United States, as well as the use of scarce agricultural land and other vital natural resources. International repercussions could result if, in a poor season, the United States could not meet the demands of importer nations (Doyle, 1982).

In more general terms, D. Bauman (personal communication, 1982) predicts that "an amount of food equal to all the food produced so far in the history of mankind will have to be produced in the next 40 years" to fulfill human food needs.

Even if individual dietary patterns are modified to include more cereals, grains, and legumes, thus making more plant foods available for direct human consumption, food production must be greatly increased. In summary, the message is clear that more food, much more food, will have to be grown to sustain the human population of the future.

VIII. SOLUTIONS?

A. Conservation

In addition to increasing food production, conservation of resources is a helpful strategy. Certainly, people around the world could and should reduce consumption of fuels, conserve land and water, reduce food storage losses, and perhaps eat a diet based more on plant than animal proteins. Some people already are making a conscious effort to do this. But conservation, although useful, will not be enough to relieve the stress on the resources of earth's natural system unless population growth is drastically slowed.

B. Technological Advances

Recent decades have witnessed many exciting and productive technological advances that have increased food supplies. For example, the advances in plant genetics focused on some major crops, and the formulation and use of agricultural chemicals, pesticides, and fertilizers have helped increase yields of food and fiber crops without expanding land use. Improved processing of foods has enabled the food supply to be safely extended beyond harvest time and the growing network of transportation has moved more food from production sites to far distant markets. In the industrialized nations, this has meant a more abundant, more nutritious, and safer food supply. People living in developing nations, however, have not been as fortunate, even though successful plant breeding products like IRRI rice have benefited millions in the far east.

Speaking in particular of the needs of the malnourished, Berg (1981) notes that past strategies that have emphasized growing more food have not been as successful as anticipated. He cautions that increased production must be accompanied by improvement in dietary patterns, which as mentioned are influenced by the distribution of income.

New technologies undoubtedly will help conserve resources and facilitate increased food production. Sufficient, reliable energy resources will be developed to take the place of the fossil fuels now being so rapidly depleted. Energy from the sun, from fission, and from the wind will become more viable resources of the future than they are at present. But relying solely on technology is depending on the unknown. These developments may not materialize as rapidly as needed to meet future foods needs.

C. Population

Thus far only factors affecting food production have been considered, but production is only one side of the food equation. The other is the rate of consumption, which is determined by the size of the human population. Ultimately, the size of the world population will determine the need for food. When human numbers exceed the capacity of the world to sustain them, then a rapid deterioration of human existence will follow. As with all forms of life, ultimately nature will control human numbers.

Problems with *increasing food production* substantially over present levels and those associated with *decreasing population growth* must be faced now. Both parts of the food equation must be brought into a balance if future generations are to have an adequate food supply and live in a world that supports a reasonably acceptable standard of living.

REFERENCES

Allee, W. C., Emerson, A. E., Park, O., Park, T., and Schmidt, K. P. (1949). "Principles of Animal Ecology." Saunders, Philadelphia, Pennsylvania.

Barer-Stein, T. (1979). "You Eat What You Are: A Study of Ethnic Food Traditions." McClelland and Stewart, Toronto.

Berg, A. (1981). "Malnourished People. A Policy View." Poverty and Basic Needs Series, World Bank, Washington, D.C.

Brown, L. R. (1981). World population growth, soil erosion, and food security. Science 214, 995–1002.

Brown, L. and Shaw, P. (1982). Six steps to a sustainable society. Worldwatch Paper No. 48. Worldwatch Institute, Washington, D.C.

Caliendo, M. A. (1979). "Nutrition and the World Food Crisis." Macmillan, New York.

Chandra, R. K. (1981). Marginal malnutrition and immunocompetence. In "Nutrition in Health and Disease and International Development" (A. E. Harper and G. K. Davis, eds.), pp. 261–265. Alan R. Liss, New York.

Clark, C., and Haswell, M. (1970). "The Economics of Subsistence Agriculture." Macmillan, London.

Coale, A. J. (1974). The history of the human population. Sci. Am. 231, 40–51.

Corsa, L., and Oakley, D. (1971). Consequences of population growth for health services in less developed countries—an initial appraisal. In "Rapid Population Growth," Vol. II. Research Papers, pp. 368–402. National Academy of Sciences, Johns Hopkins Press, Baltimore, Maryland.

Council on Environmental Quality (1980). "The Global 2000 Report to the President." Council on Environmental Quality and the Department of State, Vol. 2. U.S. Govt. Printing Office, Washington, D.C.

Deevey, E. S., Jr. (1960). The human population. Sci. Am. 203, 195–204.

Doyle, J. (1982). American agriculture: force feeding the world. CNI Weekly Report XII (34), Community Nutrition Institute, Washington, D.C.

Environmental Fund. (1979). World population estimates. The Environmental Fund, Washington, D.C.

Food and Agriculture Organization. (1970). "Production Yearbook 1969." Food and Agriculture Organization of the United Nations, Rome.

Food and Agriculture Organization (1973a). "Energy and Protein Requirements; Report of a Joint FAO/WHO Ad Hoc Expert Committee." FAO Nutr. Meet. Rep. Ser., No. 52. Food and Agriculture Organization of the United Nations, Rome.

Food and Agriculture Organization. (1973b). "Production Yearbook 1972," Vol. 26. Food and Agriculture Organization of the United Nations, Rome.

Food and Agriculture Organization (1974). "Assessment of the World Food Situation." United Nations World Food Conference, November. Food and Agriculture Organization of the United Nations, Rome.

Jiler, H. (1972). "Commodity Yearbook." Commodity Research Bureau, New York.

Kellogg, C. E. (1967). World food prospects and potentials: a long-run look. In "Alternatives for Balancing World Food Production Needs" (E. O. Heady, ed.), pp. 98–111. Iowa State Univ. Press, Ames.

Keyfitz, N. (1976). World resources and the world middle class. *Sci. Am.* **235**, 28–35.

Keys, A., Brozek, J., Henschel, A., Michelson, O., and Taylor, H. L. (1950). "The Biology of Human Starvation," Vol. I. Univ. of Minnesota Press, Minneapolis.

Kovda, V. A., Rozanov, B. G., and Onishenko, S. K. (1978). On probability of droughts and secondary salinisation of world soils. *In* "Arid Land Irrigation in Developing Countries" (E. B. Worthington, ed.), pp. 237–238. Pergamon, Oxford.

Linden, H. R. (1980). Importance of natural gas in the world energy picture. *Int. Inst. Appl. Syst. Anal.* (Conf. Proc.), June 30–July 4, Laxenburg, Austria.

Malthus, T. R. (1959). "Population: The First Essay." Ann Arbor Paperbacks, Univ. of Michigan Press.

National Academy of Sciences (1975). "Population and Food: Crucial Issues." National Academy of Sciences, Washington, D.C.

National Academy of Sciences (1977). "World Food and Nutrition Study." National Academy of Sciences, Washington, D.C.

National Academy of Sciences (1980). "Recommended Dietary Allowances," 9th ed. National Research Council, National Academy of Sciences, Washington, D.C.

New York Times. (1982). Wider hunger foreseen by World Food Council. June 22, p. A–5.

Pao, E. M., and Mickle, S. J. (1981). Problem nutrients in the United States. *Food Technol.* **35**, 58–69.

Perisse, J., Sizaret, F., and Francois, P. (1969). The effect of income on the structure of the diet. *Nutr. Newslett. (FAO)* 7(3).

Pimentel, D., ed. (1980). "Handbook of Energy Utilization in Agriculture." CRC Press, Boca Raton, Florida.

Pimentel, D., and Pimentel, M. (1979). "Food, Energy and Society." Resource and Environmental Sciences Series. Arnold, London.

Pimentel, D., and Burgess, M. (1980). Energy inputs in corn production. *In* "Handbook of Energy Utilization in Agriculture" (D. Pimentel, ed.), pp. 67–84. CRC Press, Boca Raton, Florida.

Pimentel, D., Dritschilo, W., Krummel, J., and Kutzman, J. (1975). Energy and land constraints in food-protein production. *Science* **190**, 754–761.

Pimentel, D., Terhune, E. C., Dyson-Hudson, R., Rochereau, S., Samis, R., Smith, E., Denman, D., Reifscheider, D., and Shepard, M. (1976). Land degradation: effects on food and energy resources. *Science* **194**, 149–155.

Pimentel, D., Oltenacu, P. A., Nesheim, M. C., Krummel, J., Allen, M. S., and Chick, S. (1980). Grass-fed livestock potential: energy and land constraints. *Science* **207**, 843–848.

Pimentel, D., Fast, S., Chao, W. L., Stuart, E., Dintzis, J., Einbender, G., Schlappi, W., Andow, D., and Broderick, K. (1982). Water resources in food and energy production. *BioScience* **32**, 861–867.

Poleman, T. T. (1982). World hunger: extent, causes and cures. *A.E. Research 82–17*. NYS College of Agriculture and Life Sciences, Cornell University, Ithaca, New York.

Political and Economic Planning (1955). "World Population and Resources." Political and Economic Planning, London.

Population Reference Bureau. (1982). U.S. population: where we are; where we're going. *Popul. Bull.* 37(2), 47 pp.

President's Science Advisory Committee (1967). "The World Food Problem," Vols. I, II, III. Report of Panel on the World Food Supply, President's Science Advisory Committee, The White House, U.S. Govt. Printing Office, Washington, D.C.

Reddy, V. (1981). Protein energy malnutrition: an overview. *In* "Nutrition in Health and Disease and International Development" (A. E. Harper and G. K. Davis, eds.), pp. 227–235. Alan R. Liss, New York.

Ritschard, R. L., and Tsao, K. (1978). "Energy and Water Use in Irrigated Agriculture During

Drought Conditions." U. S. Department of Energy LBL-7866. Lawrence Berkeley Lab., Univ. of California Press, Berkeley.

Roberts, L. W. (1976). Improving the production and nutritional quality of food legumes. *In* "Nutrition and Agricultural Development" (N. S. Scrimshaw and M. Behar, eds.), pp. 309–317. Plenum, New York.

Rochereau, S., and Pimentel, D. (1978). Energy tradeoffs between Northeast fish production and coastal power reactors. *J. Energy* **3**, 575–589.

Russell, B. (1961). "An Outline of Philosophy." World Publishing, Cleveland.

Ruthenberg, H. (1971). "Farming Systems in the Tropics." Oxford Univ. Press (Clarendon), London and New York.

Sanjur, D. (1982). "Social and Cultural Perspectives in Nutrition." Prentice-Hall, Englewood Cliffs, New Jersey.

Tandon, B. N., Ramachandran, K., Sharma, M. P., and Vinayak, V. K. (1972). Nutritional survey in rural population of Kumaon Hill area, North India. *Am. J. Clin. Nutr.* **25**, 432–436.

United Nations (1957–1971). "Statistical Yearbooks." Statistical Office of the United Nations, Department of Economic and Social Affairs, New York.

United Nations (1979). "World Population Trends and Prospects by Country, 1950–2000. Summary Report of the 1978 Assessment." United Nations, New York.

U. S. Bureau of Census (1981). "Statistical Abstract of the United States." 102nd ed. U.S. Bureau of the Census, U.S. Dept. of Commerce, Washington, D.C.

U.S. Department of Agriculture (1974). "The World Food Situation and Prospects to 1985." Foreign Agr. Econ. Rep. No. 98, Department of Agriculture, Washington, D.C.

U.S. Department of Agriculture (1981a). National Food Research. Economic Research Service. *NFR–15*, Summer. p. 43.

U.S. Department of Agriculture (1981b). "Agricultural Statistics 1981." U.S. Govt. Printing Office, Washington, D.C.

U.S. Senate. (1977). Dietary goals for the United States. Select Committee on Nutrition and Human Needs. U.S. Govt. Printing Office, Washington, D.C.

U.S. Water Resources Council (1979). "The Nation's Water Resources. 1975–2000," Vols. 1–4. Second National Water Assessment. United States Water Resources Council. U.S. Govt. Printing Office, Washington, D.C.

Webb, M., and Jacobsen, J. (1982). U.S. carrying capacity, an introduction. Carrying Capacity, Inc., Washington, D.C.

Wendorf, F., Schied, R., and Close, A. E. (1982). An ancient harvest in the Nile. *Science* **82**, 68–73.

World Health Organization (1963). Expert Committee on Medical Assessment of Nutritional Status. *W. H. O. Tech. Rep. Ser.* No. 258.

Wilson, E. D., Fisher, K. H., and Garcia, P. A. (1979). "Principles of Nutrition." 4th ed. Wiley, New York.

Wren, C. S. (1982). China plans a new drive to limit birth rate. *N. Y. Times*, November 7, p. 8.

Chapter 5

Energy Use in Crop Systems in Northeastern China

WEN DAZHONG* AND DAVID PIMENTEL

Department of Entomology
Cornell University
Ithaca, New York

I. INTRODUCTION

Leaders of governments, scientists, and the people of the world have become concerned about energy and other environmental resources that are essential for food production. The world population is presently 4.6 billion and is projected to reach 6.5 billion by the year 2000 (Council on Environmental Quality, 1980). Obviously, the rapid growth in the human population is resulting in increased demand for food (National Academy of Sciences, 1977). Augmenting food supplies is not easy; producing food will become a greater challenge as energy and environmental resources become increasingly scarce.

The people of China account for one-fifth of the world's population. The energy and other environmental resources of this nation are being conserved to supply food and other needs of the people of China. Although effective efforts are being made to limit the growth of the population, the population is projected to grow from a current 1 billion to 1.2 billion by the year 2000 (Zao, 1982).

*Present address: Institute of Forest and Soil Science, Chinese Academy of Science, P.O. Box 417, Shenyang, China.

FOOD AND ENERGY RESOURCES

China, like many nations, is attempting to improve its use of energy and other environmental resources for agriculture. The first step before any changes in policy are considered for improving energy and environmental resource use in agriculture is to understand the current flow and use of resources in the agroeco-system of China. In this report, an assessment is made of the energy, land, and labor inputs in several major crop systems in northeastern China. Then, based on these assessments and recognizing the resource limitations of China, various technologies are assessed that might improve energy, land, and labor use in the agricultural system.

II. CROP REGION OF NORTHEASTERN CHINA

Northeastern China lies between latitudes 38° and 53°35' north and between longitudes 120° and 135° east and includes Liaoning Province, Jilin Province, and Heilongjiang Province. The total area of this region is about 990,000 km², which accounts for 10.3% of total area of China (Agricultural Almanac of China, 1980). There are the Shunghuajiang–Nenjiang Plain, the Shunghua-jiang–Liaohe Plain, and the Shanjiang Plain with gently rising and falling to-pography. The soils are thick and fertile in the midwest and the northeast region. These plains are one of the most important bases for crop production in China. Total farming land area in northeastern China is approximately 16.6 million ha, accounting for one-sixth of the total farmland area of China (Agricultural Alma-nac of China, 1980). About 8.6 million ha in the region are cultivatable waste-lands. The total population for the region is about 88 million, of which 64% live in rural areas and are involved in agriculture.

The frost-free periods range from 100 days in the northern region to 180 days in the southern region (Agricultural Almanac of China, 1980). The precipitation ranges from 300 mm in the northwest to 1000 mm in the southeast. The rainfall during June, July, and August provides about 60% of the total precipitation. The annual average temperatures range from −1° C in the north to 10° C in the south.

The major crops in the northeast region are corn, soybean, wheat, millet, and sorghum. In the north, wheat and soybean are the dominant crops, whereas corn and sorghum are the dominant crops in the south. The total cereal crop produc-tion in 1979 was 30.6 million metric tons, which was 10.7% of the total cereal crop yield in China (Agricultural Almanac of China, 1980).

Data on the energy inputs for corn, soy, wheat, millet, and sorghum systems were obtained from Dawa County of Liaoning Province, Faku County of Liaon-ing Province, and Hailuen County of Heilongjiang Province (see Fig. 1). Dawa County of Liaoning Province is in the lower reaches of the Liaohe River, on the coastal plain of the Bohai seaside. It is about 200 km south of Shenyang City, at

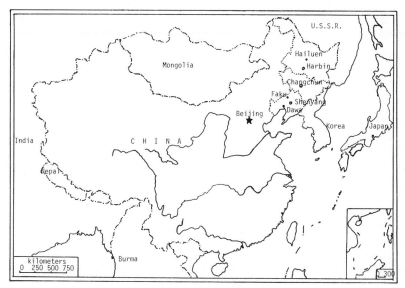

Fig. 1. Map of China.

the latitudes of 40–41° north and longitudes of 121–122° east. The annual precipitation is 637 mm and the annual average temperature is 9.6° C. The soil is seaside saline and the major crop is rice (Agricultural Almanac of China, 1980).

Faku County of Liaoning Province is in the middle reaches of the Liaohe River area with a part of Shunghuajiang–Liaohe Plain covered with alluvial soil. The county is about 100 km north of Shenyang City and is located at the latitude of 42°16′ north and the longitude of 122° east. The annual precipitation is 550–600 mm and the annual average temperature is 6.5° C. The major crops are corn, soybean, sorghum, and millet (Agricultural Almanac of China, 1980).

Hailuen County of Heilongjiang Province is located on the Shunghua-jiang–Nenjiang Plain, about 250 km north of Harbin City. It is situated at the latitude of 47°26′ north and longitude of 126°38′ east. The annual precipitation is 500–600 mm, with an annual average temperature of about 2° C. The soil is rich and black. The major crops are wheat, soybean, corn, potato, and sugar beet (Agricultural Almanac of China, 1980).

III. ENERGY INPUTS IN CROP SYSTEMS OF NORTHEASTERN CHINA

In those counties, the data on inputs for corn, rice, sorghum, wheat, soybean, millet, potato, sugar beet, and sunflower production were obtained from (1) average local agricultural production statistics and (2) individual crop production data for specific crops associated with each agricultural system in the three agricultural regions.

Energy requirements for various inputs in crop production are as follows: (1) labor = 515 kcal/hr (Pimentel and Pimentel, 1979); (2) horse power = 4576 kcal/hr. It is assumed that the average weight of a horse in northeastern China is 400 kg (Barney, 1982); (3) steel tools and other implements = 20,712 kcal/kg (Pimentel, 1976); (4) machinery = 18,000 kcal/kg (Doering, 1980); (5) diesel fuel = 11,414 kcal/liter (Cervinka, 1980); (6) electricity = 2863 kcal/kW·hr (Cervinka, 1980); (7) nitrogen fertilizer = 12,000 kcal/kg (Lockeretz, 1980); (8) phosphorus = 3000 kcal/kg (Lockeretz, 1980); (9) herbicides = 99,910 kcal/kg (Pimentel, 1980a); (10) insecticides = 86,910 kcal/kg (Pimentel, 1980a); (11) transportation = 257 kcal/kg (Pimentel, 1980b), (12) seeds = energy content of the seeds themselves.

A. Corn (Maize)

The total area of corn sown in northeastern China was 5.0 million ha in 1979, accounting for 25% of the total corn sown area of China and 35% of total cereal crop sown area of northeastern China (Agricultural Almanac of China, 1980). The total corn production in northeastern China was 17.4 million metric tons, accounting for 29% of total corn production of China and 49% of total cereal crop production of the northeastern region. Corn is the main food for people in this region, especially for those living in the central portion of the region.

Energy inputs in corn production vary, depending on production methods utilized. Before the 1950s, traditional corn production used hand and horse power, the farmer's own seeds, and organic fertilizers. Traditional corn production has now changed to include combined hand–animal–machinery production systems. In addition, synthetic chemical fertilizers and pesticides as well as hybrid seeds are utilized. Compared with traditional systems, these combined production systems have almost doubled the yields (Tables I and II).

The energy inputs of the traditional corn production system in the 1950s included the following: labor, horse power, and tools such as hoes, spades, plows, and carts (Table I). The total energy input, including labor, was 1,918,300 kcal/ha. The only fossil energy inputs were the tools and horse-drawn implements. The tools accounted for only 1.3% of the total energy input. All the other inputs were renewable bioenergy that came from the agroecosystem itself. The output/input ratio was 2.44, but the output/fossil energy input ratio was 182.3:1.

In comparison, Mexican corn production using hand labor and oxen power required less energy than the traditional system in Hailuen County but also had a

TABLE I
Energy Inputs per Hectare for Corn Production in Hailuen County, Heilongjiang Province, China (Annual Average, 1952–1954)

Item	Quantity/ha	kcal/ha
Inputs		
Labor	841.85 hr	433,553
Horses	301.75 hr	1,380,808
Tools and animal draft equipment	1.24 kg	25,683
Seeds	22.50 kg	78,300
Total		1,918,344
Outputs		
Corn yield	1345.65 kg	4,682,862
kcal output/kcal input	2.44	

lower output than that in Hailuen County (Table I and Chapter 1, Table III). The output/input ratio in Mexico was 4.34, or better than the 2.44 ratio in the more intensive production system in Hailuen.

Energy inputs in corn production in Hailuen County have increased significantly since the 1950s (Tables I and II). By 1980 the energy inputs for labor and horse power had decreased to 83% and 70%, respectively, of those of the traditional system of the 1950s. However, fossil energy inputs for tools, machinery, oil, fertilizers, and pesticides increased to about 44 times those of the 1950s (from

TABLE II
Energy Inputs per Hectare for Corn Production in Hailuen County, Heilongjiang Province, China (1980)

Item	Quantity/ha	kcal/ha
Inputs		
Labor	701.64 hr	361,345
Horses	214.00 hr	979,264
Tools and horse draft equipment	3.47 kg	71,871
Machinery	2.71 kg	48,780
Diesel	29.46 liter	336,256
Nitrogen	44.85 kg	538,200
Phosphorus	3.23 kg	9,690
Insecticide	1.50 kg	130,365
Seeds	30.00 kg	104,400
Transportation	31.22 kg	8,024
Total		2,588,195
Outputs		
Corn yield	2700.00 kg	9,396,000
kcal output/kcal input	3.63	

TABLE III

Energy Inputs per Hectare for Corn Production in Faku County, Liaoning Province, China
(Average, 1980 and 1981)

Item	Quantity/ha	kcal/ha
Inputs		
Labor	1252.40 hr	644,986
Horses	443.60 hr	2,029,914
Tools and animal draft implements	3.22 kg	66,693
Machinery	3.99 kg	71,820
Diesel	38.66 liter	441,265
Electricity	13.37 kW·hr	38,305
Nitrogen	146.91 kg	1,762,920
Phosphorus	80.28 kg	240,840
Insecticides	1.50 kg	130,365
Seeds	37.50 kg	130,500
Transportation	40.07 kg	10,298
Total		5,567,906
Outputs		
Corn yield	5013.75 kg	17,447,850
Protein yield	446.22 kg	
kcal output/kcal input	3.13	

25,683 kcal/ha to 1,143,186 kcal/ha) (Tables I and II). Note, however, that corn yield was doubled from 1346 kg/ha to 2700 kg/ha. The output/input ratio for 1980 was 3.63. The increased yield was probably due to the use of additional energy inputs, especially of synthetic chemical fertilizers, as well as hybrid seeds. Note that the output/fossil energy input ratio was reduced from 182.8 in the 1950s to 8.2 (Tables I and II).

Corn production in Faku County is more intensive than that in Hailuen County (Tables II and III). In Faku County, the labor input is nearly twice that of Hailuen County; however, the corn yield in Faku County is also nearly twice that of Hailuen. The output/input ratio is 3.13 and the output/fossil energy input ratio is 6.3. The amounts of total energy input and output are similar to those for corn in southeastern Pennsylvania (Table IV), but the labor input in Faku County is nearly 100 times greater than the labor input in southeastern Pennsylvania. Nitrogen and phosphorus fertilizer inputs in Faku County are also larger. However, the fossil energy input is only 60% of that in southeastern Pennsylvania. The output/fossil energy inputs ratio in Faku County is 6.32, compared to 3.85 in southeastern Pennsylvania.

B. Rice

In 1979 the total area sown in rice in northeastern China was 0.84 million ha (Agricultural Almanac of China, 1980). The total rice yield was 3.86 million metric tons, which accounted for 2.7% of the total Chinese rice production and 11% of the total cereal crop production in northeastern China. The major rice production area in northeastern China is Dawa County in the southern part of Liaoning Province.

Rice was produced in Dawa County using a combined hand–animal–machinery production system (Table V). The major power sources were labor and horse power. Only a few operations, such as plowing, threshing, and irrigating, used machine power. The labor input was 3046 hr/ha. This labor input was 2.5 times the labor input for corn production in Faku County and 130 times greater than the labor input for rice production in Sacramento Valley, California (Tables III, V, and VI). Labor inputs for rice were also 3.7 times larger in Dawa County than in the Philippines (Tables V, VII, VIII).

Of the fossil energy inputs, the 191 kg/ha of nitrogen (2,292,600 kcal) accounted for 41% of the total fossil energy inputs of Dawa County rice production (Table V). This 191 kg/ha of nitrogen is 45% greater than the amount of nitrogen applied in Sacramento Valley rice production (Tables V and VI). The irrigation energy input in rice production in Dawa County was 1,170,013 kcal/ha, which accounted for 21% of the total fossil energy input (Table V). Even though the irrigation energy input was less than that in Sacramento Valley, the amount of irrigation water (183.9 cm) was high.

TABLE IV
Energy Inputs per Hectare for Corn Production in Southeastern Pennsylvania, U.S.A.[a]

Item	Quantity/ha	kcal/ha
Inputs		
Labor	13.31 hr	6,855
Machinery	55 kg	990,000
Gasoline	57.29 liter	579,145
Diesel	72.18 liter	823,863
Electricity	24.70 kW hr	70,716
Nitrogen	88.03 kg	1,056,360
Phosphorus	64.15 kg	192,450
Potassium	50.68 kg	81,088
Lime	381.27 kg	120,272
Seeds	16.53 kg	413,250
Insecticides	1.04 kg	90,386
Herbicides	1.90 kg	189,829
Drying	2057.73 kg	—
Transportation	175.51 kg	45,106
Total		4,659,320
Outputs		
Corn yield	5138.17 kg	17,897,713
kcal output/kcal input	3.84	

[a] Adapted from Pimentel and Burgess (1980).

TABLE V
Energy Inputs per Hectare for Rice Production in Dawa County, Liaoning Province, China
(Annual Average, 1979–1981)

Item	Quantity/ha	kcal/ha
Inputs		
Labor	3045.40 hr	1,568,381
Horses	331.55 hr	1,517,173
Tools and animal draft equipment	4.50 kg	93,204
Machinery	14.62 kg	263,160
Diesel	72.91 liter	832,195
Electricity	121.87 kW·hr	348,914
Nitrogen	191.05 kg	2,292,600
Phosphorus	96.73 kg	290,190
Insecticides	0.90 kg	78,219
Herbicides	1.88 kg	187,831
Seeds	163.55 kg	482,800
Irrigation[a]	183.90 cm	1,170,013
Transportation	81.09 kg	20,840
Total		9,145,520
Outputs		
Rice yield	8094.40 kg	23,906,477
kcal output/kcal input	2.61	

[a]45 m³ water per kW·hr electricity, based on actual value.

The total energy input for rice production in Dawa County was 9,145,520 kcal/ha, which was 83% less than the total energy input in Sacramento Valley production (Tables V and VI). The total fossil energy input in Dawa County, however, was about half that of Sacramento Valley. The rice yield in Dawa County was 8098 kg/ha, which was 1.2 times larger than rice yield in Sacramento Valley (Tables V and VI). Dawa County's output/input ratio was 2.61, which was nearly 50% more than the ratio of 1.75 in Sacramento Valley rice production.

Rice production in the Philippines uses about one-third less labor than in Dawa County (Tables V, VII, and VIII). The yield in Dawa County was more than double that of the Philippines, even though rice production in Dawa County has only one harvest per year compared to the double cropping system in the Philippines.

C. Sorghum

In 1979, sorghum was grown on 1.2 million ha in northeastern China (Agricultural Almanac of China, 1980). This area accounted for 39% of total sorghum grown in China. Total sorghum production in this region was 3.8

TABLE VI
Energy Inputs per Hectare of Rice, Sacramento Valley, California, U.S.A. (1977)[a]

Item	Quantity/ha	kcal/ha
Inputs		
Labor	23.6 hr	12,154
Machinery	37.7 kg	742,460
Gasoline	55.2 liter	558,017
Diesel	225.4 liter	2,572,716
Electricity	29.7 kW·hr	85,031
Nitrogen (units N)	132.3 kg	1,944,810
Phosphate (units P_2O_5)	56.0 kg	168,000
Zinc	9.8 kg	49,000
Furadan	0.5 kg	42,650
Parathion	0.085 kg	7,387
Molinate	3.4 kg	294,440
MCPA	0.6 kg	59,946
Copper sulfate	11.2 kg	56,000
Seed	180.5 kg	722,000
Irrigation	250.0 cm	2,138,886
Drying	6969.0 kg	1,393,800
Transportation	451.3 kg	115,984
Total		10,963,281
Outputs		
Rice yield	6513.0 kg	19,226,376
kcal output/kcal input	1.75	

[a]Adapted from Rutger and Grant (1980).

TABLE VII
Energy Input per Hectare of Rice, Wet Season, Philippines (1972–1973)[a]

Item	Quantity/ha	kcal/ha
Inputs		
Labor	814.4 hr	419,416
Machinery	4.5 kg	81,000
Gasoline	131.3 liter	1,327,312
Nitrogen	33.0 kg	485,100
Herbicide	0.7 kg	69,937
Insecticide	3.2 kg	255,664
Seed	88.0 kg	352,000
Irrigation	15.0 cm	227,090
Total		3,217,519
Outputs		
Rice yield	3232.0 kg	9,540,864
kcal output/kcal input	2.97	

[a]Adapted from Rutger and Grant (1980).

TABLE VIII
Energy Input per Hectare of Rice, Dry Season, Philippines (1972–1973)[a]

Item	Quantity/ha	kcal/ha
Inputs		
Labor	814.4 hr	419,416
Machinery	4.5 kg	81,000
Gasoline	131.3 liter	1,327,312
Nitrogen	88.0 kg	1,293,600
Herbicide	0.3 kg	26,073
Insecticide	0.7 kg	69,937
Seed	103.9 kg	415,600
Irrigation	30.0 cm	454,180
Total		4,087,118
Outputs		
Rice yield	4175.0 kg	12,324,600
kcal output/kcal input	3.02	

[a]Adapted from Rutger and Grant (1980).

million metric tons, which was 49% of the total sorghum production in all of China.

Faku County of Liaoning Province is the major sorghum production region of northeastern China. In Faku County, the average energy inputs for sorghum production and corn production during 1980–1981 were quite similar (see Tables III and IX).

The labor input for sorghum production in Faku County was 1313 hr/ha; this was 83 times greater than the labor input in western Kansas. The nitrogen input in Faku County's production system (147 kg/ha) was also 1.3 times greater than the input in western Kansas. However, the fossil energy input of 2,292,180 kcal/ha in Faku County was only 16% of the energy input used in western Kansas. Thus, energy inputs in Faku County totalled 5,380,900 kcal/ha, which was only one-third of the total energy input for western Kansas sorghum. Sorghum yields in Faku County (4384 kg/ha) were slightly higher than yields in western Kansas (4170 kg/ha) (Tables IX and X). The output/input ratio of 2.67 for Faku County was significantly higher than the 0.95:1 of western Kansas.

A comparison of the sorghum production of Nigeria (Table XI), which utilized the combined hand–animal system, and Faku County, with its combined hand–animal–machinery system, showed that the Faku County system required a larger labor input (1313 hr/ha). This input was 11 times greater than the Nigerian labor input. The sorghum yield in Faku County, however, was 6 times larger than that of Nigeria.

D. Wheat

In 1979, wheat production in China totalled 62.7 million metric tons, which was 15% of the world's total wheat production (Agricultural Almanac of China, 1980). The wheat area of northeastern China was 2.1 million ha with a total wheat production of 3.6 million metric tons. The wheat area and the production in Heilongjiang Province of northeastern China accounted for 90% of total wheat acreage and 93% of wheat produced in northeastern China; this was primarily spring wheat.

Hailuen County is the major wheat production area of Heilongjiang Province and employs a combined hand–animal–machinery system. Compared to other cropping systems in Hailuen County, this system uses the least labor and horse power and the most fossil energy input (Table XII). The labor and horse power inputs for wheat production were 45% and 40%, respectively, of labor and horse power inputs for corn production (Tables II and XII). However, the total fossil energy input of 1,398,200 kcal/ha was 1.2 times greater than that of corn production. The energy output of the wheat produced (6,553,575 kcal/ha), however, was only one-third of corn energy output. The wheat output/input ratio of 2.44 was also less than corn output/input ratio of 3.63 (Tables II and XII).

North Dakota, which is at the same latitude as Hailuen County, has a wheat

TABLE IX
Energy Inputs per Hectare for Sorghum Production in Faku County, Liaoning Province, China (Annual Average, 1980 and 1981)

Item	Quantity/ha	kcal/ha
Inputs		
Labor	1312.85 hr	676,118
Horses	511.10 hr	2,338,794
Tools and horse draft equipment	3.22 kg	66,693
Machinery	3.16 kg	56,880
Diesel	4.11 liter	46,912
Electricity	17.54 kW·hr	50,217
Nitrogen	146.91 kg	1,762,920
Phosphorus	80.28 kg	240,840
Insecticides	0.75 kg	65,183
Seeds	22.50 kg	73,800
Transportation	9.87 kg	2,537
Total		5,380,894
Outputs		
Grain sorghum yield	4383.75 kg	14,378,700
kcal output/kcal input	2.67	

TABLE X
Energy Inputs per Hectare for Irrigated Grain Sorghum in Western Kansas, U.S.A.[a]

Item	Quantity/ha	kcal/ha
Inputs		
Labor	15.9 hr	8,189
Gasoline	34.7 liter	351,000
Diesel	64.9 liter	741,000
LP gas	15.8 liter	122,000
Natural gas	902.8 m³	10,644,000
Nitrogen	111.4 kg	1,337,000
Phosphorus	2.9 kg	9,000
Herbicide	1.4 kg	121,000
Insecticide	2.0 kg	160,000
Seed	6.7 kg	94,000
Machinery	9.0 kg	162,000
Irrigation equipment	57.55 dollar	691,000
Transportation	126.3 kg	32,000
Total		14,472,189
Outputs		
Grain sorghum yield	4170 kg	13,678,000
kcal output/kcal input	0.95	

[a]Adapted from Bukantis (1980).

production yield similar to that of Hailuen County (Tables XII and XIII), but the labor input of 6.0 hr/ha is only 1.9% of the labor input in Hailuen County wheat production. The total energy inputs are similar for both wheat regions; however, the fossil energy input of 1,398,200 kcal/ha in Hailuen County was only 44% of the fossil energy input in North Dakota. The output/fossil input ratio of 4.69 in Hailuen County is 75% greater than that in North Dakota.

TABLE XI
Energy Inputs per Hectare for Grain Sorghum in Nigeria Using Draft Animals[a]

Item	Quantity/ha	kcal/ha
Inputs		
Labor	116 hr	59,740
Equipment	2.0 kg	41,000
Oxen (pair)	365 hr each	2,555,000
Seeds	19.0 kg	63,000
Total		2,718,740
Outputs		
Grain sorghum yield	749 kg	2,457,000
kcal output/kcal input	0.90	

[a]Adapted from Bukantis (1980).

TABLE XII

Energy Inputs per Hectare for Wheat Production in Hailuen County, Heilongjiang Province, China (1980)

Item	Quantity/ha	kcal/ha
Inputs		
Labor	314.70 hr	162,071
Horses	85.40 hr	390,022
Tools and animal draft equipment	3.47 kg	71,871
Machinery	9.55 kg	171,900
Diesel	44.42 liter	507,581
Nitrogen	44.85 kg	538,200
Phosphorus	3.23 kg	9,690
Herbicide	0.86 kg	85,923
Seeds	225.00 kg	739,125
Transportation	50.82 kg	13,061
Total		2,689,444
Outputs		
Wheat yield	1995.00 kg	6,553,575
kcal output/kcal input	2.44	

TABLE XIII

Energy Inputs per Hectare for Other Spring Wheat Following Fallow in North Dakota U.S.A.[a]

Item	Quantity/ha	kcal/ha
Inputs		
Labor	6.03 hr	3,105
Machinery	22.97 kg	413,460
Gasoline	27.90 liter	282,041
Diesel	73.49 liter	838,815
Electricity	13.34 kW hr	38,192
Nitrogen	28.04 kg	336,480
Phosphorus	25.79 kg	77,370
Potassium	25.79 kg	41,264
Seeds	106.53 kg	319,590
Insecticides	0.30 kg	26,073
Herbicides	0.71 kg	70,936
Transportation	212.89 kg	54,713
Total		2,502,039
Outputs		
Wheat yield	2022.32 kg	6,683,470
kcal output/kcal input	2.67	

[a] Adapted from Briggle (1980).

Wheat production in Hailuen County requires more energy than in Uttar Pradesh, India (Tables XII and XIV). The labor and animal inputs in Hailuen County were lower (50% and 17%, respectively) than those in Uttar Pradesh. A large amount of fertilizer was used in Hailuen, and this caused an increase in the value of the total energy inputs but probably also contributed to a wheat yield that was 2.4 times greater than the output in Uttar Pradesh. The output/input ratio in Hailuen County was also twice that in Uttar Pradesh.

E. Soybean

Soybean is a major food protein and food oil source for the people of China (Agricultural Almanac of China, 1980). Northeastern China has the largest soybean acreage (2.8 million ha) in China, and in 1979, 40% (3.0 metric tons) of the total Chinese soybean production was grown in this region. A major production area is on the plains region along the Shenyang–Hairbin–Kesan Railway.

Faku County and Hailuen County are the major soybean production areas. These two counties employ a combined hand–animal–machinery system (Tables XV and XVI). The energy inputs for soybean production and corn production in Faku County were similar (Tables III and XV). The total energy input in soybean production was only 70% that of corn production. Soybean production uses much less nitrogen than corn production. The soybean yield of 6,484,830 kcal/ha was about one-third of the corn yield of 17,447,850 kcal/ha; the soybean output/input ratio of 1.64 was nearly one-half of the corn output/input ratio of 3.13. However, soybeans are produced for protein, not calories, and the protein output/kcal input for soybean production was 73% greater than the protein yield per kilocalorie for corn.

For soybean production in Faku County, both the inputs and the yield were

TABLE XIV
Energy Inputs per Hectare for Wheat in Uttar Pradesh, India, Using Bullocks[a]

Item	Quantity/ha	kcal/ha
Inputs		
Labor	615 hr	316,725
Bullock (pair)	321 hr each	2,247,000
Machinery	41,400 kcal	41,400
Seeds	65 kg	214,500
Total		2,819,625
Outputs		
Wheat yield	821 kg	2,709,300
kcal output/kcal input	0.96	

[a]Adapted from Pimentel (1976).

TABLE XV
Energy Inputs per Hectare for Soybean Production in Faku County, Liaoning Province, China (Annual Average, 1980 and 1981)

Item	Quantity/ha	kcal/ha
Inputs		
Labor	1061.35 hr	546,595
Horses	454.05 hr	2,077,733
Tools and animal draft equipment	3.22 kg	66,693
Machinery	0.47 kg	8,460
Diesel	7.55 liter	86,176
Nitrogen	29.38 kg	352,560
Phosphorus	80.28 kg	240,840
Insecticides	2.40 kg	208,584
Seeds	90.00 kg	361,944
Transportation	9.93 kg	2,552
Total		3,952,137
Outputs		
Soybean yield	1612.50 kg	6,484,830
Protein yield	548.25 kg	
kcal output/kcal input	1.64	

TABLE XVI
Energy Inputs per Hectare for Soybean Production in Hailuen County, Heilongjiang Province, China (1980)

Item	Quantity/ha	kcal/ha
Inputs		
Labor	431.29 hr	222,114
Horses	158.45 hr	725,076
Tools and animal draft equipment	3.47 kg	71,871
Machinery	2.50 kg	45,000
Diesel	19.06 liter	217,551
Nitrogen	22.43 kg	269,160
Phosphorus	3.23 kg	9,690
Insecticide	0.79 kg	68,659
Seed	105.00 kg	422,268
Transportation	22.17 kg	5,598
Total		2,056,987
Outputs		
Soybean yield	1260.00 kg	5,067,216
Protein yield	428.40 kg	
kcal output/kcal input	2.46	

higher than in Hailuen County (Tables XV and XVI). Faku County's labor and horse power inputs were nearly double those of Hailuen County, and fossil energy inputs were about 40% greater. The soybean yield in Faku County, however, was only 28% greater than that of Hailuen County. The output/input ratio of 1.64 in Faku County was less than the ratio of 2.46 in Hailuen County.

The total energy output/input ratio in Faku County was similar to the ratio in soybean production in Georgia (Tables XV and XVII). Faku County's soybean production uses much more labor and horse power than Georgia's, but the fossil energy inputs in Faku County were only 27% less.

F. Millet

In 1979 millet was planted on 1.52 million ha in northeastern China and accounted for one-third of total millet sown area in China (Agricultural Almanac of China, 1980). Millet production in this region was 2.3 million metric tons and accounted for 37% of the total millet produced in China.

Millet is especially suitable for regions with short growing seasons and low rainfall because it has a relatively short growing period and uses little water.

TABLE XVII
Energy Inputs per Hectare for Soybeans in Georgia, U.S.A.[a]

Item	Quantity/ha	kcal/ha
Inputs		
Labor	11.86 hr	6,108
Machinery	11.69 kg	210,420
Gasoline	68 liter	687,412
Diesel	62 liter	707,668
Nitrogen	27 kg	324,000
Potassium	67 kg	107,200
Phosphorus	51 kg	153,000
Lime	314 kg	99,051
Herbicide	2.94 kg	293,735
Insecticide	4.92 kg	427,597
Seed	73 kg	584,000
Transportation	188 kg	48,316
Total		3,648,507
Outputs		
Soybean yield	1664 kg	6,691,942
Protein yield	566 kg	
kcal output/kcal input	1.83	

[a]Adapted from Scott and Krummel (1980).

Because horses are used widely to power agriculture in northeastern China, millet is grown extensively in that region for its excellent forage value.

Millet production utilizes a combined hand–animal–machinery system (Table XVIII). The inputs for millet production are about one-half of those for corn production (Tables III and XVIII); however, millet yield was only about one-third of the corn yield. The output/input ratio for millet is 1.99, about two-thirds that of corn (Tables III and XVIII). If the feed value of millet forage were added to its grain yield value, millet would have an output/input ratio of 6.7. It would then be quite profitable from an energy standpoint.

G. Potatoes

About 65% of the potato production in northeastern China is in Heilongjiang Province. In 1979, 4.9 million metric tons of potatoes were produced in the region, which accounted for 28% of the total potato production in China (Agricultural Almanac of China, 1980). Potatoes are an important vegetable of the people of this region, especially during the winter.

Potatoes are produced in Hailuen County using a traditional production system of primarily hand and horse power (Table XIX). The only machines employed in field operations were small 12-horsepower tractors used for collecting and transporting manure. Fossil energy inputs in potato production are only 4.5% of the total energy input.

TABLE XVIII
Energy Inputs per Hectare for Millet Production in Faku County, Liaoning Province, China. (Annual Average, 1980 and 1981)

Item	Quantity/ha	kcal/ha
Inputs		
Labor	702.71 hr	361,896
Horses	180.00 hr	823,680
Tools and animal draft equipment	3.22 kg	66,693
Machinery	3.20 kg	57,600
Diesel	44.89 liter	512,374
Nitrogen	73.46 kg	881,520
Phosphorus	40.14 kg	120,420
Insecticides	1.13 kg	98,208
Seed	15.00 kg	50,250
Transportation	44.58 kg	11,457
Total		2,984,098
Outputs		
Millet yield	1770.00 kg	5,929,500
kcal output/kcal input	1.99	

TABLE XIX
Energy Inputs per Hectare for Potato Production in Hailuen County, Heilongjiang Province, China (1980)

Item	Quantity/ha	kcal/ha
Inputs		
Labor	937.20 hr	482,658
Horses	274.59 hr	1,256,524
Tools and animal draft equipment	3.47 kg	71,871
Machinery	0.69 kg	12,420
Diesel	3.80 liter	43,373
Seeds	1500.00 kg	920,700
Transportation	7.39 kg	1,899
Total		2,789,445
Outputs		
Potato yield	9900.00 kg	6,076,620
Protein yield	167.31 kg	669,240
kcal output/kcal input	2.18	

The labor input of 937.2 hr/ha and the horse power input of 1,256,524 kcal/ha were about one-third greater and 28% greater, respectively, than the inputs for corn production (Tables II and XIX). The fossil energy input of 129,563 kcal/ha was only 11% of the fossil energy input in corn production. The total energy input of 2,789,445 kcal/ha in potato production was slightly more than that in corn production, but the potato energy output of 6,076,620 kcal/ha was two-thirds of the corn energy yield. Thus, the potato output/input ratio of 2.18 was much less than the ratio of 3.63 in corn production (see Tables II and XIX).

The total energy inputs and fossil energy inputs in potato production in Hailuen County were only one-fourth and one-tenth, respectively, of those in South Carolina potato production (Tables XIX and XX). The potato yield in Hailuen County was only one-half of that in South Carolina. Even though potato production in Hailuen County uses 22.5 times more labor than in South Carolina, the output/input ratio of 2.18 in Hailuen County was much better than the ratio of 1.01 for South Carolina. Potato production in Heilongjiang Province could be doubled if additional fertilizers and improved varieties were utilized.

H. Sugar Beets

In 1979, sugar beets were planted on 0.21 million ha in northeastern China and the sugar beet production of 1.88 million tons in this region was 61% of the total sugar beet production in China (Agricultural Almanac of China, 1980).

TABLE XX
Energy Inputs and Outputs per Hectare for Potatoes in South Carolina, U.S.A.[a]

Item	Quantity/ha	kcal/ha
Inputs		
Labor	42 hr	21,630
Machinery	14 kg	252,000
Gasoline	178 liter	1,799,402
Diesel	101 liter	1,152,814
Nitrogen	188 kg	2,256,000
Phosphorus	225 kg	675,000
Potassium	225 kg	360,000
Lime	560 kg	176,652
Seeds	2020 kg	1,240,434
Insecticides	32 kg	2,781,120
Herbicides	6.7 kg	669,397
Transportation	2253.4 kg	579,124
Total		11,963,573
Outputs		
Total yield	19,648 kg	12,059,898
Protein yield	332.9 kg	1,331,824
kcal output/kcal input	1.01	

[a] Adapted from Schreiner and Nafus (1980).

Hailuen County is located in the major sugar beet production area of Heilongjiang Province. The energy inputs in sugar beet production were similar to those for potato production (Tables XIX and XXI); a traditional production system of hand and horse power was used. The labor input for sugar beet production was 911.7 hr/ha. The total energy input was 1,985,958 kcal/ha, of which fossil energy inputs 662,680 kcal/ha accounted for 33%. The fresh sugar beet yield output was 5,846,925 kcal/ha, with an output/input ratio of 2.94.

The labor input for sugar beet production with horse power in northern Germany in 1950 was similar to the labor input in Hailuen County, but the horse power input in northern Germany was seven times greater than that in Hailuen County (Tables XXI and XXII). The sugar beet yield in Hailuen County, however, was only 45% of that in northern Germany.

Sugar beet yields in Hailuen were one-fourth as large as yields in California, although the fossil energy inputs in Hailuen County were less than one-half of those in California (Tables XXI and XXIII).

I. Sunflowers

Sunflowers can be produced on poor soils and are grown primarily in the western region of northeastern China (Agricultural Almanac of China, 1980).

TABLE XXI

Energy Inputs per Hectare for Sugar Beet Production in Hailuen County, Heilongjiang Province, China (1980)

Item	Quantity/ha	kcal/ha
Inputs		
Labor	911.70 hr	469,526
Horses	171.50 hr	784,784
Tools and animal draft equipment	3.47 kg	71,871
Machinery	0.69 kg	12,420
Diesel	2.53 liter	28,877
Nitrogen	44.85 kg	538,200
Phosphorus	3.23 kg	9,690
Seed	22.50 kg	68,968
Transportation	6.31 kg	1,622
Total		1,985,958
Outputs		
Sugar beet yield	13,597.50 kg	5,846,925
kcal output/kcal input	2.94	

The sunflower acreage in this area was 0.24 million ha, with a total production of 0.22 million metric tons in 1979. Both in terms of acreage and yield, northeastern China accounted for two-thirds of the sunflower production of China as a whole.

Faku County was the major sunflower production region and a combined hand–animal–machinery system was utilized (Table XXIV). The energy inputs for sunflower production were similar to the energy inputs for millet production

TABLE XXII

Energy Inputs per Hectare for Sugar Beet Production in Northern Germany Using a Team of Two Horses for Production and Transport (1950)[a]

Item	Quantity/ha	kcal/ha
Inputs		
Labor	873.00 hr	449,595
Horses	311.00 hr	5,417,761
Machinery	19.50 kg	403,884
Seed	32.00 kg	98,088
Total		6,369,328
Outputs		
Sugar beet yield	30,000.00 kg	12,900,000
kcal output/kcal input	2.03	

[a]Data based on values given by Chancellor *et al.* (1980).

TABLE XXIII
Energy Inputs per Hectare for Sugar Beet Production in California, U.S.A.[a]

Item	Quantity/ha	kcal/ha
Inputs		
Labor	37.25 hr	19,184
Machinery	23.90 kg	430,200
Gasoline	68.00 liter	689,912
Diesel	209.00 liter	2,385,526
Nitrogen	190.00 kg	2,280,000
Phosphorus	31.00 kg	93,000
Seeds	4.50 kg	58,293
Irrigation	114.00 cm	7,615,832
Insecticides and herbicides	1.91 kg	190,821
Transportation	236.15 kg	60,691
Total		13,823,459
Outputs		
Sugar beet yield	53,644.00 kg	23,066,920
kcal output/kcal input	1.67	

[a]Data based on values given by Chancellor *et al.* (1980).

TABLE XXIV
Energy Inputs per Hectare for Sunflower Production in Faku County, Liaoning Province, China (Annual Average, 1980 and 1981)

Item	Quantity/ha	kcal/ha
Inputs		
Labor	845.81 hr	435,592
Horses	306.40 hr	1,402,086
Tools and animal draft equipment	3.22 kg	66,693
Machinery	2.73 kg	49,140
Diesel	35.53 kg	405,539
Nitrogen	14.70 kg	176,400
Phosphorus	40.14 kg	120,420
Seeds	30.00 kg	168,300
Transportation	36.15 kg	9,291
Total		2,833,461
Outputs		
Sunflower seed yield	1098.75 kg	6,163,988
Protein yield		
kcal output/kcal input	2.18	

(Tables XVIII and XXIV). The sunflower energy yield per hectare was also similar to millet production (Tables XVIII and XXIV).

IV. DISCUSSION OF ENERGY UTILIZATION IN CROPPING SYSTEMS IN NORTHEASTERN CHINA

The current combined hand–horse–machinery cropping systems in north-eastern China are at a stage of evolution between the old traditional cropping systems of China and the highly mechanized cropping systems of the indus-trialized nations, such as the United States. The combined hand–horse–machinery systems are capable of producing crop yields similar to or greater than those of the mechanized systems. In some cases, the combined systems accomplish this with half of the fossil energy inputs that are utilized in mechanized agricultural systems.

China has a long history and a great deal of experience in traditional farming practices that depend primarily on organic resources for soil nutrients. At the same time, China is insufficiently industrialized to supply a fully mechanized farming system. The combined systems that have evolved in present day China depend most heavily on human labor and horse power; only a small amount of machinery is utilized.

China has a substantial labor force. About 800 million people live in the rural areas and, of these, an estimated 300 million people are directly involved in agricultural production. The horses used in agricultural production are often fed residues from millet, sorghum, and corn crops so that little extra land is required to produce forage for these draft animals. Manure is the primary source of soil nutrients. Crop rotations are utilized extensively to improve soil fertility and control weeds, insect pests, and plant pathogens (Nongkenbu, 1982).

Thus, it was natural that China has developed a combined hand–horse–machine cropping system. This has helped make use of their abundant labor force while at the same time effectively recycling organic wastes in the agricultural system. Although the combined system is the dominant agricultural technology, there are a few small farming systems that rely primarily on older traditional cropping methods.

The combined cropping system has helped China to increase crop yields nearly fourfold since 1949. For example, the average cereal crop yield in China during 1949 was 1283 kg/ha whereas 30 years later the average cereal crop yield had risen to 4110 kg/ha [counted on base of cropping land area (Agriculture Almanac of China, 1980)], a tremendous achievement. Because of the increased crop yields provided by the combined cropping systems, China, with only 8.3% of the world's cereal cropland, is able to produce 18.2% of the world's cereals.

The prime difficulty with the combined system is the low level of labor productivity because of the large human labor input. For example, in Faku County about 4 kg of corn are produced per labor-hour whereas in Pennsylvania 395 kg of corn are produced per labor-hour, a level nearly 100-fold greater. A significant improvement in the yield per human labor-hour would help improve agricultural labor productivity in China, although it is doubtful that China, with its abundant labor force, would ever want to move anywhere near the production level of 395 kg/hr of corn production.

A. Improving China's Agricultural Productivity

Currently, the population of China is 1.032 billion (Xinhua, 1982a) and is expected to reach 1.2 billion by the year 2000. This increase is projected despite the full adoption of the "one child per couple" program (Zao, 1982). Therefore, to maintain the current per capita cereal grain level of 325 kg, cereal grain production of 335 million metric tons (MMT) will have to rise to 390 MMT (Xinhua, 1982b). This is more than a 16% increase in total production. Because cropland is extremely limited in China, most of the food yield increase will have to come by increasing the crop yields per hectare.

Although the people of China receive an adequate diet, there is a need to improve the diversity of food, including animal protein in the diet (Tong, 1980). At the same time long, heavy work in the agricultural fields might be reduced to improve the productivity of the agricultural labor force.

B. A Strategy to Improve Crop Yields

The agricultural production system in the United States and other developed nations has become highly mechanized. The high productivity per man hour and high crop yield levels are outstanding accomplishments of U.S. agriculture. However, relying heavily on fossil energy, especially petroleum, is a concern for U.S. agriculture. Pimentel (1980c) estimated that 1500 liters of oil equivalents are expended in the United States food system to feed 1 person per year. If petroleum were the only source of energy for food production and if we used all petroleum reserves solely to feed the world population, the known petroleum reserves of 86,912 billion liters in the world would last a mere 11 years. We also can use this calculation to estimate that if China used the United States food system to feed its 1 billion people, fossil energy consumption in China's food system each year would be almost three times the total fossil energy production in 1980, which was 0.62 billion metric tons of coal equivalents in China in 1980 (Gao, 1981). It is impractical for China to develop an agricultural system similar to that of the United States; more energy would be used just for food than the nation produces.

Fossil fuel prices that rose 5- to 10-fold during the past decade are influencing agricultural systems in both developed and developing countries. In the United States, for example, scientists are searching for alternative agricultural technologies to reduce the fossil energy inputs in their agricultural systems. China, too, is developing its agricultural systems and investigating new methods that will improve energy, land, water, and other resource use in crop production. These ecologically sound approaches will be suitable for the specific environmental and social conditions of China.

C. Fertilizers

In general, fertilizer input in crop production is the major limiting factor restricting crop yields in China. In traditional crop systems, organic manures supplied the crop with important nutrients. In crop rotation systems, crops such as soybeans are grown; these legumes supply the soil with some nitrogen by fixing nitrogen from the atmosphere. However, the scarcity of organic manures and the necessity of harvesting soybeans limit the use of these nutrient sources. Only one-third of the nitrogen is available for the following crop after the harvest of soybeans.

Several studies have demonstrated that adding soil nutrients in crop production could significantly increase crop yields (Table XXV). For example, application of soil nutrients such as nitrogen increased corn yields. Corn receiving nitrogen at rates of 45, 90, and 268 kg/ha had yields of 1346, 2700, and 5014 kg/ha, respectively (Table XXV). In China some crops, such as rice in Dawa County and corn in Faku County, do receive heavy applications of fertilizers, but the average levels of fertilizers and crop yields throughout the rest of China are much lower than in Dawa County and Faku County. In 1979, the average cereal crop yield output in China was 2783 kg/ha, and the average nitrogen input was 111 kg/ha [counted on base of sown area (Agricultural Almanac of China, 1980)]. From the data on average cereal crop yields and average chemical fertilizer inputs in China during past 3 decades, the relationship between nitrogen and crop yield is

$$y = 1365.83 + 14.6 x \qquad r = 0.9724$$

Where

y = average cereal yield   (kg/ha)
x = average chemical fertilizer (pure nitrogen: kg/ha)

The formula suggests that the average cereal yield in China would be 1366 kg/ha if no chemical nitrogen fertilizer were used. The average cereal yield increase is thus 14.6 kg/ha per kilogram of nitrogen added.

The average cereal yield in northeastern China in 1979 was 2890 kg/ha, with an input of 111 kg/ha of nitrogen. Thus, a large potential exists for increasing

TABLE XXV
Chemical and Organic Fertilizer Inputs in Some Crop Systems in Northeastern China

Crop	Site	Fertilizer inputs (kg/ha)										Crop yield outputs		Source
		Chemical fertilizers			Organic fertilizer (compost[a])			Total			kg/ha	kcal/ha	
		N	P	K	N	P	K	N	P	K			
Rice	Dawa	191.05	96.73	0	84.38	41.25	108.75	275.43	137.98	108.75	8098.40	23,906,477	Table V
Corn	Faku	146.91	80.28	0	121.50	59.40	156.60	268.41	139.68	156.60	5013.75	17,447,850	Table III
Sorghum	Faku	146.91	80.28	0	121.50	59.40	156.60	268.41	139.68	156.60	4383.75	14,378,700	Table IX
Corn	Hailuen	44.85	3.23	0	45.00	22.00	58.00	89.85	25.23	58.00	2700.00	9,396,000	Table II
Wheat	Hailuen	44.85	3.23	0	33.75	16.50	43.50	78.60	19.73	43.50	1995.00	6,553,575	Table XII
Millet	Faku	73.46	40.14	0	0	0	0	73.46	40.14	0	1770.00	5,929,500	Table XVIII
Soybean	Faku	29.38	80.28	0	90.00	44.00	116.00	119.38	124.28	116.00	1612.50	6,484,830	Table XV
Soybean	Hailuen	22.43	3.22	0	42.30	20.70	54.52	64.73	23.69	54.52	1260.00	5,067,216	Table XVI
Corn	Hailuen	0	0	0	45.00	22.00	58.00	45.00	22.00	58.00	1345.65	4,682,862	Table I

[a]Nutritional element contents in compost: N = 0.45%, P. = 0.22%, K = 0.58% (He, 1981).

corn yield in northeastern China if larger amounts of nitrogen, phosphorus, and potassium were used.

Increased soil fertility of cropland in northeastern China might be achieved by the following methods:

1. Increase the Legume–Nonlegume Crop Rotation Systems

The following crop rotation systems are currently used in northeastern China: wheat–soybean–wheat–corn (sorghum or millet); wheat–corn (sorghum or millet)–soybean; wheat–corn–soybean–wheat–wheat–soybean; and corn–soybean–sorghum (millet or corn). In 1979, soybeans were planted on 2.75 million ha in northeastern China, which was 16.6% of the total cropping area. Soybean acreage should be increased to at least 4.14 million ha to provide suitable legume crop rotations. These rotations, as well as increased soybean acreage, will not only improve soil fertility but also increase plant protein production that is important for nutrition of the people.

2. Increase Organic Nitrogen Production and Improve Manure Management

Organic matter supplies valuable soil nutrients for crop production. It also improves soil structure, reduces soil erosion, and improves the water-holding capacity and tilth of the soil. In China, organic fertilizers are important sources of soil fertility. Specifically, organic manure provided about 45% of the total required nitrogen, 42% of the total required phosphorus, and 100% of the total required potassium in northeastern China (Table XXV). Unfortunately, about 80% of crop residues are burned for cooking and heating in northeastern China. Burning crop residues wastes the nitrogen and the sulfur nutrients by releasing them to the atmosphere. If some alternative energy source, such as solar energy or methane, could be used and stoves improved, fewer crop residues would be burned and more residues would be utilized as organic fertilizer. If more animals, such as milk cows and sheep, were fed forage produced from noncropland and crop residues, more manure would be available for use on crops.

Manure management should also be improved to conserve the available soil nutrients. Manure management in northeastern China, in general, is not as good as that in southern China. In northeastern China about 50% of the nutrient elements in manure are estimated to be lost before crops can make use of them. One possible solution is to store the manure solids and urine in plastic-lined ponds until just before the crop is planted. At that time the manure and urine mix would be injected into the soil behind the plow or be covered up by soil. The nutrients in the manure would then be conserved. Note, open-air composting of manure should be avoided because a large portion of the nitrogen in the manure is lost by this procedure.

Manure collecting and composting require large amounts of labor and horse power. About 25 labor-hours and 13 horse-hours are required to collect, compost, and transport 1-metric ton of organic compost. About 35% of the total labor input and 50% of total horse power input in crop production are employed for just the organic compost input. Thus, more efficient storage and handling of manure is clearly needed. Special pumps and new manure application equipment can be developed to reduce the labor and horse power inputs in crop production.

3. Increase Chemical Fertilizer Inputs

In addition to increasing the nutrients available in organic fertilizers, there is a need to increase synthetic chemical fertilizer inputs in crop production, at least before more efficient organic fertilizer production systems are established. It has been shown in an earlier section that, on average, each additional 1 kg of nitrogen increases cereal crop output by about 14.6 kg. Thus, an input of about 12,000 kcal in nitrogen will provide about 52,000 kcal in food energy. This output/input ratio of 4.3 is very profitable from the standpoint of energy use and food production.

D. Labor, Horse Power, and Machinery

The combined hand–horse–machinery cropping systems in China are perhaps some of the most intensive labor and horse power systems found in the world today. Some increased machine use appears to be advantageous to reduce labor and horse inputs in crop production. If some machinery were utilized to reduce some labor and horse inputs, this would improve labor productivity and the well-being of the people. However, it would be unwise to use machines to reduce labor and horse inputs to the level of that of U.S. agriculture because of the current availability of human resources in China.

In corn production in Faku County, about half of the labor input, or 557 hr, is hand labor in the field (Table XXVI). Of these 557 hr, 54 hr are required for thinning seedlings and 180 hr for hoeing. Tractors are only used for plowing, harrowing, and ridging; otherwise they remain in storage. If tractors were used for a few critical field operations, the inputs of labor and horses could be significantly reduced. For example, using precision seed planters and cultivators attached to tractors would increase the fossil energy input of 164,000 kcal/ha (14,000 kcal/ha for machinery and 150,000 kcal/ha for 13.2 liter/ha of diesel fuel). This is only a 3% increase in total fossil energy inputs in current corn production. This small amount of fossil energy would reduce the labor input by

TABLE XXVI
Labor and Horsepower Inputs in Corn Production in Faku County, Liaoning Province, China
(Annual Average, 1980–1981)

Operation	Labor (hr/ha)	Horsepower (hr/ha)
Plowing by machine	3.43	0
Harrowing by machine	1.72	0
Ridging by machine	0.81	0
Sowing by hand and horsepower	67.50	13.5
Thinning seedlings by hand	54.00	0
Hoeing by hand	180.00	0
Intertilling by horsepower	20.25	40.5
Topdressing by hand	81.00	0
Spreading pesticides by hand	27.00	0
Harvesting by hand	155.30	0
Transporting harvest by horsepower	40.50	81.0
Threshing by machine	53.5	0
Stubbing by hand	60.00	0
Collecting, composting and transporting organic manure by hand and horsepower	507.40	308.6
Total	1252.40	443.6

403 hr/ha, or one-third of total labor input, and would reduce the horse input by 54 hr/ha of 247,104 kcal/ha. If we assume that the labor force consumed at least 3000 kcal of food per working day, then the amount of energy saved is about equal to the fossil energy used.

Most of horse power inputs are used to transport organic manure and the crop harvests. In Faku County corn production, for example, 81 horse-hours per hectare are used to transport ear corn and straw from the field to the farmyard. About 309 horse-hours per hectare are used to collect and transport organic manure from the farmyard to the field. These two activities account for 88% of the horse power input in corn production.

Although horses produce valuable manure and are fed residues from agroecosystems, these horses also consume a large amount of grain that is also suitable for human consumption. If some other transportation vehicles replaced horse-drawn carts, more fodder would be available to feed to milk cows and sheep. This would increase milk and meat resources for people.

Increasingly, the peasants in northeastern China are using small 12-horse-power tractors for farm transport instead of horse-drawn carts. Using 12-horse-power tractors to transport organic manure and crop harvests in Faku County corn production would increase the use of fossil energy by 373,399 kcal/ha (64,080 kcal/ha for machinery and 309,319 kcal/ha for 27.1 liter/ha of diesel fuel). This is a 13.5% increase in fossil energy input in current corn production; but this fossil energy input would reduce current horse power input by 1,782,810 kcal/ha. Thus, the 3% increase in fossil energy input for planting and weeding plus the 13.5% fossil energy increase for transport would reduce the labor input by one-third and replace all horse power. The total energy input in Faku County corn production would be reduced from 5,567,900 kcal/ha to 3,323,000 kcal/ha, and the output/input ratio would increase from 3.13 to 5.25. However, the output/fossil energy input ratio would decline from 6.30 to 5.29. The fodder previously consumed by the horses could be used to develop animal husbandry and increase the production of meat, milk, and eggs. Overall, the productivity of labor in agriculture, forestry, and industry would be increased and the well-being of the people improved.

REFERENCES

Agricultural Almanac of China. (Zhong gue Nongye Nianjian). (1980). Agriculture Press, Beijing.

Barney, G. O. (1982). Horses of horsepower? Soft Energy Notes 5, 70–73.

Briggle, L. W. (1980). Introduction to energy use in wheat production. In "Handbook of Energy Utilization in Agriculture" (D. Pimentel, ed.), pp. 109–116. CRC Press, Boca Raton, Florida.

Bukantis, R. (1980). Energy inputs in sorghum production. In "Handbook of Energy Utilization in Agriculture" (D. Pimentel, ed.), pp. 103–107. CRC Press, Boca Raton, Florida.

Cervinka, V. (1980). Fuel and energy efficiency. In "Handbook of Energy Utilization in Agriculture" (D. Pimentel, ed.), pp. 15–21. CRC Press, Boca Raton, Florida.

Chancellor, W. J., Alvani, P. K., Cervinka, V., and Alexander, J. T. (1980). Energy requirements for sugar beet production and processing. In "Handbook of Energy Utilization in Agriculture" (D. Pimentel, ed.), pp. 137–153. CRC Press, Boca Raton, Florida.

Council on Environmental Quality (1980). "The Global 2000 Report to the President," Vols. I–III. Council on Environmental Quality and the Department of State, U.S. Govt. Printing Office, Washington, D.C.

Doering III, O. C. (1980). Accounting for energy in farm machinery and buildings. In "Handbook of Energy Utilization in Agriculture" (D. Pimentel, ed.), pp. 9–14. CRC Press, Boca Raton, Florida.

Gao Y. (1981). About energy resource of China. Energy Resource (Nengyuan) 1, 2–9.

He W. (1981). "General Data of Agriculture." Agriculture Press, Beijing.

Lockeretz, W. (1980). Energy inputs for nitrogen, phosphorus and potash fertilizers. In "Handbook of Energy Utilization in Agriculture" (D. Pimentel, ed.), pp. 15–21. CRC Press, Boca Raton, Florida.

National Academy of Sciences (1977). "Supporting Papers: World Food and Nutrition Study." National Academy of Sciences, Washington, D.C.

Nongkenbu S. (Production Bureau of Ministry of Agro-reclaim). (1982). "Handbook of Agricultural Technique for State Farms (Gueyeng Nongchang Nongyie Jushu Souche)." Science and Technology Press, Shanghai.

Pimentel, D. (1976). The energy crisis: its impact on agriculture. In "Enciclopedia deno Scienza e della Tecnica." Annuario delca EST. Mondadori, Milan.

Pimentel, D. (1980a). Energy inputs for the production, formulation, packaging and transport of various pesticides. In "Handbook of Energy Utilization in Agriculture" (D. Pimentel, ed.), pp. 35–42. CRC Press, Boca Raton, Florida.

Pimentel, D. (1980b). Energy used for transporting supplies to the farm. In "Handbook of Energy Utilization in Agriculture" (D. Pimentel, ed.), pp. 55. CRC Press, Boca Raton, Florida.

Pimentel, D. (1980c). Food, energy and the future of society. Presented at the Reuben G. Gustavson Memorial Lecture. Colorado Associated Univ. Press, Boulder, Colorado.

Pimentel, D., and Burgess, M. (1980). Energy inputs in corn production. *In* "Handbook of Energy Utilization in Agriculture" (D. Pimentel, ed.), pp. 67–83. CRC Press, Boca Raton, Florida.

Pimentel, D., and Pimentel, M. (1979). "Food, Energy and Society," Resource and Environmental Sciences Series. Edward Arnold, London.

Rutger, J. N., and Grant, W. R. (1980). Energy use in rice production. *In* "Handbook of Energy Utilization in Agriculture" (D. Pimentel, ed.), pp. 93–97. CRC Press, Boca Raton, Florida.

Schreiner, I. M., and Nafus, D. M. (1980). Energy inputs for potato production. *In* "Handbook of Energy Utilization in Agriculture" (D. Pimentel, ed.), pp. 195–201. CRC Press, Boca Raton, Florida.

Scott, W. O., and Krummel, J. (1980). Energy used in producing soybeans. *In* "Handbook of Energy Utilization in Agriculture" (D. Pimentel, ed.), pp. 117–121. CRC Press, Boca Raton, Florida.

Tong D. (1980). Chinese agriculture begins a new turning point. *In* "Agricultural Almanac of China," pp. 183–184. Agriculture Press, Beijing.

Xinhua (China News Agency). (1982a). Chinese Statistic Bureau published the results of census of China. Renmin Ribao (People's Daily), Oct. 28, 1982.

Xinhua (China News Agency). (1982b). The cereal grain production in China in 1982 will be 335 million metric tons. Renmin Ribao (People's Daily), Dec. 2, 1982.

Zao Z. (1982). Report about the sixth five-year plan. Renmin Ribao (People's Daily), Dec. 14, 1982.

Chapter 6

Energy and Food Relationships in Developing Countries: A Perspective from the Social Sciences

GEORGE H. AXINN*'‡ AND NANCY W. AXINN†'‡

Department of Agricultural Economics*
Bean/Cowpea Collaborative Research Support Program†
Michigan State University
East Lansing, Michigan

‡Present address: Food and Agriculture Organization of the United Nations, G.P.O. Box 25 Kathmandu, Nepal.

121

FOOD AND ENERGY RESOURCES

I. INTRODUCTION

Energy and food relationships are manifested in a variety of patterns in the contemporary world. Energy transformation systems in the so-called "developing" countries are significantly different from those in other countries.

The urbanized countries of Europe and North America have developed in interaction with the more rural nations of Africa, Asia, and Latin America. The former group colonized the latter, used the latter as a source of raw material for its manufacturing, dominated the exchange with the latter, and built the dependency relationships that underlie the present situation.

An example of the difference is illustrated by the types of farming systems now found in these two general areas. In the so-called "modern," "developed," or "Western" countries, there is a tendency for farming systems to be on a large-scale basis and highly specialized (if not mono-crop). These systems convert large quantities of "added" energy, have relatively small numbers of people per farm, and have a high capital investment. These systems produce commodities in the marketing chain for sale off the farm.

The typical farming system in the other countries—the "traditional," "under-developed," or "non-Western"—tends to be on a small-scale basis, with low capital investment and with mixed crops and livestock (unspecialized). The typical system has relatively large numbers of people per farm, uses small quantities of "added" energy, and produces food and fiber for subsistence home consumption.

In addition to these small farming units are the large-scale plantations, which often claim the best tillable lands of Africa, Asia, and Latin America. Usually owned and operated by Europeans and North Americans, the large-scale plantations produce specialized crops for export to the more industrialized countries. Such farm products as sugar, rubber, jute, coffee, tea, cocoa, and beef are featured on these "extractive" farming systems.

There are exceptions to this generalization, of course, in both groups of nations. But the difference persists and is the subject of this chapter.

II. FARM FAMILY ECOSYSTEM

The farm family ecosystem may be viewed as a converter of solar energy into food, fiber, and fuel wood. Thus the size of the farm unit, or solar energy collector, is directly related to the relative power of the people who control it. The larger the number of hectares controlled by one human group, the greater will be the economic, social, and political power of that group over others. Similarly, the more efficient the technology employed by a human group in managing the solar collector (farm), the greater will be the relative power.

Both types of farming systems described above have the potential of converting solar energy in direct proportion to their land area. The commercial type also converts large quantities of other energy "added" to the system, while the subsistence type converts relatively smaller quantities of "added" energy. "Added" energy includes such other energy "inputs" as: human labor, draft animal power, electricity, diesel fuel, gasoline, firewood, fertilizers, pesticides, feeds, and seeds, all of which may be brought to the farming system from outside.

III. ENERGY TRANSFORMATION AND SOCIAL DIFFERENTIATION

The following sections discuss energy transformation and social differentiation as indicators of change in rural social systems, which is summarized in the development cycle. A description of materials flow and energy transformation in a typical small farm family ecosystem follows. Then the *recycling ratio* is presented as an instrument for measuring and comparing subsistence agriculture with commercial agriculture. Finally, the authors suggest implications of this type of energy analysis for (1) food and agriculture, (2) fuel for the family, and (3) rural development strategies and international development assistance.

IV. DEVELOPMENT AND CHANGE

Rather than use the ideals of the United States (the authors' country) as the "standard" for development, with those most like it described as "most developed," and those least like it defined as "least developed," this chapter takes a different approach. The writers assume that change is a characteristic of every human group. Whether a particular change is defined as "development" depends on who benefits from that change and who defines "development." It is suggested that quantities of energy transformed can serve as a more neutral proxy for measurement of change as compared to conventional approaches. Also, the extent of social differentiation, or specialization, can be used as an indicator of change, as will be discussed.

The approach used for understanding change is similar to the human ecology perspective of McKenzie, which emphasized the aggregate in an environmental context, with attention to the system as a whole (Hawley, 1968). Consideration of social differentiation and quantities of energy flow springs from such an ecosystem approach.

Fred Cottrell (1955) wrote, "The amounts and types of energy employed condition man's way of life materially and set somewhat predictable limits on what he can do and how society will be organized."

A. Rural Social System

Any rural social system may be characterized by the flow of materials and energy within it. Change in the total system can be identified at different points in time, using both social differentiation and materials and energy flows as critical variables. Each rural social system is also dependent on the larger eco-system of which it is a part, which has social, political, economic, cultural, and physical characteristics. The nature of the system may be understood both in terms of its internal relationships and exchanges and its interactions with that larger ecosystem.

Assuming that it is possible for humanity to come into some sort of equilibrium state with its environment, it is conceivable that: (1) human groups that are underutilizing the resources of their ecosystem in enhancing their own levels and styles of living may be considered to be underdeveloped; (2) human groups that are overutilizing the resources of their ecosystem in enhancing their own levels and styles of living may be considered to be overdeveloped; and (3) human groups that are in equilibrium with the resources of their ecosystem with respect to their own levels and styles of living may be considered to be appropriately developed.

Viewed over a time perspective, each human group may move through a cycle with stages of underdevelopment, balanced development, and over-development, going on to balanced development, underdevelopment, etc. This phenomenon has been labeled "the development cycle" (Fig. 1).

The rate of change varies from group to group, with some apparently static or at equilibrium and others moving quite rapidly. A given group may go through periods of rapid change, periods of very gradual change, and periods when change may not be apparent at all.

B. Relative Balance of Human Groups

One way to assess the relative balance of a particular human group with its environment is in terms of its transformation of energy. If a group is transforming relatively little energy (petroleum, electricity, firewood, etc.) per capita in en-hancing its own style of living, then it may be considered to be underdeveloped. If a group is transforming relatively high amounts of energy in enhancing its own level and style of living, compared to what its own ecosystem will sustain over time, it may be considered to be overdeveloped. And, if a group has balanced its conversion and transformation of energy, i.e., its technology and its level and style of life, with what its ecosystem can sustain over time, it may be considered

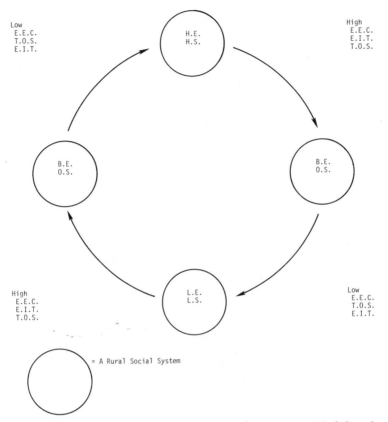

Low
E.E.C.
T.O.S.
E.I.T.

High
E.E.C.
E.I.T.
T.O.S.

H.E.
H.S.

B.E.
O.S.

B.E.
O.S.

High
E.E.C.
E.I.T.
T.O.S.

Low
E.E.C.
T.O.S.
E.I.T.

L.E.
L.S.

= A Rural Social System

Fig. 1. The development of cycle. H.E., high energy use; L.E., low energy use; B.E., balanced energy use; H.S., high specialization; L.S., low specialization; O.S., optimum specialization; E.E.C., efficiency of energy conversions; T.O.S., transactions with outside systems; E.I.T., efficiency of internal transactions. (From Axinn, 1978.)

to be appropriately developed. Different degrees of development could be represented by two different groups with the same resources.

C. Change of Human Group

Change can also be measured in terms of social differentiation, the specialization of performance of human functions. Given that several functions, such as production, supply, marketing, governance, learning, personal maintenance, and health care are performed in every rural social system, a progression may move from systems where one individual performs all functions for himself/herself to a stage where members of a family specialize in specific functions to a stage where different families in a village might specialize in certain functions, increasing their dependency on other families for other functions (Axinn and Thorat, 1972).

For example, in undifferentiated poultry production, a family may keep some hens and roosters. The family may eat some eggs, but as the hen gets toward the end of her period of egg production, her eggs will be left in the nest. She will hatch these for the next batch of baby chicks. Feed for such chickens is found by the birds themselves by scratching the ground, with perhaps some supplementation from family-grown crops or family table scraps. As the family itself becomes more specialized, one person may take responsibility for feeding the chickens, another for gathering the eggs, and perhaps a third person for occasional preparation of poultry meat for the family table. In a still more differentiated social system, the farm family may purchase baby chicks once a year from another family that manages a hatchery. Poultry feed may be purchased from a third family that manages a feed mill. Members of a fourth family may collect eggs each week and carry them to a distant market for cash sale. The last system reflects greater social differentiation than the first system described.

D. Specialization and Development

The concept of a development cycle suggests the possibility that human groups may overspecialize as they become overdeveloped and, at a later time, broaden functions to less specialization.

There is a tendency for those rural social systems that are transforming relatively little energy (in relation to what that ecosystem can provide) to also tend to be the least differentiated with respect to the seven functions mentioned above. At the opposite side of the development cycle, those systems that are transforming the highest amounts of energy also tend to have the highest degrees of social differentiation and functional specialization.

The intermediate position of balance in energy transformation vis-à-vis the environment seems to be accompanied by an optimum level of social differentiation. The extent of energy conversion vis-à-vis what the ecosystem can sustain over time and the extent of social differentiation tend to be positively related.

V. MATERIALS FLOW AND ENERGY TRANSFORMATION IN A FARM FAMILY ECOSYSTEM

The farm family is a convenient and relevant unit for analysis. Shifts in both social differentiation and energy transformation are illustrated using the family ecosystem as the basic unit.

The majority of people in Asia, Africa, and Latin America live on small pieces of land and subsist by consuming what they produce and producing what they consume. Further, current census data from Asia indicate that the total numbers and relative proportion of such families are increasing.

Different from the large-scale, commercial, capital-intensive farming systems of North America and Europe, which are specialized in the *production* function, these farming systems in Asia, Africa, and Latin America are small-scale, non-commercial, land- and labor-intensive units that perform *supply* and *marketing* functions as well as production functions. Further, these systems are also heavily involved in personal maintenance, health care delivery, governance, and learning.

Since they are less differentiated, these farming systems also tend to produce a great variety of cereal grains, livestock, and fruits and vegetables. From an agricultural economic perspective, these farming systems are integrated both vertically and horizontally. Their production is much less specialized than that of the large-scale farming systems.

A. Cash Flow

Whereas cash flow may provide an adequate indicator of the total flow of materials through the large-scale commercial farming system, cash flow is less useful as a proxy for the total flow of materials in the small, mixed farming systems. In a unit that sells its outputs for cash money and purchases its inputs with the same currency, the flow of cash tends to correlate with the total volume of other activity. Cash flow is a measure of relative wealth and may serve as descriptive proxy for the entire system. In the subsistence unit that tends to *recycle* more materials than it *exchanges* with other systems, the flow of cash sometimes accounts for a small proportion of the materials flow and provides a misleading measure.

For example, a small, mixed subsistence farming system will be assessed by international agencies as in "relative" or "absolute" poverty if the annual cash income is below a certain amount. However, the same system may have a large kitchen garden, may provide its human members with more than adequate quantities of fresh milk and dairy products, meat, and eggs, and may actually be so wealthy that the nuclear family that owns and operates it does little physical work. They may have servants and farmhands to help do the work.

Since the "shadow production" that is consumed within tends not to be reflected in cash flow measures, the higher the proportion of materials flow that is internal, the less adequate a proxy (such as cash income) is as an indicator of the nature of the system.

B. Energy Transformation

Energy transformation is an alternative proxy that can be a useful indicator of change over time, both for large-scale commercial farming systems and for small-scale subsistence farming systems, as well as transitional units in various stages between these two extremes.

Just as a monetary value can be assigned to any sort of item, so can an energy value. And the two types of evaluations can be exchanged. Thus, there is no special "magic" about energy values that makes them better than money values. However, as descriptors of materials flow and other activities in a farming system, the use of energy values as a proxy offers some advantages.

One advantage of an energy measure, like kilocalories (kcal), British thermal units (BTU), or joules in comparison with such money measures as rupees, pounds, pesos, or dollars, is that the relative values are defined and generally accepted as unchanging. The ratio of U.S. dollars to Indian rupees changes from day to day, but 1 kcal equals 3.968 BTU by international convention, and the ratio tends not to change.

A second advantage is that while the cash price of 1 kg rice, for example, varies from one place to another on any given day, and the world price of rice varies from day to day and from year to year, the kilocalories in 1 kg are relatively standard. Even with variation in the type of rice, its moisture content, and the method in which the energy value is to be transformed (burned, eaten by humans, eaten by ruminants), the energy values are relatively more standardized than the money values.

Third, in systems that utilize cash for a relatively low proportion of all transactions, the assignment of cash values may be even less valid than assignment of energy values. However, in both cases, such proxies assigned to a variety of materials should be considered as only approximations of relative value and not as precise measures of reality. Thus the calorie (kcal) is used as an indicator of estimated relationships and nothing more.

Just as social phenomena described by money values are subject to certain economic "laws," the energy descriptor is conditioned by the "Laws of Thermodynamics" (Georgescu-Roegen, 1975). Thus the engineering concepts related to energy transformation can be as useful to the social analysis as the economic concepts, and by combining both, the analysis may be strengthened.

C. Materials and Energy Transformation

As will be demonstrated with data describing small farm family ecosystems in Nepal, the flow of materials and transformation of energy can be estimated in such systems. Out of rudimentary efforts has emerged a conceptualization of the farming system that provides a base for sociological analysis of continuity and change and for demonstration of a relationship between social differentiation and energy transformation.

The conceptual framework for the materials and energy transformation perspective of small farm family ecosystems is illustrated in Fig. 2. Here a farm

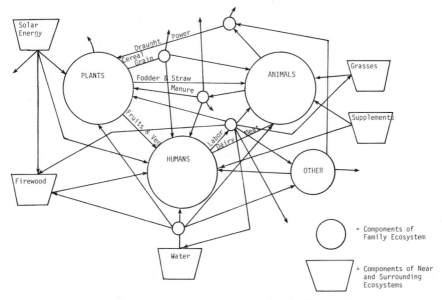

Fig. 2. Energy flow in a small subsistence farm family ecosystem.

family ecosystem is viewed as a component of a larger, rural social system. The larger system has many similar farm family ecosystems, and all are seen as part of a still larger social, political, economic, religious, cultural, and physical surrounding environment.

VI. FARM FAMILY ECOSYSTEMS—THREE MAJOR COMPONENTS

Within farm family ecosystems, the three major components are humans, animals, and plants. This perspective is similar to that suggested by Koenig and Tummala (1972) and the model developed by Tummala and Connor (1973), which provides a technique for accounting for the mass and energy flows into and out of commercial agricultural systems. The approach is also similar to analyses made by Thomas (1974, 1976). While the analytical techniques are similar, this model differs in that it allows analysis of a basic *subsistence* ecosystem, in which most materials and energy are recycled within the system rather than exchanged outside the system.

The major flows of materials and transformation of energy in this model are among the plant, animal, and human components. The "other production" component includes such "subsistence industry" activities as the manufacture of tools, clothing, and housing. Major flows to the farm family ecosystem from the surrounding environment are solar energy, water, firewood, grass cut and grazed, and small supplements to health and diet (such as salt and spices). There is a significant exchange of both human labor and animal draft power among the farm family ecosystems in such a rural social system. Within the farm family ecosystem, inputs go to each component from the other components within the system, as well as from other systems in the society.

A. Human

Major inputs to the human component of such a system are cereal grains, fruits and vegetables, milk and dairy products, meat, firewood, and water. Principal energy outputs are in the form of labor. Learning and controlling (deciding and allocating) reflect small energy transformations, serving as "triggering" mechanisms as described by Adams (1974).

B. Animal

The animal component of the farm family ecosystem may include such livestock as cattle, buffaloes, goats, swine, and poultry. Inputs to the animal component are straw and fodder, cereal grain or grain by-products, human labor, tools and facilities (including stables and barns), and grazing grass. Major outputs from the animal component include draft power, manure, milk and dairy products, meat, and eggs.

C. Plant

The plant component is the major energy source for the small subsistence farm family ecosystem. It can be likened to the system's powerhouse, as it converts solar energy into nutrients that can be transformed by both the humans and the animals and that supply the bulk of their calorie requirements. In addition to solar energy, other inputs to this component include draft power, manure (or other fertilizer), human labor, tools, seed and water, along with other potential inputs such as insecticides, fungicides, and herbicides. However, the magnitude of solar energy available on each hectare of land is so much larger than all other energy sources combined that the entire system can be viewed as one that takes a small fraction (estimated at 1–3%) of the available solar energy and converts this as the resource for all other activities.

By combining the major components of such a system, the differences between farm family ecosystems on different pieces of land and the relationship among farms of various sizes in a rural social system can be illustrated. Such a model offers a useful conceptualization to those who study the whole farming system. For example, costs and benefits of production can be evaluated in relationship to all inputs and outputs for any particular plant or animal commodity as it flows through the system.

To illustrate, one variety of cereal grain can be compared to another not only on the basis of grain production but also in terms of the use of straw and other by-products, as well as costs of seed, human labor, manure, and draft power.

Further, in addressing such questions as the potential substitution of small-scale garden tractors for animal draft power, such a conceptualization permits the inclusion of several variables, which may be overlooked by conventional studies of this issue (Axinn and Axinn, 1979; Axinn and Axinn, 1980).

VII. THE FAMILY AS AN ECOSYSTEM

Rural families are the core of the rural social system. In every farm family ecosystem, there is an intimate relationship between organisms and the environment. In subsistence societies, this relationship includes the humans, who are the main actors. It also includes other organisms, such as draft animals, other large and small farm animals, and a broad array of plants. The microbes of disease and the microbes of nitrogen fixation are also organisms that interact with other organisms and with the environment. The environment is critical in a farm family ecosystem. It provides the resource base of solar energy, water, terrain, and soil fertility (or lack of it). The climatic ranges of each area become a part of the environment and constrain the interaction of plants, animals, and people within that ecosystem.

A. Near Environment

The family, an intimate group of individuals, shares the same near environment. In rural families, understanding the relationship between the family members and their natural environment (ecological niche) is essential to understanding the transaction processes occurring within the family system.

The near environment usually includes shelter, water and food sources, a waste disposal system, and provisions for cooking, light, and heat, if needed. Domestic animals and some form of transportation are frequently included in the near environment. Information is an important input into the family system, and an information system exists in this near environment.

B. Beyond the Near Environment

Environments beyond the nearest support environment to the family expand to ever-larger ecosystems, all of which have an information input for the rural family ecosystem as well as energy and material exchanges with it. The dynamics of the flow of materials and energy through the family system can be conceptualized in this perspective. Inputs flow to the rural family, transformation occurs within the family system, and outputs result from the family.

Affective inputs into any particular family ecosystem come from the social, religious, and cultural systems. The transformation of physical inputs within the system is based on the combination of the inputs with the resources of the near environment. How these inputs are combined frequently depends on the skills and abilities of the humans nurtured in any particular family ecosystem. Within this setting, human resources are developed. Individual skills and abilities, as well as energy outputs from human labor, become potential outputs from the system.

C. Commercial Market Agriculture

Commercial market agriculture has focused on the dynamics of the organisms in farm family ecosystems: the education of the farmer, the substitution of mechanical power for draft power, and the laboratory development of new inputs of seeds, fertilizer, fungicides, and insecticides. Subsistence agriculture must recognize the environmental constraints that exist. These define the ecological niche within which the organisms interact with each other and with the environment. Each niche is a unique combination of the terrain, the weather, and the source of land and water that can support some level of human life and productive activity.

D. Small Mixed Subsistence Farms

On small, mixed subsistence farms in Nepal, units of different sizes are in a symbiotic relationship with each other, enhancing each other's survival and completely dependent on each other. The smallest farms do not produce enough to feed their own human and animal populations, forcing the humans to seek off-farm employment and requiring the animals to graze the roadsides and other public areas or to have forage brought to them from outside. Similarly, the largest farms do not have enough human and draft animal power to do the work necessary on their plant component. Thus the larger farms employ the surplus human and animal labor available from the smaller farms.

Almost all of the farm families produce most of their own inputs and consume most of their own outputs. Most materials and energy recycle within the farm. These families do some commercial marketing and purchase some supplies such as seed, feed, and fertilizer. All men, women, and children contribute to the work of the family farm.

VIII. THE HUMAN COMPONENT

The human component is a natural beginning for the analysis of the farm family ecosystem in the subsistence agricultural sections of Nepal.

In order to compare and relate the human component of the farm family ecosystem with the other components, the authors made an estimate of the average number of kilocalories converted per person per day in a selection of Nepalese farm family ecosystems (Axinn and Axinn, 1979). To make that estimate, it was assumed that each person utilizes approximately 2,000 kcal of energy per day. This was used on all sizes of the farms in two districts.

These estimates were inserted into flow charts for each component of various sizes of farms. As an example, Fig. 3 illustrates the quantity of kilocalories transformed in the human component of farm family ecosystems averaging about 0.39 ha in size in Lamjung District.

IX. THE PLANT COMPONENT

The plant component is the major energy transformer in the small subsistence farm family ecosystem. In addition to solar energy, other inputs to the plant component on the Nepalese farms include draft power, manure, human labor, tools, seed, and water.

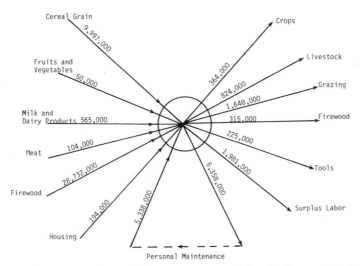

Fig. 3. Materials and energy flow in the human component of farm family ecosystems in Sundar Bazaar area of Lamjung District, Nepal, 1977. Average farm size, 0.39 ha. (Energy transformations are presented in kcal/ha/year.)

Analysis of various materials and energy flows into and out of the plant component of farm family ecosystems is illustrated in Fig. 4. This figure is based on data from farms averaging 0.39 ha in size in Lamjung District, Nepal.

In Lamjung District, the proportion of land actually used for cropping was higher on the smaller farms and less on the larger farms. As might be expected, the input of energy (kcal) to the total farming system from the plant component was largest per hectare on the smallest farms and smallest per hectare on the largest farms. The proportion of the total solar energy that was transformed by the plant component into forms usable to the other components was greatest on the smallest units and least on the largest units.

X. THE ANIMAL COMPONENT

The role of livestock in rural family ecosystems (Axinn, 1977) of Africa, Asia, and Latin America is often neglected in recent economic and social analyses. Scholars have tended to give little recognition to the importance of draft animals, both as a supplement to human energy *and* as a critical source of fertilizer. However, recently, several authors have identified the important interrelationships that exist between livestock enterprises and cropping systems on a farm. Among these, Harwood (1976) developed a generalized model of the farming system showing these interrelationships. A recent study of one small ethnic group in Nepal recognizes this critical component of the whole energy balance

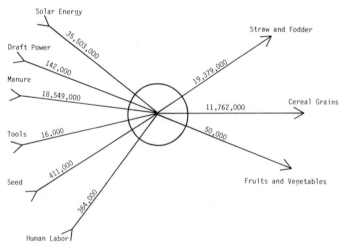

Fig. 4. Materials and energy flow in the plant component of farm family ecosystems in Sundar Bazaar area of Lamjung District, Nepal, 1977. Average farm size, 0.39 ha. (Energy transformations are presented in kcal/ha/year.)

by identifying the ecosystem linkages of animals and forests to sustain human life. "Wood and fodder flow from the high slopes above Thak, through the village where most of it is absorbed, down onto the cereal fields. On its way it produces many of the necessities of Gurung life: heat, housing material, protein, energy with which to work in the fields, and manure with which to produce cereals (calories)" (Macfarlane, 1976; Fig. 5).

On these farm family ecosystems, the total human labor per hectare required to take care of the animals varies inversely with the size of farm, and the total calories required per hectare for feeding the animals also varies inversely with the size of the farm.

Bullocks, or oxen, are of special importance in rural life in Nepal. Next to human power, bullocks supply most of the power for agriculture. Male cattle and male buffalo, castrated at about 1 year of age, are used to plow the soil, level the land, thresh grain, pull carts, and perform various other tasks.

Since those with the smallest land holdings have larger numbers of bullocks (and other large animals) per unit of land, they have some advantage in available manure. Each bullock produces approximately 5400 kg of fresh manure each year (Gotaas, 1956). However, those with very small holdings typically drive their cattle to public pastures and water sources, during which it is estimated that 20–30% of the manure is lost.

The bullock, being a ruminant, consumes coarse forage and fodder, which cannot be utilized as a source of human nutrition. Thus, some of this energy input is readily available at low cost and unusable except to ruminants. Further, the high human population per rural household provides labor that would be underutilized were it not for the opportunity to provide care, feeding, and watering to these animals.

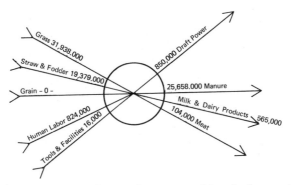

Fig. 5. Materials and energy flow in the animal component of farm family ecosystems in Sundar Bazaar area of Lamjung District, Nepal, 1977. Average farm size, 0.39 ha. (Energy transformations are presented in kcal/ha/year.)

XI. COMPONENTS LINKED IN FARM FAMILY
   ECOSYSTEM

When the three major components (human, plant, and animal) are combined for analysis, contrasts between large and small farm family ecosystems
become apparent. One example based on the smallest farms in Chitwan District
in Nepal, averaging 0.34 ha per farm, is given in Fig. 6. These farms do not
produce enough feed and fodder per hectare to supply the humans and the
animals. Assuming that the cereal grain goes to the humans until their needs are
satisfied and that total straw and fodder plus whatever surplus grain there might
be go to the animals, there is still a deficit of 26.3 million kcal/ha-year for the
animal component. The deficit is made up by cutting grass outside the farm and
by grazing animals along the roadside or on public pastures, for which the
human energy cost per year has been estimated at 730,000 kcal/ha.

Since the high population of animals on the smallest group of farms in the
Chitwan study produces a surplus of manure (estimated at 13,980,897 kcal/ha-
year), the family has a disposable surplus that can be sold to neighbors with larger
land holdings. Similarly, the bullocks on the smallest farms in that district
produce more draft power than can be utilized on those farms. Thus the surplus
of bullock power (amounting to 601,603 kcal/ha-year) is another output that can
be exchanged with neighbors. Also, since the population of humans per hectare
on these farms is relatively high, they can supply all of the labor inputs to plant
and animal production, supply, and marketing within the farm, as well as
personal maintenance; they can also supply the energy costs of gathering firewood, manufacturing tools, buildings, and facilities and still have a surplus of
human labor of 3,980,745 kcal/ha-year, which can be made available to other
farms.

By contrast, the largest sized group of farms in the study of that district had
8.11 ha per farm. These had an annual surplus from grain of 14,386,556 kcal
and a surplus of straw and fodder of 10,707,410 kcal/ha-year. The surplus is the
quantity produced in excess of that consumed within the farm family ecosystem.
Such a farm family is estimated to have an annual grain surplus of 117 million
kcal that could be marketed outside the family ecosystem or outside the rural
social system.

That largest type of farm, however, has an average annual deficit of calories
from manure of 1,094,797 kcal/ha or 8,878,804 kcal for the whole farm. Similarly, the largest farm has a deficit of human labor and a deficit of draft power.
On the average, such farms bring in 157,468 kcal of draft power per hectare per
year and 175,383 kcal/ha-year of human labor from other nearby farms. By the
type of estimation used in this study, that would be equivalent to 87.7 person-
days per hectare or 711 person-days per farm per year.

The smallest units seem to be the most "efficient" when comparing energy

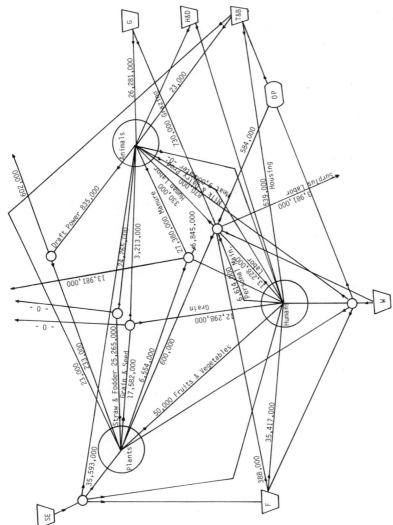

Fig. 6. Energy flow among major components of a farm family ecosystem in Chitwan District, Nepal, 1977. Data are given in kcal/ha/year. F, firewood; G, grass; H & D, health and dietary supplements; OP, other products; SE, solar energy; T & B, tools and buildings; W, water.

inputs and energy outputs. The larger units convert more energy per farming unit than smaller farms, and the larger units drain the surrounding ecosystems of more calories per hectare than do the smaller farms. However, the smaller units seem to transform a higher quantity of the solar energy available than do the larger units.

Analysis of energy flows suggests that large farms tend to be more specialized than small farms. The large farms absorb human labor and draft power from the surrounding environment, send cereal grain to the larger social system, and supply straw and fodder to the surrounding environment. These are more highly differentiated than the small farms, which consume all they produce and exchange only human and animal energy with other farms. One can infer that even at this microlevel of analysis, there is a tendency for the quantity of energy conversion to be directly related to the level of social differentiation. The efficiency of energy conversion appears to be inversely related to the level of social differentiation.

From the perspective of the people's actual work on the very smallest farms, the smaller the size of the farm, the more labor must be employed outside; this is simply because not enough is produced inside to feed the family. In that sense, the smaller the farm, the smaller the proportion of available family energy that can be recycled within the family farm ecosystem. Or, the smaller the farm, the larger the proportion of available family member energy that must be marketed off the farm.

XII. TYPES OF FARMING SYSTEMS

Estimates of materials flow and energy transformation in farm family ecosystems can be used as indicators of functional differentiation. The supply, production, and marketing functions, in particular, can be compared among different farming systems. Farming systems that specialize in production will tend to have greater proportions of materials and energy flows from outside (input supply) and greater proportions of such flows to the outside (output marketing). Less differentiated farming systems tend to have a higher proportion of total flows *within* the farm family ecosystem.

This perspective on social differentiation may be used as an indicator of change. Most strategies for rural development have been strategies designed to increase functional differentiation in farming systems. One reason that many international attempts in rural development have not been more successful may have been that designers of such projects have tended to use such economic indicators as cash flow rather than assessments of such social phenomena as functional differentiation.

Similarly, farming systems that are less specialized in function tend to carry on more different types of operations. A family that supplies its own inputs and consumes its own outputs will not specialize in one crop. Rather, the family will tend to produce cereal crops, livestock, fruits, and vegetables. Conversely, in the highly differentiated large-scale dairy farm of mid-America, for example, although milk from 300 cows may be produced daily, 100% of that milk is likely to be sold to a separate firm. If the farm household requires a quart of milk, it is likely to be purchased from an outside supplier.

Figure 7 provides a diagrammatic illustration of what might be termed a "pure" type of commercial farming system. Materials and energy flow in as inputs (arrow A) and flow out as outputs (arrow B). If 100% of the materials and energy flow were describable by the total flows on arrows A plus B, that would be, by definition, a "pure" type commercial farming system where the production function dominated all other functions.

If a "pure" type of subsistence farming system were to be described with a similar diagram, it would look like Fig. 8. In Fig. 8, arrow C represents the materials and energy flow that is both produced by the farm family ecosystem and consumed by that same farm family ecosystem. If zero inputs were supplied from outside systems and zero outputs were marketed to outside systems, 100% of the materials and energy flow would be on arrow C, and that would be a "pure" type of subsistence farming system.

Neither of these "pure" types exists among the rural social systems of the world. Even the most remote and undifferentiated farm family ecosystems tend to exchange some materials and energy with outside systems, and even the most commercially specialized farm family ecosystems tend to produce some kinds of "outputs" that are consumed within the system.

XIII. THE RECYCLING RATIO

The extent of this specialization (or functional differentiation) may be measured by a *recycling ratio*. The higher the proportion of materials and energy flow that is *within* the farm family ecosystem and its near environment, the higher the

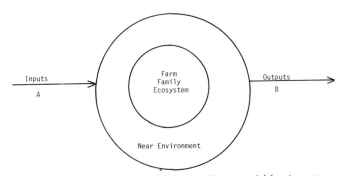

Fig. 7. Diagrammatic illustration of "pure type" commercial farming system.

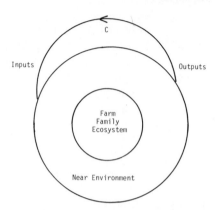

Fig. 8. Diagrammatic illustration of "pure type" subsistence farming system.

recycling ratio. The higher the recycling ratio, the less the farm family exchanges materials and energy with outside systems. Farms with a high recycling ratio are usually called subsistence farms. Farms with a low recycling ratio are referred to as commercial or market-oriented farms.

The diagram in Fig. 9 was constructed by putting together the diagrams in Figs. 7 and 8 to illustrate a typical farm family ecosystem. Materials and energy flow in (arrow A), materials and energy flow out (arrow B), and the system also recycles some of its materials and energy (arrow C). The recycling ratio represents the proportion of the total flow that is recycled (internal). It is calculated by adding an estimate of the total flow in from other systems (A) to an estimate of the total flow out to other systems (B) and to an estimate of the total quantity of

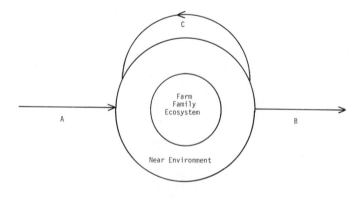

$$\text{RECYCLING RATIO} = \frac{C}{A + B + C}$$

Fig. 9. Materials flow and energy transformation in a farming system (simplified diagram). Recycling ratio = C/(A + B + C).

flow that is recycled within the system (C) and then by dividing that sum into the total quantity of flow that is recycled within the system. The recycling ratio equals C/ (A + B + C). Farming systems that recycle larger proportions of materials and energy within the system are, by definition, more independent of other outside systems. Conversely, farming systems that recycle a smaller proportion and receive greater quantities of materials and energy from outside, while marketing greater proportions of their production to others outside, are more dependent on those outside the family farm ecosystem.

In the large-scale, mono-crop, capital-intensive, commercial market-oriented farming systems of North America, the recycling ratio tends to be very low. Most inputs are purchased from outside the farm family ecosystem (seeds, feed, fertilizer, and fuel for traction). Most outputs are sold in the market in exchange for cash.

By contrast, in the small scale, mixed crop plus livestock, labor-intensive, subsistence-oriented farming systems of Africa, Asia, and Latin America, the recycling ratio tends to be much higher. Most inputs are produced within the farming system and most outputs are consumed within the farming system.

XIV. IMPLICATIONS OF ENERGY ANALYSIS FOR FOOD AND NUTRITION

In individual farm family ecosystems, examination of the recycling ratio leads to a focus on consumption rather than a focus on production. Strategies to increase consumption of appropriate mixtures of foods may or may not require increases in production. Often, increases in the production of one commodity result in decreases in production of other commodities because of competition for land, season, human labor, and other factors. The farm family ecosystem approach can identify the competitive relationships. Sometimes, strategies to improve storage of seed, for example, can have a positive impact on grain supplies, on grain production, and also on consumption. Strategies to reduce losses to rodents, insects, and microorganisms can lead to increases in consumption without increases in production.

In the larger rural social system, relationships among farm family ecosystems can be illuminated by the recycling ratio. Small mixed farming systems, particularly in the tropics, tend to convert a higher proportion of the available solar energy than do the larger, more specialized farming systems in the same location. The small mixed farming systems use a higher proportion of the land for a higher proportion of the year. The smaller units tend to have a lower labor efficiency but a higher land efficiency and higher energy efficiency as solar converters. When an entire rural area converts from units with high recycling ratios on many small farms to lower recycling ratios on fewer larger farms, food available to the human population in that area may be reduced. Thus, while this type of shift may be viewed as successful development by some (usually where there are low populations with excess of land and capital), it does not seem to be a long-run, viable option on the high-population rural areas that characterize most of Asia and parts of Africa and Latin America.

XV. IMPLICATIONS OF ENERGY ANALYSIS FOR FUEL FOR THE FAMILY

Even in remote rural areas among subsistence farm families the energy inputs in food preparation are greater than the energy values of the food being prepared. In more specialized social systems, the food preservation and food preparation energy inputs are even higher in relation to the energy value of the food itself.

Farm family ecosystems with high recycling ratios tend to use renewable energy sources for cooking fuel. Firewood is the most significant cooking fuel, with animal manure and crop residue being burned in some areas of extreme shortage of fuelwood. Biogas is also generated on a few larger family ecosystems. The efficiency of woodburning stoves can be increased using refinements. Also, solar cookers may replace woodstoves in some ecosystems. In some locations where coal or peat is readily available, it is a source of cooking fuel. These cooking systems give families significant independence from outside social systems.

As farm families increase their reliance on such fuels as kerosene, electricity, purchased coal, or gas, they have lower recycling ratios and less independence. Changes in outside price levels force adjustments within the family system.

From the perspective of the larger rural social system, group pressure for rotation forestry or evolution of mini-hydroelectric generators is developed when there are changes in the relative rates of transformation of locally available energy sources. For example, local forests tend to be managed much more effectively by a community that uses the fuelwood from that forest than by outside representatives of government agencies. Biogas generators, which may require relatively large numbers of users to be economic units, will be accepted in an area when the need is sufficiently evident, even if it requires changes in social organization.

XVI. IMPLICATIONS OF ENERGY ANALYSIS FOR RURAL DEVELOPMENT STRATEGIES AND INTERNATIONAL ASSISTANCE

The recycling ratio can be useful as an indicator of rural development, but the normative issues of good and bad will depend on the society values in terms of its lifestyle. Thus, the community where each farm family has a high recycling ratio may not be benefited at all by the introduction of technologies that would reduce this ratio. On the other hand, if that community wants more of the goods available from the outside, its goals may be a reduction of the recycling ratio; and technologies that will lead to that reduction may, in fact, be appropriate. Thus, the recycling ratio can be used as an *indicator of change* in rural social systems but not as the *goal for rural development*, which is normative. Each family and each society may determine its own goals. The recycling ratio can be used as a measure of where they are in development and as an indicator of change in the directions they have chosen. Development goals can be stated in terms of the optimal levels of recycling ratios.

A. Perspectives of Insiders and Outsiders

Similarly, the recycling of materials and energy in the human component, plant component, animal component, or other component can be separated from each other. Thus, a recycling ratio in the human component will demonstrate differences between families that must work as laborers (or servants) for others in order to sustain themselves and other families that have sufficient power to be served by outside laborers. This type of indicator allows a human group to fix developmental goals for themselves that are less likely to be skewed by "outsider's criteria" and the typical economic indicators.

By observing activities in farm family ecosystems, it is possible to estimate the recycling ratio. This, in turn, permits comparison between individual families and between rural groups of different cultures, different types of agriculture, and different religions.

Both from the perspective of insiders, who might systematically organize for their own "development," and from the perspective of outsiders, determined to assist with "development," different strategies are likely to be appropriate for farming systems with high recycling ratios than for farming systems with low recycling ratios. Thus, programs of technology development, extension education, and market infrastructure building would be quite different for the farming system with a high recycling ratio than for the farming system with a low recycling ratio.

B. Cooperatives

To illustrate, cooperatives that supply credit have been attempted in areas where farms have a high recycling ratio. Since farmers in those areas tend not to buy and sell on the market, they tend not to need outside credit of the type that such cooperatives can provide. Thus, credit cooperatives usually fail in those types of situations. Conversely, farms with a low recycling ratio and a high potential market output may have need for credit sources such as can be supplied by cooperatives.

In evolving strategies for rural development, identification of "target groups" by the relative size of their recycling ratios might provide a useful focus for programming.

C. Open versus Closed Systems

The recycling ratio for any group of farms indicates which farming systems are more "open" than others. Those with a high recycling ratio would be characterized as relatively more "closed." As they recycle most of their materials within the farm family environment, information supplied by tradition tends to be adequate to maintain the system. These farmers tend not to look to society's bureaucratic system to provide inputs for information via extension services, for instance, or material/energy such as seeds and fertilizer. Those with a lower recycling ratio would indicate more "openness" for new information that might be provided by outside systems. It could be assumed that those whose low recycling ratio reflects labor energy surplus would be responsive to information about alternative employment opportunities, training for different occupations, or intensive agriculture options. Those farmers whose low recycling ratio reflects surplus production available to the market might be open to information on credit and marketing as well as to information on alternative energy sources, such as mechanization and fertilizer, which would reduce their dependency on other farmers in labor surplus situations.

Additionally, this group of farmers tends to be more specialized and hence look to the bureaucracy of the society to provide organizational management to expedite exchanges among specialized commodity producers.

D. Support Services

Ultimately, those with the higher recycling ratios make the least demands for support services or material/energy inputs and are the least likely to be motivated to use those which are offered.

Implications for agricultural research relate to the farm family ecosystem as a "system." Instead of focusing research strategies around single commodities, the use of materials flow and energy transformation patterns to identify functional relationships within a farming system points to strategies in which each potential change in any particular component of the system is studied in terms of the impact of that change on all other components of that system.

Agricultural extension education can also be made more relevant to small, mixed farming systems by such an approach. This has implications both in the so-called "developing" countries and in the United States, where the Cooperative Extension Service has tended to focus on large-scale commercial agriculture. Since expanding cash income has been assumed to be the major universal goal for rural families, extension personnel and programs have been notably unsuccessful with noncommercial agriculturalists. The farm family ecosystem approach, using energy flow as a proxy rather than cash flow, can open new program strategies.

International development assistance can also be informed both by the cyclical perspective and by the farm family ecosystem approach. The extent of functional differentiation, the quantities of energy transformation, the recycling ratio, and the nature of materials flows all offer clues to outsiders as to what types of interventions are likely to be seen as "development" by insiders. This approach may also provide strategic help in determining what is likely to succeed and what is more likely to fail. Examples of the failure to use this approach are much more plentiful than examples of success.

The normal international development assistance assumption, whether it be by host country nationals, by "donor" country staff, or by international organizations, has been that since development and modernization vary together along the straight line of advancing technology, whatever comes from the more "advanced" countries is obviously better for the so-called "less-developed" countries. The fallacy is that in most cases a technology invented in one system to solve some of its problems is not likely to "fit" very well in another, very different system. If the technology is introduced, like an animal organ transplant that is not appropriate for the new system, it is likely to be rejected and may cause damage to the remainder of the system into which it is introduced.

Typical examples are petroleum-powered tractors being introduced into small mixed farming systems of Asia and Africa. These technological "improvements" in large-scale, mono-crop, capital-intensive farming systems tend to be rejected after introduction to small-scale, multiple-crop and livestock, labor-intensive farming systems.

E. Rural–Urban Relationships

The recycling ratio also has implications both for rural–urban competition within a nation–state and for international diplomatic relationships. If rural people are well off, enjoying high levels of consumption but with high recycling ratios, cities in their region are likely to be small and few in number. Where cities are very large in size and number, pressures tend to be exerted on rural people to lower their recycling ratios. Public policy tends to favor cheap food in the cities and combinations of taxes and prices that press farms to become larger in size, more specialized, and involve fewer people per hectare. Development strategies that require increased urbanization pressure rural people to lower their recycling ratios. This type of "efficiency" benefits urban people at the expense of rural people. A few may stay on the land and improve their wealth, but the majority must either migrate or starve.

Similarly, there is an international competition among nation–states. Rich, industrialized, urbanized nations can afford high prices for farm products imported from poor rural nations. This pressure forces large-scale plantation agriculture to replace many small, mixed farming systems. A few farms with low recycling ratios replace many farms with high recycling ratios. This deprives the majority of families of their source of food and of purchasing power.

REFERENCES

Adams, R. N. (1974). The implications of energy flow studies on human populations for the social sciences. In "Energy Flow in Human Communities," pp. 21–31. Proceedings of U.S. International Biological Program and Social Science Research Council, University Park, Pennsylvania.

Axinn, G. H. (1978). "New Strategies for Rural Development." Rural Life Associates, East Lansing, Michigan.

Axinn, G. H., and Axinn, N. W. (1979). Materials flow and energy transformation on small farms of Nepal: a new approach to comparative analysis of rural family ecosystems. Staff Paper No. 79-23, Center for International Programs. Michigan State University, East Lansing, Michigan.

Axinn, G. H., and Thorat, S. S. (1972). "Modernizing World Agriculture: A Comparative Study of Extension Education Systems." Praeger, New York.

Axinn, N. W. (1977). Rural development and education: a family ecosystem approach. In "Proceedings of the International Conference on Rural Development Technology: An Integrated Approach," pp. 535–544. Asian Institute of Technology, Bangkok, Thailand.

Axinn, N. W., and Axinn, G. H. (1980). The recycling ratio: an energy approach to planning rural development. World Congr. Rural Sociol. 5th, Mexico City, Mexico.

Cottrell, F. (1955). "Energy and Society, The Relation between Energy, Social Change, and Economic Development." McGraw-Hill, New York. (Reprinted by Greenwood Press, Westport, Connecticut. 1970, 1974.)

Georgescu-Roegen, N. (1975). Energy and economic myths. S. Econ. J. 41, 347–381.

Gotaas, H. B. (1956). "Composting." World Health Organization, Geneva, Switzerland.

Harwood, R. R. (1976). Farming systems in hill agriculture. In "A Study of Hill Agriculture in Nepal" (A. H. Moseman, ed.), pp. 93–119. The Rockefeller Foundation, New York.

Hawley, A. H. (1968). "Roderick D. McKenzie on Human Ecology." Univ. of Chicago Press, Chicago, Illinois.

Koenig, H. E., and Tummala, R. L. (1972). Principles of ecosystem design and management. IEEE Trans. Syst., Man, Cybernet. SMC-2, 449–459.

Macfarlane, A. (1976). "Resources and Population. A Study of the Gurungs of Nepal." Cambridge Univ. Press, London and New York.

Thomas, R. B. (1974). Human adaptation to energy flow in the High Andes: some conceptual and methodological considerations. In "Energy Flow in Human Communities" (P. L. Jamison and S. M. Friedman, eds.). Pennsylvania State University, University Park, Pennsylvania.

Thomas, R. B. (1976). Energy flow at high altitude. In "Man in the Andes" (P. T. Baker and M. A. Little, eds.), Chap. 19. Dowden, Hutchinson and Ross, Stroudsburg, Pennsylvania.

Tummala, R., and Connor, L. J. (1973). Mass-energy based economic models. IEEE Trans. Syst., Man, Cybernet. SMC-3, 548–555.

Chapter 7

Ethics, Economics, Energy, and Food Conversion Systems

Department of Agricultural Economics
Michigan State University
East Lansing, Michigan

> *Wisdom is the principle thing; therefore get wisdom: and with all thy getting get understanding.*
>
> *Proverbs 4:7*

A chapter dealing with ethics, energy, and food might deal with codes of conduct or the evaluation of decisions about energy and food or both. Codes of conduct have been developed for the legal and the medical professions, and some thought has been given to codes of conduct for agriculturalists. Although such codes are important, this chapter does not deal primarily with such a code; instead, it deals with an equally important or more important role for ethics— that of clarifying what various value theories, philosophies, and economics have to say about decisions involving energy and food conversion systems.

FOOD AND ENERGY RESOURCES

Ethics is conceived in this chapter as being useful in evaluating decisions and decision processes. It is regarded as the study, among other things, of "rightness" and "wrongness" of decisions and acts as well as of the goodness and badness of conditions, situations, and things. So conceived, the ethics of using energy in food conversion systems has to do with the adequacy of information, with the generation and evaluation of knowledge about goodness and badness as well as positivistic knowledge concerning energy and food. It is also concerned with the appropriateness of decision rules used to process such information into prescriptive decisions about what ought or ought not to be done to solve problems involving the use of energy in food conversion systems. In this chapter most of what stress there is on conduct centers on honesty in acquiring and using information about energy and food.

I. PHILOSOPHIC VALUE THEORY, ETHICS, AND ECONOMICS

It should not come as a surprise to educated people that economics is closely related to ethics and philosophic value theory. The optima defined by production, consumption, and welfare economics indicate "what ought to be done"— about what it is right to do—on the basis of (1) knowledge of nonmonetary as well as monetary values, (2) knowledge of positive characteristics of reality; both are processed through a decision rule. The classical literatures of philosophic value theory and economic theory include the writings of such well-known scholars as Adam Smith, Henry Sidgwick, Jeremy Bentham, John Stuart Mill, Karl Marx, and Vilfredo Pareto. The late C.I. Lewis, Professor of Philosophy at Columbia University, can be classified as an economist because of his conception of rightness as optimal and wrongness as less than optimal (1955). Currently, Nobel Laureate Kenneth Arrow, an economist, can also be assigned philosphic status because of his work on social choices and individual preferences (1951). The econometrician Georgescu-Roegan (1971) has made important contributions to economics and energy ethics in his book on entropy and economic processes (Johnson, 1973).

We all become practicing ethicists (and economists) when we accept responsibility for producing useful information about the utilization of energy in food conversion systems and make, advocate, or imply recommendations to solve practical problems in such systems. As such, we have much to gain from what ethics, economics, and the underlying field of epistemology have to say about generating, validating, and using knowledge about values, along with positive knowledge to generate prescriptive decisions as solutions to problems that involve the use of energy in food conversion systems.

II. THE MEANINGS OF SOME TERMS

In order to be sure that the reader will be encouraged to familiarize himself with the terminology followed in this chapter, these definitions are put here in the main body of the chapter rather than in a more easily neglected appendix. The reader is urged to study it. Such a glossary of terms is especially necessary in view of the special meanings assigned to these terms by philosophers and others, the more so since there is considerable variation in the meanings assigned to these terms among economists (Machlup, 1969) and even among philosphers, including ethicists and epistemologists. This section explains the meanings of selected terms used in this chapter, some defined and others undefined. In this chapter, the following terms will have the indicated meanings.

Good and Bad   These are relatively undefined terms. Their meanings are known largely from experience. Goodness or badness are regarded as characteristics of conditions, situations, and things.

Value   The meaning of a proposition about the goodness or badness of a condition, situation, or thing. There are both monetary and nonmonetary values (Sinden and Worrell, 1979).

Normative Knowledge   Knowledge about goodness and badness, i.e., about values. A normative fact is the meaning of a normative proposition deemed to have an acceptable degree of veracity with respect to what is.

Positive Knowledge   Knowledge about characteristics of conditions, situations, and things other than about their goodness and badness. The most basic positive knowledge can be regarded as relatively undefined and mainly experiential in nature. However, complex positive knowledge may be defined in terms of more primitive, less-defined positive terms. A positive fact is the meaning of a positive proposition deemed to have an acceptable degree of veracity with respect to what is.

Intrinsic Value   The value of a condition, situation, or thing under consideration in and of itself rather than as a means of attaining another condition, situation, or thing that has value.

Instrumental Value   A condition, situation, or thing that derives its value from being a means of attaining a condition, situation, or thing that has either intrinsic or further instrumental value.

Value in Exchange   The value of the last unit of a condition, situation, or thing given up when it is sacrificed in order to attain more of another condition, situation, or thing. Alternatively, it is the value of another unit of a condition, situation, or thing that is acquired by giving up some of a different condition, situation, or thing. All exchange values are instrumental but not all instrumental values are exchange values.

Right and Wrong Right and wrong are defined terms. Their definition requires both positive and normative knowledge processed through a decision rule into decisions about what is right or wrong to do. Rightness and wrongness are prescriptive in nature, i.e., they deal with what "ought" or "ought not" to be or to have been done, not with what is or was.

Prescriptive Knowledge Knowledge about what "ought" or "ought not" to be done in order to solve a problem, knowledge about right and wrong.

Tests of Truth There are four tests for the truth of a proposition or concept: logical consistency, consistency with experience, clarity (lack of ambiguity or vagueness), and workability when a proposition or concept is used to solve a problem. (See also Objective Proposition or Fact, which follows.)

Objective Proposition or Fact A proposition (normative or positive) that has been adequately tested (for purposes at hand) according to the four tests listed previously and has not yet failed. An objective proposition or fact is not regarded as having been *proven* to correspond to reality and is not regarded as absolute truth; instead, there is always the possibility that what is accepted as true today will be disproven tomorrow.

An Objective Investigator An investigator willing to subject his concepts and propositions to the above tests of truth and to abide by the results.

Logical Positivism A philosophy that holds that descriptive truth is based on experience and logic. Experience is viewed as generating undefined primitive terms that are used, in turn, to transform analytical (logical) sentences into synthetic (descriptive) propositions. As positivism presumes that there are no experiences of normative reality, undefined primitive normative terms, and hence, normative synthetic propositions are ruled out by positivism, but not in this chapter. Nonetheless, the techniques and methods of logical positivism are highly productive in generating positive knowledge. They are also effective in generating normative knowledge if not constrained by the untested presupposition that there is no normative reality to be experienced.

Normativism A group of philosophies and philosophic points of view concerned with normative knowledge, i.e., with the nature of goodness and badness and with the origin and possible verification and validation of normative propositions about a normative reality.

Pragmatism A philosophy that holds that the truth of concepts and propositions depends on their consequences. It holds, for instance, that when one knows all of the differences between the consequences of two concepts or propositions, one knows all the truth that is knowable about the difference between the two. As normative and positive propositions condition the prescriptive consequences of each other, they are interdependent for pragmatists in the context of the problems they are used to solve, and the test of workability in solving a problem becomes a relevant test of truth.

Product   The concept of product is normative. Technically, all inputs that enter a production process come out. Part of the output possesses the property of goodness; this part is called product. Those parts that are valueless are called wastes. Those parts that possess the property of badness are also called wastes but are further identified with such terms as pollutants, noxious wastes, etc.

Efficiency   Efficiency is defined as the ratio between the value of the outputs of a production process and the value of the inputs it uses. To define efficiency as the technical ratio (one devoid of values) between output and input is meaningless to economists, ethicists, and technicians as such ratios are always one (Knight, 1933; Boulding, 1981).

III. PROBLEM-SOLVING PROCESSES AND DECISION MAKING

Ethicists are concerned with the evaluation of decisions. Economists are concerned with the decision rules used to make decisions as to the optimum act to perform. In evaluating decisions, it helps to understand decision making as a part of problem solving. This section uses some of the terms explained previously to present the view of problem solving followed in this chapter. The view presented here is similar to that of Sinden and Worrell (1979); however, they involve economics more specifically and, in doing so, do not differentiate between intrinsic and exchange values and do not treat the question of whether there may or may not be a normative reality that is experienced in developing value propositions.

Although a problem-solving process is continuous, it can be partitioned and analyzed in several ways. The view of the problem-solving process followed in this chapter is represented in Fig. 1, which portrays six problem-solving steps. Making a decision about a problem is one of those steps. All of the arrows among the six steps in Fig. 1 are two-way arrows, to represent the information feedbacks and various successive iterations that occur in the process.

In addition to the six steps, there are two information banks in Fig. 1. One bank contains the normative information so important in decision making and ethics. The other contains positive information. The legitimacy of these two banks varies among positivistic, normativistic, and pragmatic philosophies. There are two-way arrows from each of the banks to each of the six steps in the process, as a problem solver may both draw on information from and deposit information in both banks at any step in the process. There is also an overarching loop labeled "pragmatic interdependence," which recognizes the pragmatic implication that positive and normative information are interdependent in the context of the problem being addressed. The observation and analysis steps

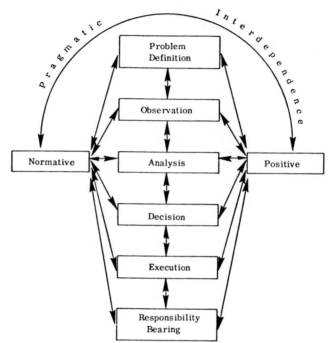

Fig. 1. Problem-solving processes and information banks showing pragmatic interaction.

include the generation, validation, and verification of positive and normative data. Honesty and competence in carrying out these processes are prerequisites for successful decision making and problem solving.

The decision step is of particular interest for this paper, which treats ethics as evaluative of decisions and decision-making processes. The output of the decision-making step is a prescription. Prescriptions are considered in more detail later in the discussion of Eq. (1).

After a decision is reached, the next step is to execute it while the final step is to bear responsibility for the consequences of the action. Responsibility lies with decision makers and with those who bear the consequences of an action taken on the basis of decisions. Responsibility bearers monitor the environment affected by the act to determine the consequences of the act. Some of these consequences are positive, others are normative. Decisions and actions can be evaluated in terms of their success in avoiding badnesses and in attaining goodness. Honesty is a prerequisite for successful evaluation of decisions and their execution.

Figure 1 appropriately stresses that solving problems requires and generates both normative and positive knowledge. Practical problems cannot be defined without both. In addition to generating positive and normative knowledge, the overall process uses both to generate prescriptive knowledge. Ethics, as noted in the first section of this chapter, involves both normative and prescriptive knowledge.

Equation 1 is of some help in envisioning the relationship between normative knowledge and the prescriptive knowledge produced in the decision-making step.

$$\text{Prescriptive} = f \text{ (normative, positive)} \tag{1}$$

The function "f" is a decision rule. It uses positive and normative knowledge to generate a prescription for solving the problem under investigation.

Under the assumption of *perfect knowledge*, economists and ethicists can use the simple decision rule of *first* subtracting badness from goodness (both of which are normative) subject to constraints specified by positive knowledge and *then* maximizing the difference as a simple application of calculus. This use of calculus to optimize presumes (1) a normative common denominator (such as money or utility) among the goods and bads involved, (2) the second-order conditions mathematically necessary to guarantee the existence of the maximum sought, (3) an interpersonally valid common denominator if the various goodnesses accrue to and the various badnesses are incurred by different individuals, and (4) an "agreed upon" decision rule, "f." In the case of *imperfect knowledge*, ethics is greatly complicated by (1) the need to establish the preconditions for optimization and (2) the existence of a number of different possible decision or maximization rules such as "maximize the expected difference between goodness and badness," "maximize the best that can happen," "minimize the worst that can happen," "satisfice," etc., one of which has to be accepted in a sort of politico-socio-economic covenant.

The ethics of making decisions in dynamic changing environments is also complicated by (1) the need to engage in learning that introduces the economics of the learning processes inherent in the first four steps of Fig. 1, (2) varying degrees of interpersonal validity in knowledge of the normative common denominator, and (3) the infinite cost of perfect knowledge. The last of these conditions (the infinite cost of perfect knowledge) makes it necessary to include various distributions of power in the decision function if conflicts are to be resolved with decisiveness. Some of the important kinds of power in decision rules include market, social, police, political, and military power. Knowledge is, itself, a source of power, particularly in the long run. At any point in time, the young members of future generations are poorly represented in the power structures of the present; this point is particularly important in considering the ethics of decisions on when to use fossil fuels.

Although this chapter is not primarily concerned with codes of conduct, it must consider honesty. In evaluating decisions and decision-making processes, it is important to know whether the positive and normative information used has been honestly tested. It is also important to know whether an agreed-on decision rule has been honestly employed. Positive and normative truth can be viewed as tested on the basis of the four criteria listed in the glossary above: internal logical consistency, consistency with experience, clarity or lack of ambiguity, and workability. Honesty requires that decision makers and investigators apply these four tests and abide by the results. Concepts or propositions can be regarded as objective and honest when they have been subjected to what is regarded as an adequate amount of testing, even if later demonstrated to be false. The avoidance of tests, falsification of test results, pretense that unconducted tests have been conducted, and the use of information known to be false are clearly forms of dishonest and, hence, unethical behavior. Honesty is considered further in Section V,C.

Some academic disciplines such as chemistry and physics concentrate on generating positive knowledge. Other academic disciplines such as the humanities (including ethics) concentrate on the generation of normative knowledge about such things as honesty, fossil fuels, life, food, justice, and pollutants. In addition to the positivistic and normativistic disciplines there are the decision disciplines and subjects that both (1) study decision-making processes formally and (2) assist in solving problems. Among the important decision disciplines and multidisciplinary subjects are ethics, engineering, farm management, medicine, architecture, business administration, dentistry, and economics, not to mention such disciplines as law, political science, and psychiatry. The decision-making disciplines may have as their objectives the creation of an optimum design for a new machine, an optimum institutional arrangement, or the optimum improvement in human beings through educational processes. Economists and others seek optima both to (1) prescribe what should be done in order to solve a problem and (2) predict the behavior of problem-solving producers, resource owners, and consumers.

IV. CONTRIBUTIONS OF ETHICS AND ECONOMICS TO SOLUTIONS OF PROBLEMS INVOLVING ENERGY USE IN FOOD CONVERSION SYSTEMS

We seek guidance from ethics and economics on the kinds of knowledge needed on energy use in food conversion systems. This section gives attention to three important kinds of research for satisfying these information needs, three kinds of knowledge (positive, normative, and prescriptive) required, and the contributions that three different philosophies make to producing the three required kinds of knowledge, two of which are prescriptive and normative and, hence, ethical in nature. Figure 2 has three dimensions dealing with the three kinds of research (in the vertical dimension), the three kinds of knowledge (in one of the horizontal dimensions) and, three important guiding philosophies (in

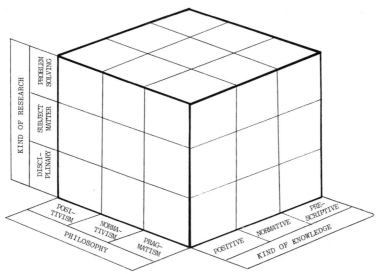

Fig. 2. Schematic showing three kinds of research, three important kinds of knowledge generated in research, and three philosophies important in research.

the other horizontal dimension). The three dimensions in Fig. 2 permit us to envision the interrelationships among three philosophies important in science, kinds of knowledge, and whether we are dealing with practical problems involving food and energy, on one extreme, or academic disciplinary questions, at the other.

A. The Three Kinds of Research That Generate Information on the Use of Energy in Food Conversion Systems

Research on energy and food can be grouped into three categories according to where they fall on the disciplinary/problem-solving research spectrum. The three kinds of research are disciplinary, subject matter, and problem solving, each of which is defined in the following three subsections.

1. Disciplinary Research

Disciplinary research is done to improve one of the basic academic disciplines such as chemistry, physics, economics, ethics, or biochemistry. It is research done to improve a discipline's basic theory, its fundamental measurements, and/or its techniques and methods. Disciplinary research can be subclassified into two categories: those of known and unknown relevance. Some disciplinary research, such as that on photorespiration and the creation of human capital, is known to be relevant for solving practical problems involving food and energy.

Disciplinary research on the use of energy in food conversion systems has been fairly extensive in the physical and biological sciences but less adequate in the decision sciences and in the humanities. Food conversion systems typically convert energy inputs of lesser value into *products* (forms of energy that have higher value), *waste* (forms of energy that have no value), and *pollutants* (forms of energy that have negative value). Although the second law of thermodynamics ensures either no net gain or a loss of low level entropy in all production processes, a production process is advantageous if there is a *net gain in value* in it.

Production, productivity, and efficiency are never purely physical or technical, as they depend crucially on values (Knight, 1933; Boulding, 1981). Therefore, energy accounting that does not take into account the value of the kinds of energy in different products (including foods) tell us little about production, productivity, and efficiency (Johnson, 1974). Before we can deal intelligently with questions of productivity and efficiency in the use of energy, we need to know much more about the value of different forms of energy and levels of entropy (Georgescu-Roegen, 1971).

Our knowledge of the intrinsic (as contrasted to the exchange) values of different forms of energy, kinds of food, and food conversion processes is particularly deficient. Means of overcoming this deficiency are considered in Section IV,B.1, which deals with normative information.

2. Subject Matter Research

Subject matter research can be defined as research of a multidisciplinary nature useful to a more or less well-defined set of practical problem solvers facing a more or less well-specified set of problems. In subject matter research on the utilization of energy in food conversion, the multidisciplinary subject being researched is regarded as important for solving a rather well-defined set of problems involving the use of energy in food conversion faced by a rather well-defined set of decision makers. Typically, subject matter research is not complete enough to solve any particular problem in the set; instead, it merely supplies a body of information useful in solving the problems of the set.

The systems that utilize energy in food conversion have institutional and human as well as technical dimensions that influence their ability to generate net increases in value. Generally, the ethical evaluation of decision processes and of decisions with respect to the use of energy in a food conversion system requires multidisciplinary analyses dealing with all three of these dimensions of the system. Systems analyses vary from informal "back of an envelope" or "seat of one's pants" analyses to highly formalized, large-scale, computerized systems science models. Research on such systems generates information badly needed by those concerned with problems involving food and energy. The next subsection considers some of our different subject matter research needs.

3. Problem-Solving Research

The third broad category of research that generates useful information on energy and food conversion systems is problem-solving research. It, like subject matter research, is multidisciplinary in nature. Problem-solving research generates or draws on positive and normative knowledge to produce prescriptions as to how to solve a specific problem for a specific decision maker (or specific set of decision makers facing the same problem). The mix of disciplines varies from problem to problem. Practical problems do not respect the disciplinary boundaries of universities.

In this connection, it is important to realize that there is no single definite "energy and food problem" that can be referred to with the definite article *the*. Instead of there being *the* problem, there exists a multiplicity of problems involving food and/or energy in greater or lesser degrees. Particular practical problems are time, space, culture, and decision-maker specific. Attempts to solve *the* food or *the* energy problem or *the* problem of using energy in food conversion systems are doomed to failure by lack of specificity as to which problem is under attack. Problem-solving research on energy use in food conversion systems is done largely in (1) the USDA/land grant colleges of agriculture, (2) the agribusiness sector (including farms) that generates inputs, produces farm products, and processes farm products into food, which it also distributes; and (3) state and federal regulatory agencies dealing with energy and food.

B. Kinds of Information Needed in Researching the Use of Energy in Food Conversion Systems

We note that both problem-solving and subject matter research are multidisciplinary. Problem-solving research necessarily generates prescriptive knowledge and, thus, is the only one of the three kinds of research specifically designed to generate prescriptive knowledge. As such, problem-solving research always has to utilize both normative and positive information.

The decision disciplines and subjects such as economics, engineering, farm management, law, medicine, dentistry, architecture, business administration, and military science are sometimes concerned with the formal study of the processes whereby problem-solving decisions are made. Disciplinarians from the decision disciplines also engage, in their applied work, in decision making, generally as part of multidisciplinary participatory exercises. The other two kinds of research, disciplinary and subject matter, do not typically provide all of the information needed to solve a particular problem and do not involve responsibility for generating a prescription to solve a particular problem involving food or energy. Disciplinary research, depending on the discipline involved, may generate positive or normative information. In this section, we are concerned with normative, positive, and prescriptive knowledge.

1. Normative Information

Normative information is needed about the monetary and nonmonetary values associated with using energy in food conversion systems. This kind of research is much neglected in researching food and energy and, when done, is often poorly done. Both the World Food and Nutrition Study (WFNS), conducted by the National Academy of Sciences at the request of President Ford, and the Commission on World Hunger (CWH), which was established by President Carter, neglected the monetary and nonmonetary values associated with food except for proceeding mainly on the basis of "self-evident" or even arbitrarily assumed values. Unfortunately, some of the values stressed in the WFNS exercises appear unobjective and self-serving for the scientists involved (Johnson, 1981). While this appeared to be less true for the political and social leaders as well as the research leaders who served on the CWH, that exercise was not entirely free of arbitrary values. Generally speaking, values were treated in these exercises as if they were intrinsic in nature. Values in exchange from the marketplace were often neglected and, in several instances, denigrated as misleading. We note that exchange values can hardly be denigrated logically while emphasizing intrinsic values inasmuch as values in exchange are derived from intrinsic values. The market establishes values in exchange (both monetary and nonmonetary in nature) as a result of marginal tradeoffs (derivatives with respect to the amount of the condition, situation, or thing having value) among values in view of what is possible given the distribution of the ownership of income producing rights and privileges. At that point, we must question the normative worth of the work done by "energy accountants," who add up various forms of energy in terms of some unit such as the British thermal unit (BTU), regardless of the values (monetary or nonmonetary and intrinsic or in exchange) of different forms of energy and levels of entropy (Johnson, 1974). There is nothing wrong with adding up BTUs so long as the result is regarded as positive and of no normative significance. This precludes their use as an indicator of efficiency (Knight, 1933; Boulding, 1981). Georgescu-Roegan's demonstration (1971) that values are related to entropy (the second law of thermodynamics) is ignored when the BTUs of energy required to produce a product are added up and interpreted as inefficient because, in accordance with the second law, they are less than the BTUs in the product except when some source of energy such as a renewable source of energy, like sunshine, is left outside the accounting system. The normative damage is done when such data are used to draw conclusions about efficiency, as efficiency is normative while the BTU data are positive (see Section II). There is a need for a common denominator such as money among the values of (1) the different kinds of energy used in food conversion and in the converted foods and (2) among the various nonfood products that are generated in a society. Ideally, this common denominator should measure intrinsic as opposed to exchange value. For exchange values there is often no better common denominator than the monetary unit. For either exchange or intrinsic values, however, the monetary unit is better than the BTU, which is positive and not normative. A BTU is a measure of an amount of energy that has legitimate positivistic uses. However, when the BTUs of energy in a pile of cow manure, a gallon of gasoline, and a bushel of corn are added to the energy in a prime steak served to one in a restaurant with a very pleasant atmosphere and in the company of an attractive member of the opposite sex, the result is normative nonsense.

Obviously, we need better measurements of *intrinsic* values, particularly of the nonmonetary values of energy for future generations associated with problems involving food and energy. It was noted above that *monetary values in exchange* have serious shortcomings but that they are a good, readily available normative common denominator if used carefully. The BTU is so poor as a normative common denominator that it should hardly be considered. A major difficulty with exchange values (money prices in some but not in all cases) from a market or a political system is that they reflect the distribution of ownership of income producing resources and other forms of power in markets and political systems. Equilibrium market prices are partially determined by income distributions. Thus the meanings of values in exchange change when (1) energy shortages redistribute the ownership of resources or (2) energy crises create demands by various antiestablishment activist groups to redistribute the ownership of income-producing rights and privileges. In a letter to this author, David Pimentel (1983), an editor and contributor of this volume, pointed out clearly and correctly that different kinds of kilocalories (kcal) have "different values to human society" and that these exchange values vary among "societies from one year to the next" and for that matter from region to region and country to country within a year. Thus, we need such knowledge of intrinsic values. Pimentel also noted that "we can also make technical evaluations of the low grade (solar radiation) energy in and the high grade energy (electricity or food) out and calculate a ratio of low grade to high grade energy output/input. This efficiency of energy conversion . . . is important information. . . ." This latter quotation nicely indicates how knowledge about the intrinsic value of different forms of energy can be used to learn something about efficiency not learnable from kilocalories. It is probably better to avoid comparisons between technical and economic efficiency (Knight, 1933; Boulding, 1981), as all measures of efficiency that have any interest are normative and not technical. In any event, Pimentel has furnished a very useful example of an instance in which knowledge of intrinsic value can be used to convert positivistic BTU or kilocalorie data into useful knowledge about efficiency, efficiency not being the unique province of either economics or technology. Knowledge of intrinsic or exchange values before and after proposed redistributions is more useful than BTU accounts.

2. Positive Information

Positive information is at least as important as normative information in the ethics of food and energy. Accurate, honest, positive information about using energy in food conversion is crucial. We need accurate positive information concerning the extent of *all* energy involved in food conversion, their rates of depletion and deterioration, requirements for energy source maintenance and augmentation, and the rates at which different forms of energy are convertible into various food and associated services. BTU accounting is a very useful kind of positivistic knowledge provided it is not misinterpreted as normative. Without accurate, honest, positive information to combine with accurate, honest information about values, there is no possibility of producing honest, accurate prescriptions to solve the problems we face with respect to food and energy.

3. Prescriptive Information

Prescriptive information is the objective of problem-solving research efforts. It contrasts to the positive and normative information discussed in the above paragraphs that can be procured through disciplinary and subject matter research. Prescriptive information is based on normative and positive knowledge [recall Eq. (1)]. Its distinguishing characteristic is that it is the logical consequence of processing positive and normative information through a decision rule. The decision rule provides the logic whereby positive and normative information are converted into prescriptive knowledge. A preliminary step in generating prescriptive knowledge is to choose a decision rule to use. Distributions of various forms of power—market, social, political, military, and police power among others— are important components of decision rules and of the subdecision rules used in choosing which decision rule to use. Many commonly advocated prescriptions to solve problems involving food and energy are based on faulty appreciation of the importance and intricacies of decision rules. Energy and food activists, academicians grinding axes for their own empires and appropriations, and "viewers with alarm" are notoriously careless in their use of decision rules and in their empirical appraisals of those power distributions so important that they must be incorporated in decision rules. The thought and practical experience of the decision disciplines and subjects—ethics, economics, law, engineering, farm management, architecture, business administration, medicine and dentistry—have much to offer. Disciplinary prescriptive information needed from the decision discipline includes information about decision rules to use in processing positive and normative knowledge into prescriptions. Currently, much work is being done on the "expected utility" decision rule (Schoemaker, 1982). This decision rule is highly specialized and is very useful but is only one among many. There is a particular need for more knowledge about the roles played by various power distributions in decision rules. Also, decision rules need to be related to optimization with respect to learning and information banking and retrieval. Another kind of knowledge needed is that about "true" risk preference and aversion, particularly for the public decision makers and the agencies concerned with food and energy utilization. Much of the current work on "risk preference and aversion" measures the curvature of utility functions for income and/or wealth rather than "true" risk preference or aversion. True risk preference and aversion involves the assignment of different values to different specific outcomes when risk and uncertainty are associated with them than when they are not.

C. Three Important Philosophies That Guide Physical and Social Scientists

Section II of this chapter discussed the meanings of various terms, including the meanings of logical positivism, normativism, and pragmatism. These three philosophies have an important bearing on our ability to generate and use the three kinds of knowledge discussed above. Each of these philosophies is discussed in the sections below.

1. Logical Positivism

As defined in Section II of this chapter, logical positivism is the dominant important philosophy underlying the generation of positivistic knowledge in the biological and physical sciences. The knowledge generated in these sciences tends to be produced in substantial part using the techniques and methods of logical positivism. These techniques and methods employ observation and experience as well as logic to generate positive knowledge about the biological and physical worlds. Because logical positivism takes the position that objective normative knowledge is impossible, there is a tendency of researchers, guided by the philosophy of logical positivism, to neglect research on values and to exercise freedom—one might better say illegitimate license—in making arbitrary assumptions about values if and when positions must be taken on values. The consequent neglect of objective research on values and the tendency to make arbitrary assumptions about values tends to (1) confine logically positivistic investigators to answering positivistic questions even with respect to subject matter research and

(2) make their problem-solving research arbitrary in the sense that its normative content is not subjected to the test of experience. In a real sense, logical positivists preclude themselves from objective problem definition and solution. Nonetheless there exists that which is known as positivistic ethics (Kaplan, 1968) and, in law, that which is called positivistic jurisprudence (Bodenheimer, 1967). Both tend to deal with whether the positivistic preconditions for an act to be ethical or lawful have been met instead of dealing with establishing the law. It should be noted that logical positivism is now regarded as passé by many philosphers (Achinstein and Barker, 1969); thus science need no longer avoid the normative and prescriptive as unscientific, which opens the way for a more objective approach to practical problems.

2. Normativistic Philosophies

The various normativistic philosophies include some that rely almost wholly on logic and others that also rely on experience. Some normativistic philosophies find the origin of values in metaphysical presuppositions. Other normativists employ both logic and experience in generating normative knowledge and are hence in a less arbitrary position than those who base their normative knowledge on assumptions and metaphysical presuppositions. Normative knowledge includes both monetary and nonmonetary values. It also includes intrinsic values and values in exchange. Quantitative techniques for measuring and working with monetary values are well developed. Various normative philosphies have also contributed substantially to the ability of ethicists and economists to work with nonmonetary values as demonstrated by research done on consumer surpluses, producer surpluses, and the estimation of utility functions with techniques associated with "expected utility analysis" (Schoemaker, 1982; Sinden and Worrell, 1979). The normative philosophies, thus, contribute substantial techniques and methods for generating and analyzing objective normative knowledge for use in both defining and solving problems involving the use of energy in food conversion systems. In doing so, they provide an essential ingredient for objective problem-solving research and for the objective generation of normative knowledge as part of various subject matter research efforts involving energy and food conversion systems. In short, various normative philosophies provide much of what is required for an objective ethics to deal with problems involved in using energy in food conversion systems (Moore, 1956).

3. Pragmatism

Pragmatism is a philosophy that tends to deal with the simultaneous generation of positive and normative knowledge as part of problem-solving activities. As such, it is remarkably well-adapted to doing problem-solving research involving the use of energy in food conversion processes. Its drawbacks involve its complexity, holism, and the view that positive and normative knowledge are mutually interdependent. Pragmatic research is problem oriented and requires attention to the multidisciplinary domains of practical problems under the presupposition that positive and normative knowledge are interdependent. It often leads to very complex approaches to problem solving and an inability, in many instances, to subdivide the problem into parts amenable to independent positive and normative investigation by specific disciplines and individual investigators. When the problematic situation really is holistic, a pragmatic approach has real advantages; however, there appear to be instances in which the interdependence between positive and normative information is not so tight as to preclude division of labor among academic disciplines in attacking the problem (Johnson and Zerby, 1973). In these latter instances, pragmatism often results in an unduly cumbersome and expensive way of attaining knowledge. A simpler, less costly alternative to pragmatism is, of course, that of using independently derived positive and normative information to solve problems.

V. INFORMATION NEEDED TO SOLVE PROBLEMS INVOLVING THE USE OF ENERGY IN FOOD CONVERSION SYSTEMS

This section concentrates on three bodies of information that the author deems important for solving significant private and public problems in the energy/food conversion sector. We need (1) to understand how to generate technical, institutional, and human change and accumulation of physical capital, (2) knowledge about the distributions of power (market, political, social, police, military, etc.) important in deciding on solutions to problems in energy/food conversion systems, and (3) knowledge about the performance of information systems serving decision makers in the food and energy conversion systems. While other kinds of knowledge about the use of energy in food conversion systems are important, these three bodies of knowledge would do much to improve and to make our decisions about energy and food conversion more ethical.

A. Information Needed on Technical, Institutional, and Human Change and on Physical Capital Accumulation

We need more knowledge on three driving forces in societies—technological advance, institutional improvements, and investments in human agents—in order to improve our decisions on the use of energy in food conversion systems.

In addition, we need better knowledge on accumulation of physical capital, a fourth driving force. In order to handle our problems involving the use of energy in food conversion more ethically, we need to utilize all four of these forces in a balanced way unhampered by biased or inadequate knowledge.

1. Technical Change

We need better knowledge about technical change in energy/food conversion systems. This is, in part, an ethical matter as research to generate new technology for using energy in food conversion needs to be guided by knowledge of the values of such technologies and of the values of the products and services (processing and marketing) they produce. We are required ethically (economically) to economize on valuable energy inputs. In this connection it is important to recognize the opportunity cost principle in establishing the value of energy inputs and of the products and services. For instance, the opportunity cost of converting edible grains into gasohol is high. Also corn stover, which appears at first blush to be a source of low-priced energy, is often seen to be very expensive when its value as a source of organic matter and fertilizer for building up soils and preventing erosion is considered. In considering the conversion of feed grains into livestock products, many deplore the BTUs not converted into human food. Unlike the gasohol conversions of grains, the exchange values of meat products produced from grain are high enough for these processes to be advantageous without subsidies. Yet, many energy activists advocate gasohol while decrying grain feeding of animals. Persons advocating the elimination of grain-fed livestock often do so without giving due attention to the alternative opportunities for using the immense quantity of feedgrain consumed in livestock production. Eliminating grain-fed livestock would greatly increase the exchange value of grain fed to livestock while forcing its diversion into uses, including exports to the world's poor. Such diversion would, in turn, only be attainable at the cost of tremendous subsidies (paid for with taxes or by inflation) while prices of grass fed livestock products would soar, to the great detriment of the same taxpayers and consumers. Clearly, the ethics and economics of deciding whether to produce gasohol and/or eliminate grain feeding requires substantial amounts of increased knowledge about exchange values (including opportunity costs). Intrinsic values and instrumental values that are not also exchange values are important. Our nutritional knowledge about the intrinsic and instrumental goods and bads associated with ingestion of plant and animal protein, vegetable oils, and animal fats is also improving. As such normative knowledge is accumulated and distributed, consumers' concepts about the exchange values and the opportunity costs of using grain to produce dairy products, aquacultured fish, eggs, poultry meat, pork, beef, lamb, and mutton change. These changes are already changing consumption patterns for grain-fed livestock products in nutritionally desirable directions without expensive regulations, taxes, and subsidies.

2. Technological Changes

Technological advance without the institutional changes necessary to create a favorable climate for the utilization of the advance makes little sense. In Nigeria, for instance, oil palm varieties were developed that were capable of harvesting two to three times as much solar energy per acre under farm conditions as can be harvested with traditional varieties. These varieties have gone almost unutilized in Nigeria because of an institutional arrangement that imposed up to a 50% tax on palm oil exports. Malaysians, with more appropriate institutional arrangements, now use the same improved oil palm varieties extensively, to their great benefit.

On the other hand, the naivete with which institutional changes are suggested with respect to energy and food conversion systems by activists and/or biological and physical scientists untrained with respect to policy and decision processes startles and disheartens persons aware of the intricacies of these processes and of the differences between the exchange and intrinsic values of different forms of energy and entropy. Examples include the proposal to make institutional changes to greatly reduce grain feeding of livestock, which was discussed previously. In this connection, it is important that we be able to see the secondary and tertiary as well as primary consequences of proposed institutional changes. The secondary and tertiary consequences are generated by the decisions reached within the freedom permitted under the new institutional proposal. Economics and ethics have much to offer in predicting the secondary and tertiary consequences of whatever freedom of choice is permitted in any institutional arrangement. Environmentalists and ecologists have a similar, although different and less complex role to play, vis-à-vis secondary and tertiary environmental effects. While the physical and biological environment is complex, its complexity is but part of the complexity of total systems including social, political, and economic dimensions. All of these dimensions must be taken into account in envisioning the secondary and tertiary impacts of institutional change in social, political, and economic systems.

3. Human Change

In turn, technological and institutional change without people capable of handling them have little value. If any of the first three types of change—technical, institutional, or human—is paramount, it is probably human change, which is often considered by economists under the rubric "capital investments in the human agent." The primacy of highly trained humans in creating technical and institutional change as well as in using them provides some basis for regarding investments in human beings as more fundamental even than technical and institutional change in the management of societies. Managing our energy producing resources and food conversion processes requires continual improvement in the human agent in order to restructure our societies technologically and institutionally in order to handle our energy and food problems. In this connection, the research of the Nobel Laureate economist, T.W. Schultz (1971) on investments in human capital is highly relevant. Neither the energy nor food industries can meet the challenges ahead without an adequate supply of well-trained people (human capital).

4. Accumulation of Physical and Biological Capital

More knowledge is also needed on the accumulation of nonhuman capital in energy/food conversion systems. In any developed society it is extremely hard to differentiate between natural resources and man-made resources. Land is a mixture of (1) the soil and energy resources given by nature and (2) the capital that man has invested to maintain, augment, conserve, and improve soils and energy resources. The resultant mixture of natural and man-made resources is land; most soil without capital is unproductive and cannot really be regarded as *land* capable of producing products of value to people other than "hunters and gatherers." Investment increases our stock of capital, including land and energy resources, by converting soil into land and unavailable energy into available energy; thus, investments also increase the accessible stocks of fossil fuels and minerals. They also improve possibilities of recycling resources. Investments also increase the rate at which we can use renewable resources, including the acreage useful in harvesting solar energy as biomass and food. Disinvestment in natural resources and man-made capital results in deterioration from undermaintenance. A perfectly maintained stock of capital (natural or otherwise) is one in which disinvestment through use is just offset by investment through maintenance. Net investment augments. Much more knowledge is needed on the impacts of investment and disinvestment in our various capital stocks, natural or otherwise, important in using energy in food conversion systems. Undoubtedly, many parts of the world have failed to make the investment required to develop and maintain their land bases. On the other hand, other parts of the world have made the investments necessary to greatly augment the supply of usable land and energy resources. Our calculations need to take into account the value of present-day investments for future generations who are not now part of today's power structures and who are beyond the short economic horizons going with present-day or even lower interest rates. We cannot do an adequate job of evaluating these processes with simple positivistic energy and soil accounting. Ethics and economics requires that we measure and understand (1) the values sacrificed when we do or do not make such investments and (2) the values gained if we do.

The impacts of technical, institutional, and human changes and of physical capital accumulations on energy/food conversion systems cannot be readily analyzed and predicted within single, isolated academic disciplines. Instead, multidisciplinary systems analyses of energy/food conversion systems are required.

Such analyses have to deal with both the normative and the positive dimensions of such systems; hence, the biological sciences, the humanities, and the decision disciplines while being individually insufficient all have valuable contributions to make. Modeling and analyzing energy/food conversion systems also requires a somewhat eclectic use of the methods and techniques associated with positivistic, normativistic, and pragmatic philosophies. Positivistic ethics along with logical positivism is passé among many philosophers. In the last 10 years several formerly positivistic authors have contributed to a book whose title puts logical positivism in the past tense (Achinstein and Barker, 1969). It follows, therefore, that the biological and physical sciences whose logically positivistic philosophy dominates the National Academy of Sciences and the National Science Foundation have important contributions to make to the study of energy/food conversion systems but are in no position to "go it alone," whatever the inclination of their leadership. The National Academy of Sciences and the National Science Foundation sorely need to (1) move beyond logical positivism to more adequate philosophic foundations and (2) form a truly coordinated relationship in which the biological and physical sciences, the social sciences, and the humanities are treated as equals.

B. Knowledge Needed on Distributions of Power Important in Food/Energy Conversion Systems

It has been noted above that distributions of power are important components of the decision rules, which indicate what should be done in order to solve problems. We are all aware of the new powers that have been exercised by OPEC in the energy markets. We are also somewhat aware of the powers claimed and sometimes exercised by activists—both those who defend and those who attack the status quo—in energy/food conversion systems. The distributions of various forms of power (market, political, social, police, military, etc.) are important in making decisions to solve energy problems. These different forms of power tend to be studied in different disciplines. Economists study the distribution and use of market power, political scientists study political power, sociologists study social power, while students of military science study the distribution and use of military power. We need integrated knowledge from the multiplicity of disciplines that study power. The information they have on power distributions is important in making more ethical decisions about the production and utilization of energy in food conversion systems. Such distributions of power indicate which solutions are feasible and which are infeasible. Importantly, knowledge of the distributions of "real power" often makes it unnecessary to learn about the distribution of power with ethically questionable tests of power, most of which are destructive and very damaging to the losers whether the test be a political, market, social, or military "shoot-out." When the author lived in Nigeria, for instance, the Nigerians engaged in a military test of power that involved, among other things, who had the power to control revenues from newly discovered petroleum resources. The military test was very destructive. It might have been unnecessary had sufficient research been carried out in an iterative manner with interactions among the conflicting parties who possessed the powers that were tested in the field of battle.

C. Performances of Information Systems Serving Decision Makers in Food/Energy Conversion Systems

Persons and agencies making decisions to solve problems in energy/food conversion systems include persons and organizations in producing, resource owning, and consuming units of our society as well as public decision makers and agencies in legislative and administrative (including regulatory) branches of government. These persons (and agencies) are served by several information systems that generate, assemble, and transmit knowledge about energy and food. This knowledge is of varying degrees of accuracy and conceptual soundness. Some of it is unbiased but inaccurate, while some is dishonest and, hence, unethical.

The ethics of decisions about the use of energy in food conversion systems includes the evaluation of these information sources. This subsection examines the following information systems: the market and price system, various political systems, the USDA/land grant college of agriculture system; the nonagricultural colleges and departments in land grant universities; non-land grant universities and various institutes; the National Academy of Sciences and National Science Foundation; the information media; and the food and energy activists, including both conservatives and radicals. We address some of both what we know about the performances of these systems and what we need to know about their performances.

1. The Market and Price System

One of the most important information systems in market-oriented economies such as ours is the market and price system. Market and price mechanisms transmit information about production, marketing, and processing costs to consumers from producers and about consumers' wants, desires, and concepts of value to producers. The market tends to generate market clearing equilibrium prices (values in exchange). Nonmonetary values and knowledge of intrinsic values are reflected in market transactions and prices as are costs including the effects of taxes, costs of complying with regulations, and subsidies. The prices (both monetized and nonmonetized) generated in a market are exchange, not intrinsic, values. Markets and prices cannot serve as an information system without both freedom of choice and constraints to protect that freedom of choice. Exchange values are, themselves, functions of the distribution of the ownership of rights and privileges and, hence, are not stable in the face of large redistributions of income such as those accompanying exhaustion of major energy resources, revolutions, wars, large educational changes, and major demographic shifts. We should note, particularly, that exchange values from the market do not reflect the values that future generations will place on fossil energy and that the planning horizon (given present interest rates) of many living persons in the market is closer than their life expectancies. Evaluation of the consequences of proposed changes in the distribution of the ownership of rights and privileges requires attention to the new market prices, which will emerge after such changes given whatever freedom of choice is left for producers, consumers, and resource owners to choose among alternatives.

The effectiveness of price and marketing information systems in generating exchange prices can be distorted with (1) subsidies and taxes from the public sector, (2) false advertising (as contrasted to much true advertising), and (3) market constraints originating in the private sector. False information from activists either defending or attacking the establishment also distort the flows of information in the market and price mechanism. Conversely, the true information distributed in advertising and by activists is not distortive whether positive, normative, or prescriptive and often serves to put important issues on the agenda for public discussion. It must also be pointed out that taxes, subsidies, and market constraints may reflect legitimate rights and privileges and that, hence, the influence of such rights and privileges cannot always be regarded as distortions. Ethical and economic analysis requires honesty and justification of distributions of power, including ownership of rights and privileges. The influence of justified (and therefore equitable but not necessarily equal) distributions of rights and privileges on decisions is not ethically deplorable. At this point we do not attempt to indicate what is "legitimate or justified" but, instead, make the general point that the legitimacy and justness of the exchange values (prices) generated in a market depend on the legitimacy and justness of the underlying power distributions.

Subject to limitations such as those noted, the market and price mechanisms are effective and honest (therefore, ethical in the important sense of honesty) information systems. Such systems should be expected to generate information about values in exchange, given the existing pattern of ownership of rights and privileges. Analysts of market price systems usually have substantial success in making useful predictions about how values in exchange change with shifts in ownership patterns. Persons who claim that market prices are measures of intrinsic value are either (1) ignorant of the natures of markets and prices or (2) dishonest and unethical. Similarly, those who claim ethical justification for market prices (exchange values) without attention to the ethical justification for the ownership patterns that partially determine those prices are also either ignorant or dishonest. Also, those who do not recognize that markets and prices constitute an important information system in the ethics of food and energy are simply uninformed. More knowledge of how markets work is greatly needed by decision makers in our energy/food conversion systems. Markets do not and should not be expected to redress ethically unacceptable (inequitable) distributions of the ownership of income producing rights and privileges. Generally, attempts to redistribute by "rigging markets and prices" without first redistributing power through actions taken outside of the market (1) fail to redistribute and (2) lessen the effectiveness of the market as an information system.

2. Political Processes

An information system provides a substantial two-way flow of information that occurs between governors and the governed of political systems. Political systems, like market and price mechanisms, are important systems for generating and transmitting positive and normative information about energy and food. Voters pass information to elected officials, sometimes emphatically. Elected officials, in turn, pass information back to their constituents, particularly at election time when competing with rivals. Political systems, like market and price systems, cannot serve as an effective information system without both freedom and constraints, the latter being necessary to protect political freedom which is, itself, a privilege. Although political processes are often denigrated as dishonest, the cross-checks within free political systems tend to keep "the game more or less honest." So do the cross-checks between the political information systems and the other information systems being considered here. Political compromises are reached by trading off marginal increments and decrements in the attainment of various values in political processes to establish "political exchange values." These political exchange values, like the exchange values or prices generated in markets, depend on distributions of power, in this case political power. As in the case of exchange values generated in the market, political exchange values do not reflect the values of future generations. Further, political planning horizons are often even closer to the present and market horizons. In one sense, political processes can be corrupted by the distribution of political power if the distribution of political power is unjustified. In another sense they cannot, since the equilibrium exchange values of politics are functions of power distributions; thus, politically motivated subsidies, taxes, and "pork barrel" appropriations "honestly" reflect the impact of such political power. Similarly, political values in exchange, even if influenced directly or indirectly by market power, "honestly" reflect the impact of market power on political exchange values. In general, political exchange values like the exchange values of the market are no more ethical than the power distributions that determine them. Thus, it is unethical to claim that political exchange values are ethical and just (or unethical and unjust) without first investigating how ethical or just are the power distributions that partially determine them.

The question of honesty in political processes also arises apart from ethical justification of the distribution of power in such processes. Politicians, for example, have been known to argue supposedly on behalf of the powerless for conclusions that favor those with power. An example includes the argument that gasoline should not be taxed because it will hurt the poor, when keeping gasoline taxes down actually benefits mainly those with one or more cars who drive many miles; the poor, who have no cars or perhaps an old car that is not driven many miles, receive negligible benefits.

Decisions to redistribute the ownership of income producing rights and privileges may be put into effect through the exercise of police and military force, the power of the state. Although market and price interventions are disruptive and are ineffective redistributors, politicians often unwisely seek redistributive objectives with market and price regulations having secondary and tertiary effects that offset their immediate redistributive effects. While the United States and other societies generally recognize the needs to redistribute in favor of the badly disadvantaged, these needs are best met by direct redistribution (progressive taxation with regressive distribution of benefits) rather than indirectly through regulation of food and energy markets and prices. Market interventions are blunt and weak instruments, while the "energy for food conversion" market is likely too small for market interventions to accommodate the needed redistributions.

3. The USDA/Colleges of Agriculture as an Information System

This information system tends to be on the practical end of the spectrum, running from disciplinary or basic research and teaching through subject matter research to problem-solving research and teaching. On this end of the spectrum, they also carry out extension work and adult education programs in farming, rural, and even nonfarm communities on farm and food related problems and subjects.

These agencies were established to work on the practical end of the spectrum because it was felt that the basic disciplines of traditional universities did not adequately serve the practical needs of agriculture. However, they found it necessary from the beginning either to draw on information from the basic biological, physical, and social sciences and the humanities or to do relevant disciplinary research themselves, as well as the subject matter and problem-solving work they were established to do. For many years these agencies were the important and almost the undisputed generators and providers of information on energy for agriculture and food. Still further, they were the authoritative information system for the rest of society as well.

The USDA/land grant college of agriculture system, however, has developed its own problems, a number of which are ethical in nature. It, like most other public agencies and systems, has become bureaucratic. As such, it sometimes seeks its own ends and those of its own personnel rather than of those it was established to serve. As part of this bureaucratic development, unfortunate competition sometimes appears (1) between the USDA and the colleges of agriculture, (2) among colleges of agriculture and, (3) among departments within the colleges of agriculture. Further, this system has displayed some tendencies to become discipline-like, not in the sense of effectively doing the relevant disciplinary research necessary to serve the practical needs in systems that use energy in food conversion but instead in the unfortunate sense of reduced interest in helping farmers, middlemen, and consumers while concentrating on its own institutional and administrative ends.

This disorientation of the USDA/land grant colleges of agriculture system has been aggravated by two other events. The first was that energy utilization in food conversion systems became so complex and important that the private sector developed an important adjunct role to the USDA/land grant college system as an information system. The second was the joint occurrence of the energy crisis (apparently long run in scope) and the food crisis (now appearing short run) in the first half of the 1970s. When energy and food became issues, grants and appropriations became available for researching food and energy. Suddenly, the USDA and colleges of agriculture had competition in the field of energy use in food conversion from agencies that would have disdained involvement in farming and food "huckstering" a few years earlier. Partly as a result of the developments summarized previously, the USDA/land grant college system is now under scrutiny while competing strenuously with other information systems for research and education budgets (Norman, 1982; New York Times, 1982; Marshall, 1982).

4. Nonagricultural Colleges and Departments in Land Grant Universities

This set of institutions constitutes an information system on energy/food conversion more or less distinct from the USDA/land grant colleges of agriculture system just discussed. They generate and provide much basic disciplinary knowledge important in making decisions concerning the use of energy in food conversion systems. The disciplinary specialization in the biological and physical science departments outside of the agricultural colleges makes it possible for them to be more effective in generating relevant disciplinary information for solving food and energy problems than the multidisciplinary departments in agricultural colleges, which have their comparative advantage in doing problem-solving and subject matter research. Most college agriculture departments are more like multidisciplinary institutes than traditional academic departments. For instance, an animal husbandry department is multidisciplinary in the sense that it must deal with animal nutrition, genetics, pathology, entomology, engineering, and economics as they pertain to livestock. Such "institute like" departments are effective in doing problem-solving and subject matter research but are often less effective in doing disciplinary research than the more traditional disciplinary departments found in colleges of arts and sciences. As mentioned above, the energy and food crises, which came to the fore in the 1970s, have stressed the need for basic disciplinary research relevant to solving problems encountered in using energy in food conversion. This has provided an opportunity for these other colleges and departments to make an important contribution to knowledge about energy and food conversion systems. Undoubtedly, there is a great need on the part of society for (1) knowledge from the subject matter and problem-solving "institute like" departments in colleges of agriculture properly combined with (2) the contributions of the more disciplinary departments from the other colleges of a land grant university. An ethical problem of concern here is to coordinate the efforts of the two kinds of departments and colleges in order to produce the appropriate mixes of the three kinds of research discussed earlier in this paper and to avoid destructive competition.

The USDA and land grant colleges of agriculture need to produce some basic disciplinary knowledge and to draw heavily on the knowledge producible in other colleges without losing their ability and comparative advantage in doing multi-disciplinary problem-solving and subject matter research on problems involving the use of energy in food conversion systems. Conversely, the departments outside the college of agriculture need to concentrate on producing relevant disciplinary research without becoming unduly involved in multidisciplinary problem-solving and subject matter research, at which they tend to be at a comparative disadvantage. Unfortunately, there has been an unethical tendency to "sell" the ability to generate needed relevant disciplinary knowledge as the ability to solve multidisciplinary practical problems and generate subject matter research. Unfortunately, some highly specialized disciplinarians have attempted to divert financial support from the USDA/land grant system to their own work, with the promise that they can deliver "more for the buck" in terms of solving the practical problems of society than the colleges of agriculture and the USDA (Norman, 1982; New York Times, 1982; Marshall, 1982). There is a great need for (1) recognition of the functions that the two kinds of agencies can perform advantageously and (2) coordination of efforts to perform these functions. Until the comparative advantage of these two groups of institutions is recognized and a more rational coordination of their activities replaces current destructive competition and bickering among them, we will continue to face grave, ethical questions with respect to the scientific information systems servicing decision makers concerned with energy/food conversion systems.

Activists and critics of the USDA/land grant establishment criticize it for neglecting the problems and needs of such groups as women, racial minorities, small farmers, consumers, the urban poor, etc., and such issues as environmental pollution, fossil energy depletion, aquifer drawdowns and malnutrition. Part of these criticisms are justified while some of them should be addressed to nonagricultural information systems. All of them indicate the importance of doing subject matter and problem-solving research and extension and resident instruction in the agricultural establishment.

5. The Non-Land Grant Universities

These universities are something like the nonagricultural colleges and departments of a land grant university. By and large, they are properly specialized along more traditional disciplinary lines and have their comparative advantage in doing relevant basic disciplinary research. These institutions often lack the intimate knowledge of agriculture found in land grant colleges of agriculture that is required to generate multidisciplinary subject matter knowledge on food conversion systems and to address practical problems in energy/food conversion systems. Just as there is an ethical problem of recognizing and exploiting the comparative advantages of agricultural and nonagricultural colleges and departments in a land grant university, so there is a problem of recognizing and exploiting the comparative advantages of the disciplinary departments in the non-land grant universities and of the land grant colleges of agriculture and the USDA.

6. The National Academy of Sciences, the National Science Foundation, and Various Research Institutes

These institutions tend to be concerned with basic disciplinary research. In a sense, they are counterparts to the disciplinary departments of the nonagricultural colleges of land grant universities and of the colleges and departments in the non-land grant universities. The National Academy of Sciences (NAS) and the National Science Foundation (NSF) place substantial emphasis on basic disciplinary research. While NSF has made excursions into problem-solving research under the rubric of Research on National Needs and other descriptive phrases, these more applied efforts have tended to "wither on the vine" relative to the sustained interests of NAS and NSF in promoting basic disciplinary research (much of it of known relevance) in the biological and physical sciences. There can be no doubt about the need for relevant disciplinary research pertaining to the use of energy in food conversion systems. Much knowledge generated by such research is relevant and crucial to the development of new technologies for generating and using energy in food conversion systems. The problem which arises is partially (1) that of failing to recognize the comparative advantages of different kinds of research agencies in doing problem-solving research, at one extreme, and basic disciplinary research, at the other, and (2) that of confusing disciplinary with problem-solving research, which traps agencies with comparative advantage in doing disciplinary research into competing for resources to do problem-solving research and even extension for agriculture. Again, the ethical problem is one of coordinating and exploiting the comparative advantages of agencies for doing problem-solving and disciplinary research, in this case, NAS and NSF, on one hand and the USDA and colleges of agriculture on the other.

7. The Information Media

Another important information system that assembles and distributes knowledge about the use of energy in food conversion systems is made up of the information media. This information system is constrained, of course, by the supply of knowledge generated by the information generating systems just discussed. Its strength is in the distribution, not in the generation, of information. As such, the knowledge distributed by the information media suffers all the shortcomings of the knowledge generated by those information systems that do generate knowledge. At times, the information media suffer from sensationalism and, at times, unwise competition for information markets. However, the information media are so diverse that there are substantial checks on the accuracy of the information distributed. With many different firms and organizations involved in radio, TV, newspapers, and journals there is a tendency for competitors to keep the "game" honest.

8. Private Firms

Information systems are maintained by private firms for their own use and for use of their clients and customers. With respect to the use of energy in food conversion, these firms generate new technology, design alternative institutional arrangements, and influence the generation of human capital by providing information and training to customers, clients, and employers. Because such firms are interested in information on the practical end of the spectrum, they tend to compete rather directly with the colleges of agriculture and extension services that are financed by the public to deal with the use of energy in food conversion systems. When it is possible for such firms to generate and appropriate the benefits of the knowledge they generate, it is entirely appropriate for such knowledge to be paid for by private agencies. In fact, it is difficult to make ethical arguments in favor of using the public monies in the USDA/land grant system to generate information for private firms. Two ethical problems do arise, however. One has to do with whether the ownership of information should be confined to a private firm, its customers, and clients or whether the interest of the public would be better served if such information were produced in a public agency and made generally available to all firms, customers, and clients. The other ethical problem that arises has to do with the honesty of information distributed by private firms to its clients and customers. In many instances, and in the long run, the interests of a firm are best served by distributing accurate, reliable information to clients and customers; however, in the short run, inaccurate information and the withholding of information may be advantageous to a private firm.

Currently, severe ethical questions are arising around campuses as the result of the formation of businesses to do applied developmental research. Some of these operations involve the utilization of energy in food conversion systems. Important ethical issues involve conflicts of interest between academic responsibility to universities and private gain (Giamatti, 1982). In the case of agriculture where experiment stations were set up to serve the public good, the ethical question arises as to whether "university blessed" satellite research institutions are seeking private and institutional gain at the expense of those who were to be served by the Agricultural Experiment Stations and Cooperative Extension Services.

9. Energy Agencies in Government

Several government agencies other than the USDA now generate substantial amounts of information on energy, some of which is relevant in food conversion systems. The federal government and several of the governments of energy producing states have had their own "energy departments," complete with research and information units (Johnson and Brown, 1980). These agencies have sought to find an appropriate balance between the initial flush of enthusiasm for their work at the onset of the energy crisis and the efforts since then to reduce their size, importance, and, particularly, their associated regulatory powers.

10. Activists as an Information System

While it may be stretching the concept of an information system, there is a more or less identifiable information system or set of information systems that can be referred to as the activist information system. Within this system or systems there are activists who attack the status quo and those who defend it. One characteristic of many activists is that they seek actively to redistribute or avoid redistribution of the ownership of rights and privileges. Because the emphasis is on advocating presently held convictions about "what ought to be done," activists tend to be persuasive, demonstrative, and hortatory. They attempt to mold public opinion and then use such public opinion as a force to promote their prescriptions. Because their prescriptive convictions are often rigidly held, activists spend relatively little time in the objective pursuit of positive and normative knowledge to process through decision rules in order to reach prescriptive decisions. Thus, at times, it is difficult to regard an activist information system as a "true" information system in the sense that an objective attempt is made to generate and distribute knowledge. However, we have noted repeatedly that other information systems are not entirely objective and that the use of various forms of power is commonplace in the decision rules used to process positive and normative information into decisions about what ought to be done to solve problems involving the use of energy in food conversion systems. Although activists (both defenders and attackers of the status quo) undoubtedly take unethical liberties with knowledge, it is also true that they have placed important ethical issues involving energy and food on the agenda for public discussion and research.

VI. SUMMARY AND CONCLUSIONS

Ethics is, among other things, evaluative of decision processes and decisions. In this chapter we have treated ethics as evaluative of decisions with respect to the use of energy in food conversion systems. In such a view of ethics and food/energy conversion decisions, ethical codes of behavior are neglected except to rule out dishonest behavior in generating and using knowledge in decision processes. Instead, the emphasis is on the generation and utilization of positive and normative information to process through decision rules into prescriptions as to which acts are right and wrong with respect to the use of energy in food conversion systems.

The classical and modern literatures of ethics and economics contain many common authors and works. Economics and often ethics define optimal or ethical acts as "right things to do" or as "what ought to be done, all things considered."

Three kinds of research generate information to improve decisions about the use of energy in food/conversion systems: basic or disciplinary, subject matter, and problem solving. These three kinds of research generate positive, normative, and/or prescriptive knowledge. Three philosophic orientations condition our ability to generate knowledge: logical positivism, normativistic philosophies, and pragmatism. Positivism, sometimes regarded as the philosophy of science, (1) undergirds the biological and physical sciences but (2) precludes the objective normative knowledge and, hence, prescriptive knowledge essential to the ethical evaluation of decisions about energy and food. Positivism is now regarded by many philosophers as passé, despite its somewhat unfortunate domination of the biological and physical sciences (Achinstein and Barker, 1969). Fortunately, normativism and pragmatism provide some foundation for objectivity with respect to normative and prescriptive knowledge.

Important normative knowledge with respect to energy and food includes knowledge of both monetary and nonmonetary values as well as both intrinsic and instrumental or exchange values. A right or ethical action with respect to energy and food conversion is viewed here as optimizing net monetary and/or nonmonetary values in both ethics and economics. Efficiency is defined as the ratio between the value of the outputs of a production process and the value of the inputs it uses. Technical ratios between the energy that goes into and comes out of food conversion processes are always one and, hence, are singularly uninteresting and of little utility as indicators of efficiency that is normative. This does not imply that positivistic data on BTUs and kilocalories are of no value. Obviously such data tell us about quantities of different kinds of energy and entropy. Such quantities are required along with normative knowledge about the value of different kinds of energy and entropy in reaching ethical judgments about energy. Together, positive and normative knowledge permit us to calculate efficiency ratios between values of what goes into and what comes out of production processes. Such efficiency ratios are no more technical than economic and vice versa; instead, they attempt to measure efficiency (see Section II).

Our normative information about energy and food is particularly inadequate. We need much more knowledge about the intrinsic and exchange values of different forms of energy and entropy. Simplistic energy accounts cannot be regarded as measures of value or as a valid basis for evaluating the efficiency of energy utilization in food conversion systems. Properly regarded as positivistic knowledge, energy accounts have considerable value in solving problems involving energy and food.

Power distributions are important components of rules for converting positive and normative into prescriptive knowledge. Objectivity requires honest, explicit attention to the roles played in decision making distributions of market, political, social, police, military, and religious power. The power of knowledge is also important, especially in the long run.

Knowledge concerning energy and food is generated by at least the following information systems: markets and prices; political; the USDA/colleges of agriculture; nonagricultural colleges and departments in land grant universities; non-land grant universities; the NAS, NSF, and various institutes; the information media; private firms; energy agencies in government; and activists. Serious ethical issues exist with respect to the honesty of some of these different information systems. Even scientific and academic information systems are observed to shade or distort truth in seeking budgetary and institutional advantage. With respect to the research activities carried out in these information systems, there are also serious ethical issues involved in attaining coordination of the comparative advantages of different agencies in doing disciplinary, subject matter, and problem-solving research on energy and food.

ACKNOWLEDGMENTS

Michigan Agricultural Experiment Station Journal Article No. 10766, Project 442. This chapter has benefited substantially from comments and criticisms advanced by James Bonnen, Larry Connor, David Pimentel, and Lewis K. Zerby.

REFERENCES

Achinstein, P., and Barker S. F., eds. (1969). "The Legacy of Logical Positivism." Johns Hopkins Press, Baltimore, Maryland.

Arrow, K. J. (1951). "Social Choice and Individual Values." Wiley, New York.

Bodenheimer, E. (1967). Analytical Postivisim. In "Jurisprudence: The Philosophy and Method of the Law," Chap. 7. Harvard Univ. Press, Cambridge, Massachusetts.

Boulding, K. E. (1981). "Evolutionary Economics," pp. 152–153. Sage Publications, Beverly Hills, California.

Georgescu-Roegan, N. (1971). "The Entropy Law and the Economic Process." Harvard Univ. Press, Cambridge, Massachusetts.

Giamatti, A. B. (1982). The University, Industry, and Cooperative Research. *Science* **218**, 1278–1280.

Johnson, G. L. (1973). Review of The Entropy Law and the Economic Process by Nicholas Georgescu-Roegan. *J. Econ. Issues* 7, pp. 494–499.

Johnson, G. L. (1974). The Roles of the Economist in Studying Problems Involving Energy and Food. In "Proceedings of the 1974 Western Agricultural Economics Association Conference." Moscow, Idaho.

Johnson, G. L. (1981). Ethical Issues and Energy Policies. In "Increasing Understanding of Public Problems and Policies—1980." Proceedings of the 30th National Public Policy Education Conference held at Vail, Colorado. Farm Foundation, Oak Brook, Illinois.

Johnson, G. L. (1983). The U.S. Presidential World Food and Nutrition Study and Commission on World Hunger—Lessons for the U.S. and Other Countries. Paper delivered at the Theodor Heidhues Memorial Seminar held at the Institute of Agricultural Economics, University of Göttingen, West Germany, November 1981 (in press).

Johnson, G. L., and Zerby, L. K. (1973). "What Economists Do About Values—Case Studies of Their Answers to Questions They Don't Dare Ask." Department of Agricultural Economics, Center for Rural Manpower and Public Affairs, Michigan State University, East Lansing.

Johnson, G. L., and Brown, J. L. (1980). "An Evaluation of the Normative and Prescriptive Content of the Department of Energy Mid-Term Energy Forecasting System (MEFS) and the Texas National Energy Modeling Project (TNEMP)" (M. L. Holloway, ed.), Texas National Energy Modeling Project, Part III. Texas Energy and Natural Resources Advisory Council, Austin, Texas.

Kaplan, A. (1968). Positivist Ethics. In "International Encyclopedia of the Social Sciences." (D. L. Sills, ed.), Vol. 12, pp. 393–394. Macmillan, New York.

Knight, F. H. (1933). "The Economic Organization," pp. 8, 50–52. Univ. of Chicago Press, Chicago, Illinois.

Lewis, C. I. (1955). "The Ground and Nature of the Right." Columbia Univ. Press, New York.

Machlup, F. (1969). Positive and Normative Economics. *In* "Economic Means and Social Ends" (R. Heilbroner, ed.), Prentice-Hall, Englewood Cliffs, New Jersey.

Marshall, E. (1982). USDA Research Under Fire. *Science* **217,** No. 4554, p. 33.

Moore, G. E. (1956). "Principia Ethica." Cambridge Univ. Press, London and New York (originally published, 1903).

New York Times (1982). "The Worm in the Bud," editorial. October 21, p. 26.

Norman, C. White House Plows into Ag Research. (1982). *Science* **217,** 1227–1228.

Pimentel, D. (1983). Personal correspondence, January 31, 1983.

Schoemaker, P. J. H. (1982). The Expected Utility Model: Its Variants, Purposes, Evidence and Limitations. *J. Econ. Lit.*, June, pp. 529–563.

Schultz, T. W. (1971). "Investment in Human Capital." Free Press, New York.

Science for Agriculture (1982). Report of a Workshop on Critical Issues in American Agricultural Research. Sponsored by The Rockefeller Foundation and the Office of Science and Technology Policy, Executive Office of the President. Winrock International Conference Center, Morrilton, Arkansas, June 14–15.

Sinden, J. A., and Worrell, A. C. (1979). "Unpriced Values: Decisions Without Market Prices," pp. 12–14. Wiley, New York.

Chapter 8

Solar Energy Applications in Agriculture

GIGI M. BERARDI

Department of Environmental Sciences
Allegheny College
Meadville, Pennsylvania

But thy eternal summer shall not fade.

Shakespeare, Sonnet 18

I. INTRODUCTION

High inputs of direct (radiant) and indirect (e.g., fossil fuels and other organic matter) solar energy are required for the industrialized agriculture that is typical of most developed countries. Direct solar energy is converted through photosynthesis into chemical energy, which is more readily usable by humans than are other forms of energy. Indirect solar energy, e.g., petroleum and natural gas, is used to produce fertilizers, farm machinery, and liquid fuels so that plants are artificially fertilized, field operations are mechanized, and drying procedures are powered. In the United States, about 1500 liters of oil per person are required to produce, process, distribute, and prepare food. The energy used for these pur-

181

poses amounts to about 17% of the total energy used in the United States (Pimentel and Pimentel, 1979).

A. Fossil Fuels

Whereas the supply of direct solar energy is essentially inexhaustible, the supply of fossil fuels is rapidly being depleted and cannot be replenished in a meaningful human time span. Thus, we are experiencing higher prices for these fuels as supply decreases and demand increases.

There is the potential in agriculture to replace or partially replace fossil fuels, a virtually nonrenewable resource, with passive and active solar energy systems,[1] wind energy, water energy, biomass conversion, and increasing the efficient use of organic matter (crop residues, human and animal wastes, and green manures[2]), all of which are renewable energy resources. The potential for replacement of fossil fuels (especially LP and natural gas) by solar energy systems is large. Currently, substantial amounts of these fuels are used in agriculture for low temperature heating and drying operations simply because they are convenient or have been economical in the past. In 1971, one-half of LP gas used in agriculture was for nonmotor purposes, i.e., crop drying and curing[3] and space heating of livestock housing (Energy Research and Development Administration, 1977a).

B. Fertilizer

Reduction in the use of synthetic fertilizer could also result in large energy savings in agriculture. In 1974, approximately 125×10^{12} kcal were used to produce fertilizers, 90% of the energy being in the form of natural gas (Nelson *et al.*, 1976). The price–supply interaction for natural gas is expected to directly affect nitrogen fertilizer price and availability within the next 5–10 years (Chancellor and Goss, 1976).

More efficient methods of using commercial fertilizers such as applying moderate amounts of fertilizer nitrogen just before the crop begins its period of maximum growth (Bouldin *et al.*, 1971) are being investigated. Also, better management of organic matter to reduce production costs for farm operators is being pursued. Such procedures will enable farmers to be less dependent on

[1]Solar energy systems refers to humanly designed, constructed, and maintained systems. Passive systems are characterized by use of natural energy flows and building designs, e.g., buildings that are made air tight and well-insulated. Active systems are characterized by arrays of fans, pumps, collectors, and tubing in which fluids are heated and transported.

[2]Crop residues, human and animal wastes, green manures, and other organic matter are examples of indirect solar energy, stored in plants and animals.

[3]Over 400 million gallons of LP gas are used annually for peanuts, forage, and tobacco alone (Butler, 1977b).

commercial fertilizers manufactured with a costly and unpredictable supply of natural gas (Lockeretz *et al.*, 1978).[4]

C. Solar Energy

This chapter will consider ways in which solar energy can be utilized more extensively in food production. In particular, passive and active solar systems to provide energy for space heating and to process heat, and management of organic matter for crop fertilization will be discussed. Environmental and safety impacts of solar system components will also be examined. Other forms of solar energy, such as biomass conversion, are treated elsewhere in this book.

II. ACTIVE AND PASSIVE SOLAR ENERGY SYSTEMS: BASIC PRINCIPLES AND COMPONENTS

Solar radiation is best suited to operations requiring low temperature heat applied in an intermittent fashion in rural areas (Energy Research and Development Administration, 1977a). Land is more likely to be available there than in urban areas, and transmission and transportation costs associated with other conventional energy sources are eliminated. The initial investment for components, however, is usually costly (Energy Research and Development Administration, 1977a).

Solar energy has been employed in U.S. agriculture primarily in passive applications. One of the main problems with widespread use of solar energy devices is the lack of dependability. If rapid response is needed, the system must have a backup heating capability. Another problem associated with solar energy is its diffuse character. Large amounts of solar energy reach the earth. For example, the amount of solar energy that arrives globally in 1–2 weeks is equivalent to the fossil energy stored in all the earth's known reserves of coal, oil, and natural gas (Eaton, 1976). However, relatively little is concentrated at any one place, i.e., the energy must be concentrated to maximize usable energy obtained from the system.

Solar energy systems used to produce heat work on the same principle, i.e., radiant solar energy is converted into thermal energy that is then applied to the heating of various products (Fig. 1). In these systems, solar radiation is absorbed by the collector and removed by a heat transfer medium. Since storage is always less than 100% efficient and increases the cost of the system, the ideal application from the standpoint of cost is one in which no storage is required and energy is used whenever available. If storage is required, then usually oil, rock, or water

[4]The unpredictability of natural gas supply was dramatically illustrated by the natural gas shortage of 1976–1977.

(perhaps with a salt solution) is used. Heat is removed from storage on demand and distributed to the process by a heat transfer medium (which may be a fluid different from that moving into the collector). Circulation through the system occurs through pumps, blowers, ducts, etc. System designs vary considerably, depending on cost of individual components and end-use of heat (Fig. 1).

A. Solar Collectors[5]

1. Shallow Ponds and Translucent Structures

These structures generally produce a working fluid below 65°C (150°F). The collector consists of an "absorber plate," which is a layer of flowing or static water 5–10 cm (2–4 in.) in depth, a plastic bag with a black bottom and a clear top, and top glazing. The top glazing is a semirigid sheet of corrugated, clear plastic arched over the water bag. A slab of heat insulating material reduces heat loss from the bag to the ground and protects the bag against pest attack. Frequent replacement of plastics, where used, may be necessary due to their low weatherability (University of Maryland, 1974). In these collector systems, heat not used immediately is transferred to a storage system through air circulation.

2. Flat Plate Collectors

This is the most common type of collector and is widely manufactured by many businesses. This system consists of a metallic absorption plate (steel, copper, aluminum) with integral or attached thermally bonded tubing and a backing of insulation. The plate may be treated with a black paint or some selective surface to increase absorption of short wave solar radiation. The plate and insulation are placed in a metal or wood container, which is covered by one or two sheets of glass or plastic and is hermetically sealed. The cover sheets are used to create a dead air space between the absorption plate and thus reduce losses through convection. The cover sheets also block longer wave radiation emitted from the absorber passing back to the outside environment.

The collectors are mounted on the ground or on the southward facing rooftops (in the northern hemisphere) and tilted at an angle usually within 10° of the latitude where they are located. The maximum temperature achievable with this system is usually 93°C (200°F). On sunny days when the collector is not in use and the transfer liquid is stagnant, temperatures inside the collector can exceed 149°C (300°F) (Midwest Plan Service, 1980).

Flat plate collectors are being experimented with in many different locations.

[5]Much of the information on system components in this section is found in Energy Research and Development Administration, 1977a.

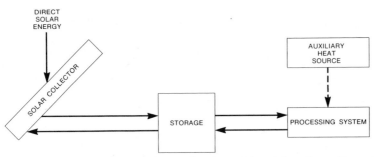

Fig. 1. Solar energy heating system used to produce heat. (Adapted from Energy Research and Development Administration, 1977a.)

Some of the collectors are being used to produce electricity as well as heat. The University of Delaware is researching collectors containing cadmium sulfide solar cells that convert solar energy into electric and thermal energy and flat plate collectors used for thermal boosting.

The level of corporate involvement in control and promotion of solar energy system components is substantial (University of Maryland, 1974). Besides corporations researching and developing components, individual homeowners and farmers are also designing and constructing them. The Young Solar Collector has been designed by a Nebraska farm couple in cooperation with the Solar Farm Energy Project (Heid, 1981). The collector is portable and tiltable, with a flexible airflow system; it is used to dry grain and to heat buildings.[6]

A compressed-film floating solar collector, consisting of a layer of insulation floating on a body of water, was developed by researchers at Texas A & M University (Harris, 1974). The top of the insulator is made of black weather- and heat-resistant material protected by several layers of plastic or glass. The body of water serves as heat storage for the system. This collector is well-adapted to large-scale installations; the cost of suitable insulation material prohibits small-scale applications (Davison and Harris, 1977).

3. Tubular Glass Collectors

Tubular glass collectors are attractive because they can be manufactured with the existing technology that is associated with fluorescent lighting. They consist of glass, tubular forms, usually two coaxial tubes, with an evacuated insulation chamber. A selective coating is applied to the outer surface of the inner tube in order to reduce radiation losses. The working fluid, either liquid or air, enters and leaves the inner tube through the same end (using a reverse flow path aided by a feeder tube or series of tubes).

[6]In 1979 the collector saved 331 gallons of propane worth $179.00. It has a payback of 5.8 years and an expected 20-year life span.

These collectors have higher efficiencies than the flat plate collectors and are useful for higher temperatures, operating at temperatures up to 149°C (300°F). Such factors as tube spacing, orientation, and wall thickness determine the level of performance. Due to the configuration of the collector, by which almost as much incoming solar radiation is intercepted during the morning and afternoon as during the midday period, a more stable efficiency is maintained throughout the day.

4. Focusing Collectors

Focusing collectors direct solar radiation to a focal point or axis where higher temperatures may be generated. These collectors should be used in areas with mostly clear skies and little air pollution because the units utilize direct rather than diffuse solar radiation.

The collectors have one of two basic shapes, either the cylindrical parabolic trough or the circular parabolic dish. The cylindrical parabolic trough uses a parabolic-shaped reflecting surface to focus direct solar radiation onto a linear absorber pipe (in the focus of the parabola) that contains the liquid working fluid. The circular parabolic dish focuses direct radiation on an absorber located at its focal point. Segmented mirrors may be used to replace the parabolic reflective surface (Steward, 1973).

B. Heat Transfer Components

Various liquids or air are used as fluids for heat transfer. Liquid systems require tubing and pumping power, whereas air systems require large ductwork and fans or blowers. Air systems are convenient because they do not freeze. Liquid systems must be treated with antifreeze solutions to prevent freezing as well as anticorrosion additives to prevent excessive corrosion of the metallic absorption plates and tubing.

C. Storage

It is desirable to store thermal energy when an excess is generated by the collector/concentrator system. The storage medium is usually oil, rock, or water,[7] which may or may not include salt solutions. The working fluid transfers heat to the oil, rock, or water and/or causes a salt solution to melt, thereby extracting and holding heat. When stored heat is required the process is reversed,

[7]Scientists at Texas A & M University have been researching the efficiency of underground storage of large quantities of chilled water to be pumped later for summer air-conditioning (Davison et al., 1975). Studies show a storage efficiency of 80–85% after initial cooling. The large-scale applications of this technology are quite promising.

TABLE I
Storage Materials[a]

Material	Weight (lb/ft³)	Specific heat[b] (BTU/lb-°F)
Water (8.3 lb/gal)	62.4	1.0
Rock (¾ in.–3 in. diameter)	100.0	.2
Glaubers salt[c]		
Solid	100.0	.5
Liquid	70.0	.8

[a]Data are from Midwest Plan Service, 1980.
[b]Specific heat is for sensible heat storage.
[c]Glaubers salt melts at 91°F and has a latent heat of fusion of 108 BTU/lb.

with the oil or rock transferring heat back to the working fluid and the salts freezing.[8] See Table I for properties of heat storage materials.

III. ACTIVE AND PASSIVE SOLAR ENERGY SYSTEMS: APPLICATIONS

A. Passive Systems

Major applications of solar energy utilized in passive solar systems include crop drying, greenhouses, and space heating of buildings.

1. Crop Drying[9]

Many of the passive solar crop drying systems currently in use are in the developing countries. The systems are usually inexpensive and reliable, constructed with local materials, and used for small- and medium-scale drying operations. Solar agricultural dryers are used in Colombia to dry coffee, maize, beans, and cocoa. The two basic types, tray and terrace, utilize natural air convection. These have been slightly modified from the traditional method of drying on trays and wooden floors to include movable carts, movable trays, mobile roofs, concrete floors and/or walls, and plastic or glass covers. The estimated life of these dryers is 5–20 years. One limitation with these systems is unfavorable weather; the rainy season coincides with the harvest period, which lengthens the sun drying process.

[8]For further information on storage materials and their advantages and disadvantages, see Butler (1977a).
[9]The Brace Research Institute (1975) provided much of the material discussed in this section.

Rack dryers are commonly used in Australia for fruit drying. In 1972, about 100,000 metric tons of fresh grapes were dried in rack dryers by natural air circulation. The racks consist of wire netting tiers with an optional sheet metal roof. The roof protects raisins from rain and excessive sun. Racks are aligned lengthwise on a north–south axis to effectively utilize early morning and late afternoon sun. The dryers are best used in areas with hot, dry weather and gentle winds. During these weather conditions, mold and pest infestation is not a problem. Labor costs are high and maintenance costs are low for this system. The estimated life of the dryer is 20–40 years.

A vertical tray dryer consisting of wire mesh that surrounds vertically stacked wooden trays is used in Colombia to dry cassava particles. The particles are dried by natural air circulation. Drying in the vertical tray dryer uses one-half the time as that for floor and wooden tray sun drying. As with most solar dryers, care must be taken to avoid exposure to excessive heat and humidity. The estimated life of the dryer is 10 years.

Small-scale chamber dryers are used in many countries, and under different climates, to dry a wide variety of agricultural products. As an example, in Syria a small-scale dryer consists of a rectangular container, insulated at its base and sides and covered with a double-layer transparent roof. Solar radiation is transmitted through the roof and is absorbed on the blackened interior surfaces. The base is perforated to permit the entry of fresh, ventilating air. Outlet ports are located in the upper parts of the side and rear panels. The life span of the dryer is substantially reduced if plastic rather than glass covers are used.

Various other chamber dryers are being tried in India and the Ivory Coast. The Indian design is similar to the one described above, which uses natural air convection. The Ivory Coast dryer consists of a rectangular wooden frame that is divided crosswise by retaining bars. The cover of the frame is made of transparent polyvinyl chloride. The dryer is operated in two positions in an east–west plane around a central axis of rotation running north–south. The drying frame can be tilted and fixed to follow the sun during morning and afternoon hours.

Solar dryers using natural air convection are in operation in Brazil and the United States. A glass roof solar dryer is used to dry cocoa in Brazil. The unit is similar to a greenhouse in design and has a roof-peak cap, which serves as a flue and protects the inside of the dryer from rain. Heated air is removed through the roof cap, allowing fresh air to enter through side shutters. The dryer consists of two parallel rows of drying platforms with a central passage for an operator. A fixed glass roof above the drying platform allows for the penetration of solar radiation. Surfaces inside the dryer are painted black to increase absorption of solar radiation. The estimated life of the dryer is about 10 years.

In the United States chamber dryers using natural air convection are used to dry various foods, ranging from fruits and vegetables to herbs and meats. Located in New Mexico, one dryer uses both indirect and direct solar radiation. Air is admitted to the base of the drying enclosure, rises through the drying racks, and is exhausted by natural convection through openings located at the top and the rear wall of the chamber. Also, direct solar radiation passes through the Plexiglass sides and the front and top panels of the dryer, warming the product.

2. Greenhouses

Solar greenhouses usually require double glazing of the glass and/or night insulation, a storage mass, and an insulated upper roof and northern wall. The solar greenhouse may be attached to another structure, replacing the northern wall of the greenhouse, which can then receive excess heat from the solar greenhouse during the day. See Albright (1980), Albright et al. (1981), Allen (1980), Kohler and Lewis (1981), McGowan (1979), and Mercier (1981) for further discussion of passive solar heating of greenhouses.

3. Space Heating of Buildings

Passive solar energy systems that are used for the space heating of buildings generally use the building as a solar collector and store heat within the mass of the building. Buildings can be constructed such that walls and floor surface areas contain materials appropriate for thermal storage such as brick, concrete, or ceramic tile. The building mass should be directly exposed to incoming solar radiation in order to admit as much solar energy as possible; it should include insulated drapes or shutters that trap the heat when solar energy is no longer available (National Academy of Sciences, 1981).

In Wahoo, Nebraska, on the Vennie Kavan farm, a warm floor is achieved by laying hollow clay tile under the concrete floor in a farrowing house (Anonymous, 1978). On the same farm, a growing–finishing building contains translucent panels that are opened in the summer to increase natural ventilation. For a further discussion of passive solar building designs see Denner and Price (1981), Intermediate Technology Group (1980), McCray (1981), MacDougall (1981), and Zornig and Godbey (1981).

B. Active Systems[10]

Major applications of solar energy that utilize active solar systems include crop drying, greenhouses, and space heating of buildings.

---

[10]This discussion is essentially limited to solar systems that produce space heat and process heat. For a discussion of systems that generate electricity see Baum and Babaev (1976), Bombay and Chary (1979), Enochian (1982), and University of Maryland (1974). Encouraging advances have been made regarding pricing and efficiency goals for solar-generated electricity. Several countries (France and the Federal Republic of Germany) and industries have established programs to meet reduced price goals for silicon-based solar cell modules. For further discussion, see National Academy of Sciences (1981).

1. Crop Drying[11]

Chamber dryers using electric fan-forced circulation are used to dry herbs and flowers in Santa Barbara, California, and coffee in Puerto Rico. The Santa Barbara solar dryer is triangularly shaped and has a set of drying drawers. The air heater consists of a clear, plastic cover, a black metal plate absorber, and a back cover. A 15-watt fan blows air on both sides of the black absorber plate of the solar collector; air is then heated and forced through a perforated bottom floor, and it is eventually exhausted at the upper rear section of the drying chamber. The dryer has a life span of over 10 years.

The Puerto Rican chamber bin dryer has been used regularly since 1962 to dry coffee beans. The roof acts as a solar collector. Other components of the system include electric fans and various air ducts. The estimated life of the dryer is about 15 years. The cost of installing the solar collector was recovered within one season of operation.

An experimental chamber bin dryer is being tested in Brookings, South Dakota. The air circulation is fan forced. The fan-drawn air enters the opening in the bin along the roof peak and moves through the collector roof down the south wall and into the outside air duct. The fan then pushes the warmed air into the inside air duct and through the grain via a perforated floor.

Applications of solar energy for soybean, corn, alfalfa, and onion drying and dehydration are discussed by the Energy Research and Development Administration (1977a). These applications include use of flat plate collectors in various modes (direct use, storage-to-dryer, and with an auxiliary heating booster). Continuous conveyor dehydrators and gas-fired rotary dehydrators are used to process over 2724 kg/hr of product in which the air is preheated by solar energy. Table II lists collector surface areas needed to dry specified quantities of product.

In many of the active solar systems, roofs are commonly used as solar collectors. Optimum construction and operating procedures for solar crop drying systems are discussed by Buelow (1976). An application of these principles and procedures is discussed in Hall (1978). For further discussion of other applications of solar energy for crop drying and curing, see Chiappini (1979), Converse et al. (1981), Cundiff (1981), Ekstrom and Gustafsson (1979), Gopalachari et al. (1980), Hellkickson et al. (1979), Henson et al. (1981), Michigan State University (1980), Misra and Kenner (1980), Olczak (1981), Shove (1979), Shove (1981), and Sydney (1981).

2. Greenhouses

The efficiency of solar energy used in a greenhouse can be increased by using

---

[11]Brace Research Institute (1975) and Butler (1977a) provided some of the material discussed in this section.

TABLE II
Collector Surface Area Needed for a 5°F, 24-hr Average Temperature Rise for Solar Stir Drying near Lincoln, Nebraska[a]

Quantity to be dried (bushels)	Collector surface area (ft²)[b]
500	90.4
1,000	180.8
2,500	452.0
5,000	904.0
7,500	1,356
10,000	1,808

[a]It is assumed that (1) the grain will be dried between October and November at 1¼ cfm/bushel; (2) the collector tilt angle is latitude +15°; and (3) the average energy available on latitude +15° surface during the dry period is 1688 BTU/day-ft² (October) and 1354 BTU/day-ft² (November).

[b]The following equation (Midwest Plan Service, 1980) was used to determine collector surface area:

$$\frac{1.1 \times \text{collector air flow (cfm)} \times \text{max. temp. rise (°F)}}{\text{Noon hour, clear day solar radiation (BTU/hr-ft}^2) \times \text{noon hour collector efficiency}}$$

specific absorption surfaces, thermal storage, and flat plate collectors. Orientation of buildings to optimize insulation and improved wall and roof materials for control of heat transfer also increase the efficiency of solar energy use (University of Maryland, 1976). The components of greenhouse solar systems include insulators, absorbing surfaces, and heat storage. Shading can be used to prevent overheating and to protect the collector from damaging high temperatures (Midwest Plan Service, 1980). For further discussion see Energy Research and Development Administration (1977a.)

One type of absorbing surface that receives increasing research attention is the solar pond (Short et al., 1979a,b). Shallow ponds are used for space heating of greenhouses and other buildings. One design uses a salt concentration gradient that absorbs heat (Short et al., 1976). Solar radiation first passes through clear water to a black liner holding the liquid. As the temperature of the black liner increases, heat is transferred to the 20% salt solution in the bottom half of the pond. As the saltwater is heated, it rises within the bottom half and is replaced by cooler water. The upper, non-circulating region acts as a partially transparent insulator. After the amount of radiation absorbed during one summer has penetrated the pond, the bottom pond temperature should be near boiling. Heat is transmitted from the pond and throughout the building by pumping the fluid through heat exchange pipes.

Solar pond heat costs are about the same as electric heating if the system is used for a single building (Short et al., 1975). Maintenance costs include replacement of salt (as it floats to the top), repair of leaks, systematic addition of water to replace that lost through evaporation, and removal of leaves and other debris that may blow into the pond. For further discussion of other solar collectors and components and modes of operation for solar greenhouses, see Bianchi and Manera (1981), Facchini (1981), Fynn *et al.* (1981), Kamal (1981), Petrescu *et al.* (1981), Sasaki *et al.* (1980), Shah *et al.* (1980), Shah *et al.* (1981a), Shah *et al.* (1981b), Takezono (1980), Yianoulis (1981), and Willets *et al.* (1981).

3. Space Heating of Buildings

Livestock shelters and residential buildings can be heated by solar systems. The principles of heating both types of buildings are the same, although livestock usually have a greater tolerance for temperature variations. Usually, space heating and waste treatment are dual functions of the system. For example, many waste disposal systems, such as lagoon or digestion tanks, provide an available mass of liquid for storage of heat that might be used for a solar energy system. Furthermore, the heat storage in waste disposal systems enhances the digestion process, especially in winter when biological processes slow down (University of Maryland, 1976). Systems currently being designed or demonstrated include shelters for dairy cows and chickens. For further discussion, see Collins (1981), Energy Research and Development Administration (1977a), and University of Maryland (1974).

C. Environmental and Safety Impacts

1. Air Quality

The impact of solar energy systems on air quality should be minimal. Any pollution will be associated with equipment needed for back-up operations such as fossil fuel-fired boilers and heaters. Pollutants from combustion include particulates, hydrocarbons, SO_x, NO_x, and CO.

2. Water Quality

High Temperature Working Fluid Release   Hydrocarbon oils and eutectic salt combinations used for heat transport and storage could be released to the environment (either due to routine system flushing or leakage) and affect local water quality (Energy and Development Administration, 1977a). Drinking such water (especially that contaminated with nitrates from fluid additives) might produce toxic effects.

Lower Temperature Water-Based Fluids   Additives are usually used for the lower temperature water-based fluids in order to prevent corrosion. Chromates, phosphates, nitrates, nitrites, sulfites, and sulfates in the fluid might cause environmental problems in aquatic systems such as eutrophication and increased salinity and pH levels (Energy Research and Development Administration, 1977a).

3. Land Use

Industrial and agricultural heating systems can require collector areas of 1 sq mile or more, thus representing substantial land use. A solar thermal electric (STE) system, in particular, is a definite land intensive technology, requiring about 1 sq mile/100 MWe (megawatt electric) capacity for central receiver plants located in the southwestern United States (Energy Research and Development Administration, 1977b). A comparable figure for an average nuclear system is .2 sq miles (assuming an average of 100 acres per plant site and underground uranium mining; Oakridge National Laboratories, 1976); for a 1000 MWe electric power plant using high-efficiency coal or oil-fired technology, the figure is 43.8 sq miles (Baranowski, 1973).

Environmental problems may also arise due to the shading by the collectors. Nonnative or pest species may thrive in the shade, and local or desirable insect, plant, and animal species may be endangered.

4. Safety Issues

Contamination of Commodities Being Heated   Commodities may be contaminated by the working fluid. Contamination by various toxic chemicals can cause the growth of fungi and bacteria and cause spoilage.

Handling of Working Fluids   The nitrite and nitrate salts of sodium or potassium can be particularly dangerous. When nitrate compounds are exposed to very high temperatures, containment vessels rupture and the compounds may fuel the intensity of an existing fire (Energy Research and Development Administration, 1977a). Hydrocarbon oils also pose a potential fire hazard. At temperatures of about 180°C, oil vapors will combust if exposed to air; at higher temperatures, the oil itself might combust.

5. Aesthetics

The visual effects of solar energy systems will be minimal in industrial areas, e.g., industrial parks. However, in rural areas the array of solar collectors and other structures will provide a sharp contrast to the rural scenery. Information on the physical changes in the rural landscape must be made available to residents of the area before large-scale systems are adopted.

6. Proper System Management

The National Bureau of Standards for the Department of Housing and Urban Development (1976) provides guidelines for the proper containment and disposal of liquid working fluids. These include requiring a list of the chemical components of the heat transfer medium in milligrams per liter, if these components comprise more than 0.10% of the medium; the organic constituents of these components must have a 5-day biochemical oxygen demand (BOD), using sewage seed, of at least 70% of the theoretical oxygen demand, and the concentration of chemical constituents must be compared with the 96-hr lethal concentration (LC)-50 bioassay value for protection of aquatic life.

By following these guidelines, pollution by working fluids should be prevented. Furthermore, proper containment of fluids and salts should be monitored at all times. Further research is needed on relative environmental impacts of various sites selected for solar system installation, toxicity of and potential problems caused by the various working fluids and their additives, reclamation of spent fluids, waste disposal, and worker safety.

D. Summary and Recommendations

1. Summary

Solar energy systems are attractive in that the supply of solar energy is essentially inexhaustible. Solar energy is available in remote areas and thus useful for agricultural applications.[12] On-site use is possible such that no distribution system is required, and availability and use are independent of the actions of other nations. Furthermore, solar energy is a "clean" energy source as compared with the solid wastes produced by fossil fuel-fired power plants. Solar process heat is relatively nonpolluting in terms of air, water, and thermal pollution. Use of solar energy provides for conservation of gas and oil, which is necessary for high temperature processes. The disadvantages of solar energy include the possible pollution effects discussed in Section III,C, high initial capital costs, and lack of dependability (due to intermittent availability).

2. Recommendations

Recognizing the advantages of solar energy relative to conventional sources, public and private support has been given to public academic institutions as well as to the private sector for research projects on potential solar energy applications. One such project has been funded by the National Science Foundation and carried out by the Agricultural Experiment Station of the University of Maryland (1976). The object of the research was to obtain information that could be used as the basis and justification of an overall research program on

---

[12]Storage facilities in the form of ponds, liquid waste systems, and stored products are also readily available in rural areas, further making agricultural applications attractive.

agricultural applications of using heat from solar energy. Recommendations were developed for an overall experimental research program that would establish the technical and economic feasibility of using solar energy in agricultural operations and for strategies to achieve adoption of solar energy components and systems in agriculture. These recommendations include the following:

1. Continue and expand currently funded categories of research and development of solar energy hardware systems and components.[13]

2. Broaden the geographical spread of funded projects in order to assure adequate consideration of local requirements and environmental variation.

3. Increase the replication of funded projects in order to accumulate performance data with a range of prevailing weather conditions as well as to provide the needed statistical confidence in results.

4. Make special efforts to develop solar systems and components that have multiple use.

Shared use of solar collectors and storage for drying and curing of crops and for farm home or livestock shelter heating provides for greater utilization of the equipment (and reduced cost) throughout the year.

5. Provide funds for designs that are amenable to retrofit applications.

6. Study and develop new total system designs for application of solar energy.

7. Increase funding for "do-it-yourself" solar applications, which will provide for more effective use of farmers' ability of practical design and construction using local materials.

8. Apply funds to develop attractive applications of solar generated shaft power for irrigation, which includes computer simulation and economic feasibility studies.

9. Continue and expand the dissemination and exchange of technical information.

10. Develop interim performance criteria for solar energy systems and components for agricultural applications.

The expertise of organizations such as the American Society of Agricultural Engineers and the National Bureau of Standards should be used to establish, maintain, and monitor interim standards for performance of solar energy systems. This is important for various evaluation activities.

11. Establish basic guidelines for collecting, analyzing, and presenting data from research and development programs. There is a lack of consistency in the collection and presentation of data. Common guidelines must be developed within each agricultural sector.

12. Plan and initiate future demonstration programs.

[13]This should include designs for medium- and small-scale operations.

13. Initiate a study of the application of solar energy to food processing.

14. Research and development programs should be coordinated with an educational program (perhaps under the guidance of the Cooperative Extension Service).

15. The U.S. Department of Agriculture should develop incentives to foster the adoption of solar energy components and systems.

16. Coordinate the domestic program of solar energy applied to agriculture and with international institutions.

17. Establish a "Center for Agricultural Energy Systems."

Activities of the Center could include supplying technical support to public and private agencies that fund solar research and development projects, maintaining a central repository of information, developing resource allocation models for energy applications to agriculture, and assisting in the development of interim performance criteria for solar energy systems and components.

These and other recommendations are discussed in greater detail by the University of Maryland (1976). Adoption of these recommendations together with the establishment of tax credits and exemptions (see, for example, the discussion of the North Dakota exemption laws for installation of solar energy systems in Martin, 1977) as economic incentives will ensure continued research and development and facilitate adoption of solar energy systems in agriculture.

IV. MANAGEMENT OF ORGANIC MATTER FOR CROP FERTILIZATION

Through photosynthesis direct solar energy is converted to an indirect form, i.e., chemical energy. In agricultural production, this indirect solar energy, stored in the bodies of macro- and microorganisms and in their waste products, is a major source of plant nutrients. Other sources of plant nutrients include commercial fertilizers and rainwater. Figure 2 shows a balance diagram indicating gains (sources) and losses for one macronutrient, nitrogen. The relative contribution of organic matter to the supply of soil nutrients necessary for crop production is determined by a variety of factors such as total quantity of organic matter, soil pH and drainage, total quantity and form of commercial fertilizer, and climate.

A. Benefits of Organic Matter

Not only does organic matter provide soil nutrients (primarily nitrogen, sulfur, potassium, and phosphorus—mineralization of phosphorus from organic sources is especially important in highly weathered soils), but it also has an

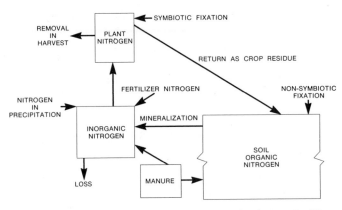

Fig. 2. Generalized balance sheet for nitrogen in a cropped soil. (From Bouldin, undated.)

important influence on soil physical properties. By improving soil structure granulation is encouraged, plasticity and cohesion are reduced, soil aggregates are stabilized, and water infiltration[14] and water-holding capacity[15] are improved. Improved soil structure by increased organic matter helps to control erosion (also by increasing the density of crop cover and slowing down surface runoff[16]). Organic matter content also influences seedling emergence, soil aeration, and root growth. Furthermore, organic matter is an important source of cation exchange capacity,[17] especially in sandy soils or soils where kaolinite is the major clay mineral.

B. Decomposition of Organic Matter

The rate of decomposition of organic matter varies greatly. Sugars and starches in the organic matter are easily decomposed and are thus readily available energy sources for soil organisms whereas lignins, fats, and waxes are very

[14]Data from experimental plots of a Holtville silty clay (Typic Torrifluvents) soil in an irrigated desert region showed that a 1% increase in organic matter decreased the time required for water to infiltrate by 31% (Meek *et al.*, 1982).

[15]Data from experimental plots with Crider series soils (Typic Palendalfs, fine-silty, mixed mesic) in Kentucky showed that plant-available water-holding capacity values (0.33 minus 15 bar soil water) for the 0- to 15-cm depth were 4% higher with soils high in organic matter. Higher clay content also accounted for the higher water-holding capacity (Frye *et al.*, 1982).

Higher water-holding capacity also accounted for statistically significant differences in soil moisture content (soil depth, 0–8 cm and 12–20 cm) in heavily manured Davidson clay loams (Typic Rhodic Palendult, clayey, kaolinite) compared with controls (Weil and Kroontje, 1979).

[16]Experiments have shown that for oxisols in Southeastern Nigeria surface runoff values of 204 mm were achieved on bare fallow plots, whereas in mulched plots the values were as low as 12 mm (Obi, 1982).

[17]Cation exchange capacity is the sum total of exchangeable cations that a soil can absorb.

resistant to decomposition. In addition to the chemical composition,[18] the quantity and vigor of microorganisms present are major determinants of decomposition rate. Soil aeration, temperature (optimal soil temperature for microbial activity is about 34°C, or 90–95°F), moisture (about one-half to two-thirds of soil pores should be filled with water), and pH (adequate supplies of calcium and a pH of 5.5 and higher) substantially affect the microbial population. These four factors must be managed properly to maximize microbe numbers.

C. Sources of Organic Matter

Sources of organic matter include current crops, i.e., stubble and root residues; composts; and animal manures and green manures, e.g., rye, buckwheat, peas, and soybeans.

1. Current Crops

Maintaining moderate to high yields of crops through adequate liming and fertilization practices will maximize the amount of stubble and root residues available for plant growth.

2. Composts

Composts are used mostly in the management of nursery, garden, and greenhouse soils. Maintaining proper temperature and moisture regimes is essential for maximum control of the biological processes involved and to produce a high-quality product. To avoid the loss of nitrogen as ammonia, wastes should be used with carbon to nitrogen (C/N) ratios between 25 and 35 (Parr and Wilson, 1980). Addition of straw can also help to reduce nitrogen loss. Experiments with composted pig and poultry waste show a nitrogen reduction of 33% for solids to which no straw has been added, 15% with those solids containing 2.3% straw, and only 7% when the solids contained 4.6% straw (Vanstaen et al., 1980).

3. Animal Manures

Today, domestic animals in the United States produce over 1 billion tons of waste per year or about 22% of the total of all organic wastes produced in the United States (U.S. Department of Agriculture, 1978). This represents 175 ×

[18]In terms of chemical composition of the organic matter, care should be taken such that materials with wide C/N ratios (for example, sawdust has a ratio of 400:1) are added only if sufficient nitrogen is available. Otherwise, microbes will outcompete higher plants for nitrogen until the C/N ratio is substantially reduced. Examples of organic matter with relatively low C/N ratios are the legumes, alfalfa (13:1), and clover (23:1), as well as well-rotted barnyard manures (20:1).

10^6 dry tons that contain 7.7×10^6 tons of nitrogen, 1.9×10^6 tons of phosphorus, and 4.2×10^6 tons of potassium. About 40% of this manure is produced under confined conditions (U.S. Department of Agriculture, 1978). Chemical composition of the manure varies with the type and age of animal and the feed ration. Estimates nutrients supplied in kilograms per ton of manure range from 14 kg of nitrogen from poultry manure to 4.5 kg of nitrogen from hog manure, 3.6 kg of phosphorus from poultry manure to .9 kg of phosphorus from dairy manure, and 4.5 kg of potassium from dairy manure to 3.2 kg of potassium from poultry manure (Benne, 1961). Nutrient content will vary substantially depending on the method of storage and the procedure used for analysis.

Large losses of plant nutrients, especially nitrogen, occur in the conventional handling and storage of manure, especially losses of the valuable liquid portion. Leaching of soluble nutrients in the solid portion is also a major loss of nutrients (Lund and Doss, 1980). Leaching losses vary with the amount of water passing through the manure and the amount of surface exposed by a given volume of manure as well as application rates. Rate of application and soil drainage conditions can also influence volatilization losses.

Even with daily removal and spreading of fresh manure, substantial nitrogen losses may be expected. Nitrogen losses of .16 to .26 kg/ha/day in the form of ammonia have been reported from the soil of grazed legume pasture (Strijdom, 1979). Field experiments in New York with manure application rates of 34 and 200 metric tons per hectare showed losses of ammonia ranging from 61 to 99% of the total ammoniacal nitrogen (Lauer et al., 1976). Additional losses occur in storage so that even under optimal conditions (manure which is well-compacted and protected and stored at low temperatures) the total loss of nitrogen is rarely less than 15% and is usually higher (Salter and Schollenberger, 1939). The U.S. Department of Agriculture (1978) reports nitrogen losses of 63% under current management and 45% under improved management, e.g., timely incorporation of the manure with soil on spreading.

Daily use of the manure spreader is impractical for some farmers and thus storage of the manure is required. Several types of storage are possible. These include storage or packing in piles (in which anaerobic and aerobic breakdown take place), aerobic liquid treatment (in which there is aerobic digestion of a liquid-manure slurry, as in an aerated lagoon), and anaerobic liquid treatment (in which no gaseous oxygen is added). Each method varies in the cost of construction, cost of maintenance, nutrient loss, and odor control. For example, aerobic liquid treatment has high construction and maintenance costs but maximum odor control. Besides method of storage, time of application in relation to planting, depth of incorporation of manure, and method of applying manure influence the amount of nutrients ultimately available for plant growth.

When manures are applied much in advance of planting, soluble nutrients such as the nitrates, phosphoric acid, and potash are lost. Results of field experiments show that for crops in their first year, manure applied in the fall produces smaller average yields than when applied in the spring (Iverson, 1931). No significant difference, however, in residual effect on later crops was observed.

4. Green Manures

Green manures are undecomposed green plant tissues that are plowed into the soil. Substantial quantities of organic matter can be returned to the soil by green manures. For example, planting sweet clover in the fall and plowing it under 1 year later will add about 168 kg of nitrogen per hectare to the soil (Willard, 1927). Estimates for the fixation of nitrogen by clover in a grass/clover mixture range from 100 to 200 kg of nitrogen per hectare per year (Strijdom, 1979). In four corn response tests, nitrogen contained in legumes was from 16 to 92% as effective as inorganic nitrogen for increasing corn yields (Stickler *et al.*, 1959). Besides supplying plant nutrients, if the green manure is succulent then microbial activity is encouraged, including activity of the nitrogen-fixing organisms. Microbial activity is necessary for organic matter decomposition, inorganic transformations, and nitrogen fixation.

Green manures that produce growth of succulent tops and roots in a short period of time should be used. Erosion control is maximized when the green manure grows on poor soils and ground cover is produced soon after establishment. Although expensive, leguminous green manures (alfalfa, red and sweet clover, soybean, Canadian field pea, cowpea) should be grown to provide added nitrogen. Possible nonleguminous crops include rye, oats, barley, millet, buckwheat, ryegrass, sudan grass, mustard, and rape. Although care must be given to avoid applying green manures with wide C/N rations and high moisture requirements (so as not to deplete soil moisture and create drought conditions), green manures are especially useful where nitrogen fertilizers are expensive or inaccessible. In the humid tropics, several crops a year can be grown using green manures.

D. Soil Management for Increasing Availability of Plant Nutrients

Whether from organic or inorganic sources, availability of plant nutrients can be regulated through careful soil management. Adequate soil drainage will help to prevent nitrogen losses (where nitrogen is usually lost through volatilization and surface runoff of soluble nitrogen). Soil and water conservation practices that control erosion will reduce potassium loss (total potassium removed by erosion generally exceeds that of any other major nutrient[19]). Adequate liming (main-

---

[19]According to Larson *et al.* (1983), the total amounts of nitorgen, phosphorus, and potassium lost each year in eroded sediments in the United States are (in thousands of metric tons), respectively, 9494, 1704, and 57,920.

TABLE III
Fertilization Methods and Results

	System 1 (conventional Corn-Belt)	System 2 (swine manure, knifed down in the fall with N-serve)	System 3 (green manures: wheat and hairy vetch)	System 4 (alfalfa incorporated into rotation; and dairy manure)
Energy cost (BTU × 10^9)	3.678	1.852	2.552	2.781
Energy output/input	6.71	13.30	8.20	8.25
Net income ($/year)	45,644	62,713	38,714	45,716

taining a pH between 6.0 and 7.0) will minimize phosphate fixation.

Soil conservation practices,[20] together with systematic applications of organic matter, will result in greater availability of plant nutrients for crop growth. In 1977, the U.S. Department of Agriculture estimated that the amounts of organic wastes returned to the land were equivalent to 85% of the nitrogen, 56% of the phosphorus, and 150% of potassium purchased as commercial fertilizers (U.S. Department of Agriculture, 1978). As the price of commercial fertilizers increases farmers will be seeking methods to fertilize crops at reasonable costs,[21] such as with organic matter application, using good management practices. Agriculturalists need to make greater use of this renewable resource.

REFERENCES

Albright, L. D. (1980). A passive solar heating system for greenhouses. In "Proceedings of the Annual Meeting of the International Solar Energy Society, American Section," pp. 54–58. University of Delaware, Newark, Delaware.

Albright, L. D., Langhans, R. W., White, G. B., and Donohoe, A. J. (1981). Enhancing passive solar heating of commercial greenhouses. In "Proceedings of the 1980 ASAE National Energy Symposium," pp. 509–512. St. Joseph, Michigan.

Allen, J. M. (1980). A 100% passive solar (heating) use underground greenhouse. Alternative Sources Energy (Sept./Oct.), pp. 9–13.

Anonymous (1978). A solar system for swine house heating, cooling. Agric. Eng. 59, 24–25.

Baranowski, F. (1973). Comparative Land Area Disturbance of Producing Uranium and Fossil Fuels. Unpublished paper, Dept. of Energy, Division of Production and Materials Management, Washington, D.C.

[20]These practices are used to control availability of nutrients from both organic and inorganic (commercial fertilizer) sources.

[21]Simulation results from a study conducted by Considine et al. (1977) give comparative energy costs, energy output/input efficiency ratios, and net income for four different cropping systems. The systems were based on similar resource endowments and 600 acres of land (for further discussion, see Considine et al., 1977). The method of fertilization for each system and the simulation results appear in Table III.

Baum, V. A., and Babaev, A. G. (1976). Development of a solar pump for lift irrigation purposes. *Ann. Arid Zone* **15**, 137–145.

Benne, E. J. (1961). Animal manures. *Mich. Agric. Exp. Stn., Circ.* 231.

Bianchi, A., and Manera, C. (1981). Richerche sperimentali, sull' impiego dei pannelli solari in apprestamenti protetti. *Colture Protette* **10**, 17–25.

Bombay, and Chary, S. T. (1979). Solar photovoltaic water pumping system. *Agric. Agro-Ind. J.* **12**, 30–32.

Bouldin, D. R. (undated). Soil Organic Matter. Department of Agronomy, Cornell University, Ithaca, New York.

Bouldin, D. R., Reid, W. S., and Lathwell, D. J. (1971). Fertilizer practices which minimize nutrient loss. *Proc. Cornell Agric. Waste Manag., 3rd*, pp. 25–35.

Brace Research Institute (1975). A survey of solar agricultural dryers. Technical Report T99. Macdonald College of McGill University, Ste. Anne de Bellevue, Quebec, Canada.

Buelow, F. H. (1976). Drying crops with solar energy. *Ann. Arid Zone* **15**, 172–176.

Butler, J. L., ed. (1977a). "Proceedings of the Solar Crop Drying Conference." North Carolina State University, Raleigh, North Carolina.

Butler, J. L. (1977b). Solar energy research for peanuts, forage and tobacco. *In* "Proceedings of the Solar Crop Drying Conference." North Carolina State University, Raleigh, North Carolina.

Chancellor, W. J., and Goss, J. R. (1976). Balancing energy and food production 1975–2000. *Science* **192**, 213–218.

Chiappini, U. (1979). Low cost experimental solar collector for hay-drying. Michigan State University Energy for Agriculture Series ENR. Michigan State University, East Lansing, Michigan.

Collins, N. E. (1981). The use of a concentrating solar collector for heating and cooling of broiler houses: Final report. Delaware Exp. Stn. and Agric. Eng. Dept., University of Delaware, Newark, Delaware.

Considine, T. J., Muller, R. E., Peart, R. M., and Doering III, O. C. (1977). The economic trade-offs of commercial nitrogen fertilizers, legumes and animal wastes in midwest agriculture. *In* "Food, Fertilizer and Agricultural Residues," pp. 299–317. Ann Arbor Science Publishers, Ann Arbor, Michigan.

Converse, H. H., Lai, F. S., Aldis, D. F., and Sauer, D. B. (1981). Application of solar energy in grain drying. *In* "Proceedings of the 1980 ASAE National Energy Symposium," pp. 131–136. St. Joseph, Michigan.

Cundiff, J. S. (1981). A renewable resources system for curing tobacco. *In* "Proceedings of the 1980 ASAE National Energy Symposium," pp. 59–65. St. Joseph, Michigan.

Davison, H. H., and Harris, W. B. (1977). Further development of the compressed-film floating-deck solar water heater: final report. Department of Chemical Engineering, Texas A & M University, College Station, Texas.

Davison, H. H., Harris, W. B., and Martin, J. H. (1975). Storing sunlight underground: the solaterre system. *Chem. Technol.* **5**, 736–741.

Denner, S., and Price, S. (1981). Passive solar heating-residential. *Ext. Bull. Wash. State Univ., Coop. Ext. Serv.*, No. 950.

Eaton, W. W. (1976). Solar energy. *In* "Perspectives on Energy: Issues, Ideas and Environmental Dilemmas" (L. C. Ruedisili and H. W. Firebaugh, eds.), 2nd ed. Oxford Univ. Press, London and New York.

Ekstrom, N., and Gustafsson, G. (1979). The application of solar collectors for drying of grain and hay. Michigan State University Energy for Agriculture Series ENR. Michigan State University, East Lansing, Michigan.

Energy Research and Development Administration (1977a). "Solar Program Assessment: Environmental Factors (Solar Agricultural and Industrial Process Heat)." ERDA 77-47/2, UC-11, 59, 62, 63A. Washington, D.C.

Energy Research and Development Administration (1977b). "Solar Program Assessment: Environmental Factors (Solar Thermal Electric)." ERDA 77-47/4, UC-11, 59, 62, 63A. Washington, D.C.

Enochian, R. V. (1982). Solar- and wind-powered irrigation systems. Agricultural Economic Report, February (482). USDA Economics and Statistics Service, Washington, D.C.

Facchini, U. (1981). Collettore solare ad aria per apprestamenti di protezione. *Colture Prottete* 10, 47–50.

Frye, W. W., Ebelhar, S. R., Murdock, L. W., and Blevins, R. L. (1982). Soil erosion effects on properties and productivity of two Kentucky soils. *Soil Sci. Soc. Am. J.* 46, 1051–1055.

Fynn, R. P., Short, R. H., and Shah, S. A. (1981). The practical operation and maintenance of a solar pond for greenhouse heating. In "Proceedings of the 1980 ASAE National Energy Symposium," pp. 531–535. St. Joseph, Michigan.

Gopalachari, N. C., Nageswara, B. R., and Sitaramachari, T. (1980). Curing Virginia tobacco with solar energy. *Tob. Res.* 6, 63–66.

Hall, M. D. (1978). Machine storage building with solar roof for heating and grain drying. M.S. thesis, Southern Illinois University, Macomb, Illinois.

Harris, W. B. (1974). A compressed-film floating-deck collector. In "Proceedings of the Solar Heating and Cooling for Buildings Workshop (Part 1: Technical Sessions)," Department of Mechanical Engineering, University of Maryland, College Park, Maryland.

Heid, W. G. (1981). The Young solar collector: an evaluation of its multiple farm uses. Agricultural Economic Report, May (466). USDA Economics and Statistics Service, Washington, D.C.

Hellkickson, M. A., Peterson, W. H., and Verma, L. R. (1979). Development and evaluation of a multiple use solar energy system for agriculture. In "Proceedings of the International Solar Energy Society, Silver Jubilee Congress" (K. W. Bhoer and B. H. Glenn, eds.), pp. 6–9. Atlanta, Georgia.

Henson, W. H., Walton, L. R., Ewen, L. S., and Parker, B. F. (1981). Energy for curing tobacco. In "Proceedings of the 1980 National Energy Symposium," p. 152. St. Joseph, Michigan.

Intermediate Technology Group. (1980). Passive solar heating-improved living conditions for a high altitude population. *Approp. Technol.* 7, 7–9.

Iverson, K. (1931). Spring vs. fall application of stable manure, 1898–1929. *Tidsskr. Planteavl.* 37, 545–613.

Kamal, A. L. (1981). Application of "bubble" and "solar still" technology. In "Advances in Food Producing Systems for Arid and Semi-Arid Lands" (J. T. Manassah and E. J. Briskey, eds.), pp. 717–735. Academic Press, New York.

Kohler, J., and Lewis, D. (1981). Passive principles: choosing your system. *Solar Age* 6, 26–28.

Larson, W. E., Pierce, F. J., and Dowdy, R. H. (1983). The threat of soil erosion to long-term crop production. *Science* 219, 458–465.

Lauer, D. A., Bouldin, D. R., and Klausner, S. D. (1976). Ammonia volatilization from dairy manure spread on the soil surface. *J. Environ. Qual.* 5, 134–141.

Lockeretz, W., Shearer, G., Klepper, R., and Sweeney, S. (1978). Field crop production on organic farms in the Midwest. *J. Soil Water Conserv.* 33, 130–134.

Lund, Z. F., and Doss, B. D. (1980). Residual effects of dairy cattle manure on plant growth and soil properties. *Agron. J.* 72, 123–130.

McCray, J. W. (1981). Passive solar and earth-sheltered residential designs: reactions of housing intermediaries sampled. *Arkansas Farm Res.* 30, 13.

MacDougall, E. A. (1981). Passive solar hen house–second year. In "Proceedings of the International Seminar on Energy Conservation and the Use of Solar and other Renewable Energies in Agriculture, Horticulture and Fishculture," pp. 365–370. Polytechnic of Central London, London.

McGowan, T. F. (1979). Commercial growers' passive solar greenhouse at the Hidden Springs

Nursery, Cokeville, Tennessee. *In* "Proceedings of the International Solar Energy Society, Silver Jubilee Congress," (K. W. Bhoer, and B. H. Glenn, eds.), pp. 1704–1707. Atlanta, Georgia.

Martin, I. (1977). The role of government in causing energy end use efficiency. *In* "Proceedings of the International Conference on Energy Use Management, Vol. II" (R. A. Fazzolare and C. B. Smith, eds.), pp. 489–518. Tucson, Arizona.

Meek, B. L., Graham, L., and Donovan, T. (1982). Long term effects of manure on soil nitrogen, phosphorus, potassium, sodium, organic matter and water infiltration rate. *Soil Sci. Soc. Am. J.* **46**, 1014–1019.

Mercier, J. R. (1981). Design and operation of a solar passive greenhouse in the south-west of France. *In* "Proceedings of the International Seminar on Energy Conservation and the Use of Solar and Other Renewable Energies in Agriculture, Horticulture and Fishculture," pp. 381–388. Polytechnic of Central London, London.

Michigan State University (1980). Solar assisted heat pump dries corn quickly and efficiently. *In* "Energy in Agriculture," pp. 2–3. Department of Agric. Eng., Michigan State University.

Midwest Plan Service (1980). "Low Temperature and Solar Grain Drying Handbook." Midwest Plan Service, Iowa State University, Ames, Iowa.

Misra, R. N., and Kenner, H. M. (1980). Engineering analysis of solar assisted low temperature in-bin fall grain drying and subsequent long-term storage in Ohio. *Am. Soc. Agric. Eng. Paper*, No. 80-3542.

National Academy of Sciences (1981). "Energy for Rural Development: Renewable Resources and Alternative Technlogies for Developing Countries," National Academy Press, Washington, D.C. (Suppl.).

National Bureau of Standards for the Department of Housing and Urban Development (1976). Intermediate minimum property standard for solar heating and domestic hot water systems. Interim report, Washington, D.C.

Nelson, L. F., Burrows, W. C., and Stickler, F. C. (1976). Recognizing productive, energy-efficient agriculture in the complex U.S. food system. *In* "Increasing Agricultural Productivity," pp. 29–44. American Society of Agricultural Engineers, St. Joseph, Michigan.

Oakridge National Laboratory (1976). Report on Design Data and Safety Features of Commercial Nuclear Power Plants 1975–1976. Oakridge National Laboratory, Oakridge, Tennessee.

Obi, M. E. (1982). Runoff and soil loss from an oxisol in southeastern Nigeria under various management practices. *Agric. Water Manage.* **5**, 193–203.

Olczak, M. (1981). Dosuszanie siana przy wykorzystaniu kolektorow slonecznych. *Mechanizacja Rolnictwa* **16**, 5–11.

Parr, J. F., and Wilson, G. B. (1980). Recycling organic wastes to improve soil productivity. *Hortic. Sci.* **15**, 162–166.

Petrescu, S., Danescu, A., and Baran, N. (1981). Combined solar power plants for irrigation and for heating greenhouses using modular cylindrical parabolic concentrators. *In* "Proceedings of the International Seminar on Energy Conservation and the Use of Solar and Other Renewable Energies in Agriculture, Horticulture and Fishculture," pp. 417–421. Polytechnic of Central London, London.

Pimentel, D., and Pimentel, M. (1979). "Food, Energy and Society." Arnold, London.

Salter, R. M., and Schollenberger, C. J. (1939). Farm manure. *Ohio Agric. Exp. Stn. Bull.*, No. 605.

Sasaki, K., Itagi, T., and Takahasi, M. (1980). Studies on the solar greenhouse heated by an earth storage heat exchange system. *Kanagawa Hortic. Exp. Stn. Bull.*, No. 27.

Shah, S. A., Short, T. H., and Fynn, R. P. (1980). A solar pond-assisted heat pump heating system for commercial greenhouses. *In* "Proceedings of the Annual Meeting of the International Solar Energy Society, American Section," pp. 67–71. University of Delaware, Newark, Delaware.

Shah, S. A., Short, T. H., and Fynn, R. P. (1981a). Modeling of a salt gradient solar pondgreenhhouse heating system. *In* "Proceedings of the 1980 ASAE National Energy Symposium," pp. 126–130. St. Joseph, Michigan.

Shah, S. A., Short, T. H., and Fynn, R. P. (1981b). A solar pond-assisted heat pump for greenhouses. *Solar Energy* **26**, 491–496.

Short, T. H., Badger, P. C., and Roller, W. L. (1975). Solar pond shows promise in energy conservation. *Natl. Hog Farmer* (October), p. 83.

Short, T. H., Badger, P. C., and Roller, W. L. (1976). OARDC's solar-heated greenhouse. *Agric. Eng.* (July), 30–32.

Short, T. H., Badger, P. C., and Roller, W. L. (1979a). The operation of a solar pond-to-greenhouse heating system. *In* "Proceedings of the Fourth Annual Conference on Solar Energy for Heating of Greenhouses and Greenhouse-residence Combination" (D. R. Mears, ed.), pp. 83–92. New Brunswick, New Jersey.

Short, T. H., Badger, P. C., and Roller, W. L. (1979b). The development and demonstration of a solar pond for heating greenhouses. *In* "Proceedings of the International Solar Energy Society, Silver Jubilee Congress" (K. W. Bhoer and B. H. Glenn eds.), pp. 1021–1025. Atlanta, Georgia.

Shove, G. C. (1979). Solar collectors integrated into buildings dry agricultural crops. Michigan State University Energy for Agriculture Series ENR. Michigan State University, East Lansing, Michigan.

Shove, G. C. (1981). Utilization of solar buildings for drying grain. In "Proceedings of the Annual Meeting of the International Solar Energy Society, American Section," pp. 35–39. University of Delaware, Newark, Delaware.

Steward, W. G. (1973). A concentrating solar energy system employing a stationary spherical mirror and movable collector. *In* "Proceedings of the Solar Heating and Cooling for Buildings Workshop (Part 1: Technical Sessions)," Dept. of Mechanical Engineering, University of Maryland, College Park, Maryland.

Stickler, F. C., Shrader, W. D., and Johnson, I. J. (1959). Comparative value of legume and fertilizer nitrogen for corn production. *Agron. J.* **51**, 157–160.

Strijdom, B. W. (1979). Legumes as suppliers of nitrogen to pasture. *Proc. Grassl. Soc. South. Afr.* **14**, 15–17.

Sydney, P. (1981). Solar energy for crop drying. *Power Farming Mag.* **90**, 14–15.

Takezono, T. (1980). A study on the solar greenhouse, using transparent-heat-insulating collecting layers. *Hokkaido Natl. Agric. Exp. Stn.-Jpn. Bull.*, No. 128, 137–139.

University of Maryland (1974). "Proceedings of the Solar Heating and Cooling for Building Workshop: Part II—Panel Sessions, March 23." Prepared for the NSF-RANN by the Department of Mechanical Engineering. University of Maryland, College Park, Maryland.

University of Maryland (1976). "Solar Energy Applications in Agriculture: Potential, Research Needs and Adoption Strategies." Agric. Res. Service - USDA, University of Maryland, College Park, Maryland.

U.S. Department of Agriculture (1978). "Improving Soils with Organic Wastes." USDA, Washington, D.C.

Vanstaen, H., Neukermans, G., Debruyckere, M., and Verstraete, W. (1980). Composting of solids from pig and poultry liquid manure. *Compost Sci./Land Util.* **21**, 46–49.

Weil, R. R., and Kroontje, W. (1979). Physical condition of a Davidson clay loam after five years of heavy manure applications. *J. Environ. Qual.* **8**, 387–392.

Willard, C. J. (1927). An experimental study of sweet clover. *Ohio Agric. Exp. Stn. Bull.*, No. 405.

Willets, D. H., Chandra, P., and Miller, C. H. (1981). A solar energy collection/storage system for greenhouses: observed and simulated performance. *In* "Proceedings of the 1980 ASAE National Energy Symposium," pp. 59–65. St. Joseph, Michigan.

Yianoulis, P. (1981). Solar energy collection and storage for greenhouse heating. *In* "Proceedings of the International Seminar on Energy Conservation and the Use of Solar and other Renewable Energies in Agriculture, Horticulture and Fishculture," pp. 567–574. Polytechnic of Central London, London.

Zornig, H. F., and Godbey, L. C. (1981). Solar heated and cooled building. U.S. Patent Office (4, 244, 519), Washington, D.C.

Chapter 9

Biomass Energy and Food—Conflicts?

WILLIAM J. HUDSON

Market Research
The Andersons
Maumee, Ohio

In this chapter three main sources of biomass energy will be considered—grain, agricultural residue, and "others" (such as wood, refuse, kelp, etc.). The potential for conflict comes in the same order. The wisdom of converting grain to fuel energy has been widely argued and will serve as the primary focus here.

I. THE MORALITY OF FOOD VERSUS FUEL

The production of gasohol from grain is not an easy subject from the viewpoint of morality, at least in the sense of yielding to clear scientific analysis. To most people gasohol from grain has moral connotations that serve to make the subject somewhat troublesome. Grain is food, and food is our life supply. Our customs, our culture, and even our morality flow in large measure from our food—and its present abundance. Food remains so abundant in America that few people think much about it. Less than 4% of Americans are involved directly in farming; the other 96% can afford to forget the subject . . . at least until there is a surge in food prices, or perhaps a story of starvation somewhere else in the

FOOD AND ENERGY RESOURCES

world, or a grain embargo, or an article saying that gasohol will increase the price of food and take food from the starving.

Gasoline has also been abundant in America, and there was a time when few people thought much about it either. "Cheap gas" seemed as much a birthright as "cheap food" to most Americans, at least until 1972, when petroleum producing countries began to control supply and to raise prices. Gasoline became more and more expensive through the 1970s, making it seem that OPEC's control was absolute and that prices would continue to rise. Then the idea came of fighting OPEC with our food, either by means of a "bushel for a barrel" or by means of the conversion of "cheap food" into "cheap gas." Can we substitute one for another and still continue to have both? Can we do this with a clear conscience? What about the world's starving?

Table I shows an estimate of how the "average American" might think through these last questions—not scientifically, but in terms of morality and common sense. In examining Table I let us now try to follow this path of thought, bringing to bear evidence from the recent history of agriculture and energy.

II. "CHEAP FOOD" IS SURVIVING THE GRAIN EXPORT BOOM

For most Americans who are used to complaining about food prices, Fig. 1 may come as a surprise. The price of our food, seen as a percentage of disposable income, has been trending steadily downward since World War II. If we have a day-to-day impression of higher prices, this probably reflects our difficulty in automatically adjusting for inflation, which can be done either with the consumer price index or (more reliably) with the method shown in Fig. 1.

A careful study of the top line in this figure shows only a couple of upward reversals since World War II in the real food price trend: one in 1962 associated

TABLE I
The Morality of Food versus Fuel—An Estimate of How the "Average American" Thinks

Conversion of food to energy is an acceptable possibility *if*:
- We can maintain abundant "cheap food" at home
- We can continue to provide food assistance to the starving people abroad
- There is a gain in the "energy balance"
- There are no hidden stumbling blocks, such as
      trade problems
      economic problems
      more erosion
      more pesticides
      more corporate farms

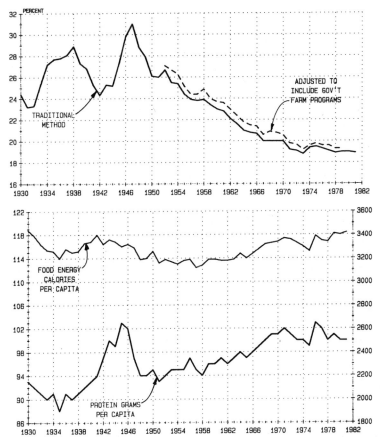

Fig. 1. Expediture for food (as a percentage of disposable income in United States), food energy, and protein.

with the Korean War and another in 1974 associated with the beginning of the export boom. By 1976 the trend is again downward, although one can also see that the 1970s, taken as a decade, represent a flattening out of the downward movement so evident in the 1950s and 1960s.

The dotted line at the top of Fig. 1 shows that farm programs introduced by the U.S. government have added very little to the consumer's bill for food. If food (including alcohol) expenditures are in the neighborhood of 19% of disposable income, this percentage is not more than $19\frac{1}{2}$–20%, with farm programs included. The impact of farm programs is less in years of strong export and strong crop prices.

The middle line of Fig. 1 is food energy calories per capita, which reached a low in the 1950s and has recently been climbing quite steeply. The dip in 1975 is associated with unusually high sugar prices, stemming from production shortfalls and leading to much greater use of grains (especially corn) in the chemical conversion to sugar substitutes. The bottom line of Fig. 1 is protein grams per capita, which declined sharply after World War II but which has been climbing steadily through the 1960s and 1970s. One can see a drop in protein in 1973–1975 that was associated with the beginning of the export boom, which led to much higher grain prices and thus to higher livestock feeding costs and resulted in less feeding, less meat, and thus higher meat prices. As the U.S. agricultural sector adjusted to the new levels of exports by doubling the production of grain and wheat, real prices for consumer protein returned to past levels, and the trend in per capita protein consumption resumed upward.

It is being argued by some that, nutritionally, the upward movement in calories and protein is not good. It is hard to argue, however, that this is not what people want. In a capitalistic sense, the U.S. food system can be seen to be performing almost ideally, providing more of what people want, for less. The U.S. food system, which permits Americans to spend less of their income for food than anywhere in the world, is surviving the continuing grain export boom that began in 1973. Having survived one boom, could the U.S. food system now withstand another, say a "gasohol boom," which would likely be much more gradual?

III. PRESERVING FOOD EXPORTS TO THE WORLD'S STARVING

It can safely be asserted that our "average American" would prefer that no one starve. As demonstrated by Public Law (P.L.) 480, the average American will *give* food away in order to prevent starvation and malnutrition. But the giving is not a bottomless well. Starvation is one thing, while living high on the hog is another. The average American would not necessarily *give* in order to permit others to eat the same quantity and quality of foods. Other peoples, in the absence of natural disasters, are seen as having a responsibility to earn their food by economic output. So while we want to acknowledge the two main conditions on converting food to fuel (maintaining cheap food at home and continuing to help the starving abroad), we look to history for guidance on how much help the American is really willing to give.

At the bottom of Fig. 2 is the world trade of all grains, along with the U.S. share of that trade and the portion of U.S. exports that are P.L. 480 "give-away." During the early 1960s, the P.L. 480 Program accounted for one-third to one-half of U.S. exports. In the 1980s P.L. 480 has dropped to less than 5% of U.S. exports.

The major explanation for the decrease in P.L. 480 shipments is no doubt the

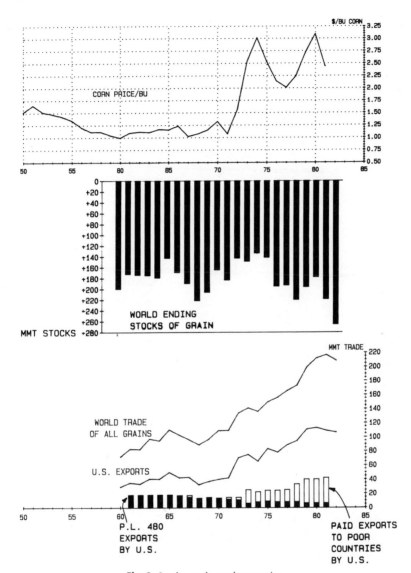

Fig. 2. Stocks, trade, and corn price.

increasing price of grains during the 1970s, as illustrated by the price of corn at the top of Fig. 2. Corn price, unadjusted for inflation, peaked in 1974 as world ending stocks dropped to lows for the modern period. The time of heightened awareness of the "world food problem" was 1974–1975. World stocks are now back to record high levels as we enter the 1980s. Corn price would likely return to even lower levels than it has, were it not for U.S. government price support programs. With P.L. 480 now costing over $1 billion, enlarging on this foreign aid expenditure is apparently not something the American taxpayer is eager to do. The policy of the Reagan administration has been to avoid enlarging public spending and the federal deficit.

Thus, food assistance in the neighborhood of 5% of U.S. exports, or about 5 million metric tons (MMT), might be taken as the practical limit of American generosity. How much is needed? Depending on how one defines "starving" or "malnutrition," the Food for Peace Administrator (1981) puts the number at about 25 MMT, which is small compared to world trade but large compared to present aid. If donations are to remain at 5 MMT, whether this seems morally adequate or not, it would be difficult to argue that such a small percentage of our total would ever be threatened seriously by even a major food to fuel conversion program.

The bar graph at the bottom of Fig. 2 shows another interesting aspect of history with respect to food for the poorer countries. The unshaded portion of the bars represents shipments to the poor countries (basically the same list of recipients as for P.L. 480) that the poor countries were able to pay for. Notice that these countries' ability to pay takes a dramatic jump in 1973 and again in 1978, coincident with the major oil price hikes by OPEC. The argument of recycled funds clearly suggests that when the "average American" pays more for gasoline, the money goes to OPEC and OPEC deposits the money with international banks. The banks then lend more freely than ever to the Third World, and the Third World buys American grain, thus helping our balance of trade, keeping our dollar stronger than it would have been otherwise, and easing the blow of higher oil prices. If this argument is true, however, the eventual loser is indeed the average American, as international debt piles up to unredeemable levels, generating ever greater demand for credit, which is followed by continuing high interest rates.

IV. THE ENERGY BALANCE VERSUS THE ECONOMIC BALANCE IN CONVERTING FOOD TO FUEL

In the 1930s, a movement called "Technocracy" arose briefly and died. The idea was to change from dollars to joules or BTUs, that is, to base the world economy on the laws of thermodynamics, which were felt to be more certain and lasting than other human coin. In the 1980s, a somewhat similar movement, although not so generalized, has arisen in connection with gasohol (generally gasohol is 10% ethanol and 90% gasoline). The "energy balance" question is, simply, "If it takes more energy to produce gasohol than it supplies, why do it?" Investigators of this question put forth data on the energy required to grow corn, the energy required to process corn into alcohol, and the road mileage obtainable from octane-boosted alcohol–gasoline blends. No scientific agreement has been reached on the question, nor is one likely.

One of the key reasons for controversy is that not all BTUs are alike: the energy in steam is different from the energy in gasoline, which is different from the energy in coal. The form of energy, its so-called "quality," matters. High-quality liquid fuels make automobiles possible. Coal, of which we have relatively abundant supplies, will not work in automobiles, unless it is first converted to liquid; that conversion process is expensive, both energetically and economically. Coal, however, is a suitable boiler fuel, and steam from boilers is required to convert corn to alcohol. Why shouldn't one, therefore, argue that gasohol is really a means for converting coal to a liquid, with corn as the medium? Only part of the energy required to grow corn is in the form of liquid, so the net gain in liquid energy is much greater than the net gain (if there is one) in total energy as measured in BTUs. The average American, especially in times of high, fast-rising gasoline prices, will probably accept the idea of corn-based alcohol as a reasonable way of bringing coal to bear on the needs for "cheap gas"; thus, the energy balance question may lose its moral sting.

The real question in a capitalistic society is whether gasohol can make money. Profit is our long-term test, and in the long term it will be the relation of corn price to gasoline price that determines how much corn gets converted to liquid fuel. Figure 3 shows this relationship, unadjusted for inflation, since 1950. As can be seen, the price of both commodities stays rather flat until 1973, when the upward swing begins.

At the bottom of Fig. 3 is the ratio of corn price to gasoline price over the same period. Since, physically, there are about 2.5 gallons of ethanol in a bushel of corn, we can expect that whenever the ratio of corn price to gasoline price dips to 2.5 or below, we might begin to see some commercial interest in processing. The figure shows a zone of commercial interest, from 1.6 to 2.0 on the ratio's scale, which derives from the simple fact that most chemical industries operate, more or less profitably, in the range of 60–80% efficiency. This zone of commercial interest is also verified by many proforma studies of gasohol feasibility, including one by the U.S. Department of Agriculture (1980).

History shows that the relationship between corn price and gasoline price first began to favor gasohol in the early 1980s. Will this continue to be the case?

V. RELATION OF GASOLINE PRICE TO CORN PRICE DEPENDS ON INTERNATIONAL POLITICS AND WEATHER

Figure 4 shows, on a monthly basis, the last 4 years of gasoline price versus corn price and the ratio between them, which twice drops into the zone of

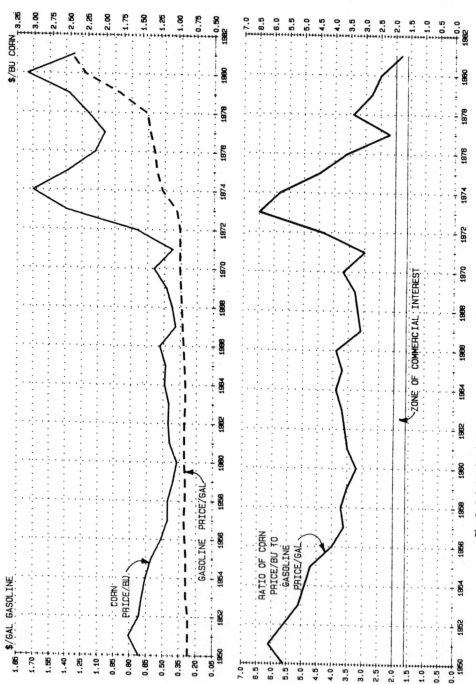

Fig. 3. Relationship between corn price and gasoline price and the ratio since 1950.

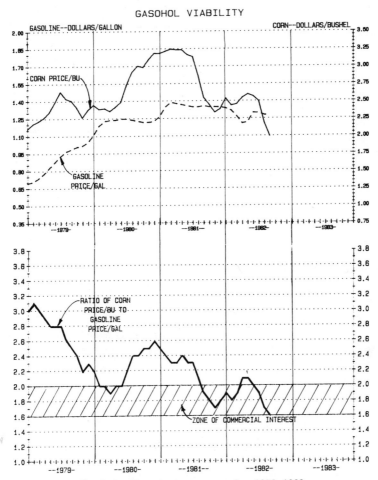

Fig. 4. Gasoline price versus corn price, 1978–1982.

commercial interest, once in early 1980 and again in late 1981. In early 1980, with gasoline prices rising due to the supply interruptions in Iran and with corn prices weak due to the Carter grain embargo on Russia, gasohol became a very hot subject. A short crop in the fall of 1980, however, strengthened corn prices and a new Republican administration began to cut government subsidies of all kinds, including gasohol, and the subject cooled off. With the crude oil glut of 1981, gasoline prices levelled off, and not even a sharp drop in corn price after the big crop of 1981 could restore vigor to the gasohol movement. Even though the ratio of gasoline price to corn price was more favorable in the winter of 1981–1982 than ever before, commercial development still apparently hinged on government support, which had largely dried up.

So history has not yet made it clear what conditions might set up sustaining viability of gasohol and, as can be seen in both Figs. 3 and 4, history seems to deny any causal link between gasoline price and corn price. Clearly, it requires gasoline (and other energy) to grow corn, but a rise in gasoline prices is not always accompanied by a rise in corn prices, or vice versa. Corn price proceeds on its bumpy path with apparent disdain for gasoline price. The gasohol investor wants to know why this might be so and whether it will continue this way.

First, let us briefly address the issue of energy input to corn. The average U.S. bushel of corn requires about 120,000 BTUs to grow, compared to 145,000 BTUs in a gallon of gasoline. We cannot conclude, however, that therefore a bushel requires three-fourths of a gallon of gasoline, because the input energies come in all different forms: a small amount of diesel fuel for the tractor, a lot of natural gas for the fertilizer, a lot of electricity for irrigation, etc. Furthermore, it must be realized that corn is grown at the end of a massive climatic lever, on which the role of weather as an energy input makes man's inputs seem puny. The scale of this lever can be seen by calculating the amount of energy involved in delivering rainfall to the U.S. corn crop. The evaporation of water (from the ocean or elsewhere) requires about 2.2 quadrillion BTUs/km^3; if 40 inches of rain falls on the U.S. corn belt each year, that would be about 3000 km^3 of water, which, in cubic kilometers, would require over 6000 quads from the sun to form clouds (let alone to circulate the clouds to the right place). This is roughly 100 times the total energy used by man (approximately 75 quads) in the United States for all purposes! It is thus no wonder that seemingly small changes in weather can affect the corn market so dramatically.

Second, we must remember the role of politics in both the price of gasoline and the price of corn; the same international episode may not act on each commodity in the same way. Table II presents a rough illustration of this thesis, taken from the author's experience in close contact with the commodity markets during the period 1978–1982. It should be noted that the impact of an international conflict, say Poland/Solidarity, on commodity prices cannot be demonstrated by quantitative methods, such as econometrics, because human conflict is not obligated to express itself quantitatively. Conflicts are what they are, however, and even the dabbler in commodity speculation knows the reality of market moves in reaction to qualitative events of the day.

A difficulty with Table II is the idea of direct effect versus indirect effect, for it can be argued that all things are connected, perhaps through the price of gold, or some might even say through the price of energy itself. The Afghanistan invasion, for instance, warranted the grain embargo as a response precisely because Persian Gulf oil was ultimately at stake. Maybe so, but such are the qualitative vagaries of international affairs. These vagaries, however, most definitely assert themselves on both gasoline price and corn price, probably differently, and the equally unpredictable but real role of climate on corn production combines with

TABLE II
Major International Conflicts and Their Direct Impact on Prices (1978–1982)

	Affected gasoline price strongly	Affected neither strongly	Affected corn price strongly
Iranian revolution	X		
Afghanistan invasion (+U.S. embargo on Russia)			X
Hostage crisis		X	
Poland/solidarity			X
Falklands Islands			X
Israel–Lebanon 1982		X	

future international politics to permit us only a blurry vision of how long the ratio of gasoline price to corn price might stay favorable to gasohol.

VI. GASOLINE MARKET SIZE VERSUS CORN MARKET SIZE

Let us consider the scale of gasoline use in the United States versus the present production of corn. In subsequent topics, we will consider how much the corn crop could be enlarged.

Table III shows the loss of nutrients involved in the conversion of a bushel of corn to $2\frac{1}{2}$ gallons of alcohol (gross) plus various by-products. Corn supplies two main things to livestock, protein and digestible energy. The ethanol conversion process has little effect on the protein, which emerges in the main by-product, called distillers dried grains and solubles (DDGS). However, the digestible energy portion of corn, the carbohydrates, or starch, is indeed the very material that is converted to alcohol, and most of what animal nutritionists refer to as total digestible nutrients (TDN) is lost to the food chain. Of the 56 lb of material in a bushel of corn, 31 lb of TDN are lost in the conversion to ethanol.

VII. PROSPECTS FOR EXPORTING CORN BY-PRODUCTS

Large amounts of gasohol from corn would result in large amounts of DDGS. The possibility of stumbling blocks to the exporting of this material must be considered should the U.S. domestic market not require or accept all of the DDGS. The argument of gasohol proponents has generally been to parallel processed cornmeal with processed soybean meal (SBM): the world needs protein

William J. Hudson

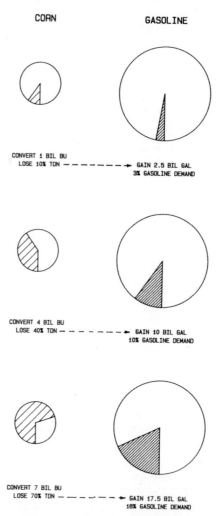

Fig. 5. Relative market size of corn and gasoline and impact of converting corn to ethanol.

most of all, so sell the world DDGS, just as we now sell SBM. In this way, the United States would increase its value-added manufacture ahead of export, instead of shipping raw materials for processing industries of other countries.

The middle portion of Fig. 6 shows the history of U.S. exports of corn by-products (primarily corn gluten meal, which is quite similar in nutrient profile to DDGS). The primary customers have been the Netherlands and West Germany, two of the most advanced industrial nations, particularly with respect to the computerized compounding of livestock feed. Neither corn protein meal nor

TABLE III
Corn Digestible Nutrients Lost in Ethanol Conversion[a]

	Total weight	Crude protein	TDN
One bushel corn	56 lb	4.9 lb	44.8 lb
DDGS from one bushel corn	17	4.6	13.6
Lost to ethanol		0.3	31.2
		6%[b]	70%

[a]Crude protein of #2 yellow corn is 8.7% (56 lb × 8.7% + 4.9 lb). TDN (Total Digestible Nutrients) of #2 yellow corn is 80% (56 lb × 80% = 44.8 lb). (From *Feed Industry Redbook*, 1981.)

[b]The Distillers Feed Research Council argues that protein *quality* is enhanced by processing to make DDGS, so that an actual gain in total protein feed value takes place. (From Isgrigg, 1980.)

soybean protein meal have been products sold extensively to undeveloped countries.

The top portion of Fig. 6 shows the relative annual export values of corn, corn by-products, and soybean meal. The value of corn by-products varies between corn and SBM, seeking a level just below halfway, a level that is less than that domestically sold. In 1981 the value of corn by-products departed from the previous pattern, turning downward even though both corn itself and SBM went up. This change in value may reflect a structural limit to corn by-product exports to members of the European Economic Community (EEC). The Common Agricultural Policy of the EEC is founded on levies that help to assure that value-added manufacture stays within the EEC. For example, there is a levy on corn imports but not on soybeans: this encourages the production of SBM in Europe. Because the available quantities of processed corn by-products were very small when the EEG began, no levy was established. Now, however, as more become available, the Netherlands and West Germany are taking advantage of the cheapness of corn protein meal as compared to corn with its import levy. But this increased use of corn by-products has incurred the resentment of France and other members of the EEC, who are proposing either import limits or a levy, both of which cause our own government to talk of a retaliatory trade war.

The bottom portion of Fig. 6 shows U.S. export tonnage by percentage for the past decade. The percentage, made up of all processed meals and feeds (from all sources: wheat, corn, soybean, etc.), has not grown. Raw feedgrains and oilseeds have increased, feedgrains have decreased, and processed meals and feeds have remained stable. History confirms that those who have an advantage want to keep it; in this case, our customers all wish to keep the value-added manufacture at home. There is one exporting country to have reversed this trend, namely Brazil, which has caused virtually all of its soybeans to be exported in the form of processed meal and oil; this is only possible, however, through the subsidization of the Brazilian processing industry when price relationships favor raw bean

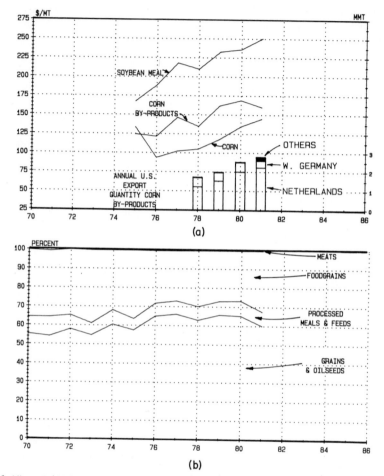

Fig. 6. History of U.S. export of corn by-products 1970–1981. (a) Annual U.S. export values. (b) U.S. export tonnage by percentage.

exports versus meal. If one outcome of a major gasohol program were to be a continuing subsidy, as in the Brazilian soybean processing case, this should surely be denoted as a severe stumbling block in forward planning.

VIII. DOMESTIC MARKET FOR CORN BY-PRODUCTS

The nutritional make-up of the two principal corn by-products, corn gluten feed (the principal remainder after high fructose wet milling) and DDGS (the remainder after ethanol wet milling) as in Table IV. The profile of either DDGS or gluten feed falls about midway between SBM and corn.

The price of DDGS in the past decade has also averaged midway between the prices of SBM and corn, as shown at the top of Fig. 7. The usage of DDGS took a major increase in 1981, as shown by the bars in Fig. 7. However, the total of gluten feed and DDGS did not rise so dramatically (roughly the levels of 1972 and 1975), even though there were 8% more livestock units to be fed in 1981.

The trend of feeding practice for the U.S. livestock industry is shown at the bottom of Fig. 7, where it can be seen that the percentage of processed feeds has been stable to slightly down, over the past decade. This trend exists in the face of the soybean processing industry, which would surely like to increase its share of total feeding but which is denied this by price relationships that flow from feeding practices and computerized nutritional analyses. The gasohol investor must recognize that the by-product, DDGS, will enter the feed ingredient market in direct competition with all the other materials, especially soybean meal, manufactured by well-depreciated commercial mills (over $1 billion in replacement value).

Isgrigg (1980), Executive Director of the Distillers Feed Research Council, published an article in which a claim is made for higher digestibility of DDGS compared to SBM. The feed industry has not in practice, however, endorsed these research findings in the form of stronger prices for DDGS. Feed nutritionists in the United States tend to view DDGS as most well-suited for dairy rations, although experience indicates a use limit due to palatability.

IX. POTENTIAL MAGNITUDE OF ACREAGE CHANGES FROM A MAJOR GASOHOL PROGRAM

Using history as the guide, there will be substantial difficulty in absorbing the DDGS from a major gasohol program in either the export or domestic markets. If such difficulty is overcome, however, we should inquire about the further changes that might be wrought in the U.S. agricultural system, especially acreage, chemical inputs, and conservation practices.

TABLE IV
Nutritional Composition of DDGS versus Other Feeds (%)[a]

	SBM	#2 yellow corn	SBM/ corn average	DDGS	Corn gluten feed
Crude protein	44.0	8.7	26.4	27.0	22.0
TDN	78.0	80.0	79.0	80.0	
Fat	.5	3.9	2.2	9.0	2.0
Fiber	6.5	2.4	4.5	10.0	10.0

[a]Data from *Feed Industry Redbook* (1981).

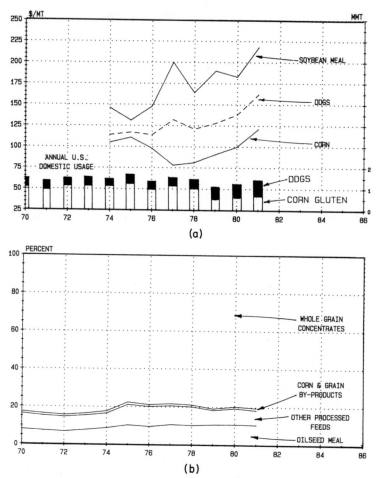

Fig. 7. Trend in prices and feed tonnage, United States, 1970–1981. (a) Annual U.S. domestic prices. (b) U.S. domestic feed tonnage by percentage.

Several expert groups have issued reports on the subject of acreage changes associated with large corn-to-ethanol conversion, using various econometric techniques. Such techniques have proven dubious in agricultural economics to date because of the strong impact on commodity markets of such qualitative factors as weather, domestic farm bills, and international politics. Using some straightforward calculations will give an idea of the potential change in acreage that might take place in two cases: (1) the conversion of 1 billion bushels of corn to 2.5 billion gallons of ethanol and (2) the conversion of 4 billion bushels of corn to 10 billion gallons of ethanol.

Table V shows the present levels of production of coarse grain (largely corn) and soybeans in the United States, along with the current usage level of DDGS. If corn is used to produce 2.5 billion gallons of ethanol, the impact on production is given in Case 1. The method is to add 7.6 MMT of DDGS to the protein and TDN supply, and then adjust soybeans and corn downward until the original tonnage and nutritional "mix" is achieved. This method treats the current U.S. output of grains and oilseeds like a large, single livestock ration, sought out by the historical flux of markets and presumably under lasting demand from the world.

Case 1 shows that 2.5 billion gallons of ethanol can be produced and the "mix" of present U.S. feed and export demand be maintained, if corn is enlarged by 10 million acres and soybeans lessened by 5.3 million acres. Case 2 shows

TABLE V
Crop Production and Acreage Levels before and after Gasohol[a]

	Coarse grains	Soybeans (in SBM equiv.)	DDGS	Mix (%)	Mix MMT[b]
Present (1977–1982) production level					
Feed and export (MMT)	223	42	.6		265.6
Protein (%)	9	44	27	14.6	38.8
TDN (%)	80	78	80	79.7	211.7
Total acres	105.8 million	65.3 million			
Future production levels to maintain same mix, after introduction of gasohol industry					
Case 1. Introduce 2.5 billion gallons ethanol					
Ethanol (MMT)	25.4	—			
Feed and export (MMT)	219.0	38.4	8.2		265.6
Protein (%)	9	44	27	14.6	38.8
TDN (%)	80	78	80	79.7	211.7
Total acres	115.8 million	60 million			
Acres change	+10 million	−5.3 million			
Case 2. Introduce 10 billion gallons ethanol					
Ethanol (MMT)	101.6				
Feed and export (MMT)	208.0	26.0	31.4		265.4
Protein (%)	9	44	27	14.6	38.8
TDN (%)	80	78	80	79.8	211.8
Total acres	146.7 million	40.6 million			
Acres change	+40.9 million	−24.7 million			

[a]Data from U.S. Department of Agriculture (1980).
[b]MMT, million metric tons.

that 10 billion gallons and the present "mix" are possible with 41 million additional acres of corn and 25 million acres less of soybeans. The feasibility of these changes needs to be ascertained.

X. AGRONOMIC IMPACT OF ACREAGE CHANGES FROM A MAJOR GASOHOL PROGRAM

The history of U.S. acres of the principal crops harvested (wheat, corn, and soybeans), which account for two-thirds of all cropland (with hay and cotton being the bulk of the remainder), is shown on the top portion of Fig. 8.

In the 40 years between 1930 and 1970, the acres of the principal crops harvested trended down very slightly. After 1972, with exports growing at 7% per year, acreage also grew dramatically at almost 3% per year. This fast growth trend relied on recapturing set-aside acreage and converting pasture and rangeland. Such a trend will probably not continue indefinitely, especially in the face of urbanization, which claims as much as 1–3 million acres per year (often of the best land) for principal crops. Furthermore, remaining hay, pasture, and rangeland that might be converted to row crops is not of the same quality as that presently in use, at least in terms of organic matter and rainfall. Some good quality land remains, however, even in the midst of the corn and wheat belt, where small plots of forest are converted to row crops when crop prices make such investments look attractive.

The 1980s promise a slower rate of growth for exports as compared to the 1970s; this is not because the growth of population has slowed but because economic growth has to catch up with the need of the population. Ideas on the rate of export growth abound, but a reasonable figure will lie between 0 and 7% per year; let us say, 3%. Allowing for continued improvement in crop yields at about the same pace as now (leaving genetic breakthroughs for later, after 1990), a 3% rate of export growth and a steady domestic demand would translate to a 1% per year growth in acreage of the principal crops. This 1% annual growth is without major gasohol programs.

In the previous topic, the magnitude of acreage increases from two gasohol scenarios was considered:

Case 1. Introduce 2.5 billion gallons ethanol. Add 10 million acres corn. Subtract 5 million acres soybeans.

Case 2. Introduce 10 billion gallons ethanol. Add 41 million acres corn. Subtract 25 million acres soybeans.

The middle portion of Fig. 8 shows the paths of both Case 1 and Case 2, when added to the 1% growth due to export demand. Neither path exceeds the growth trend of the late 1970s, but this was primarily possible through the recapture of set-aside acres.

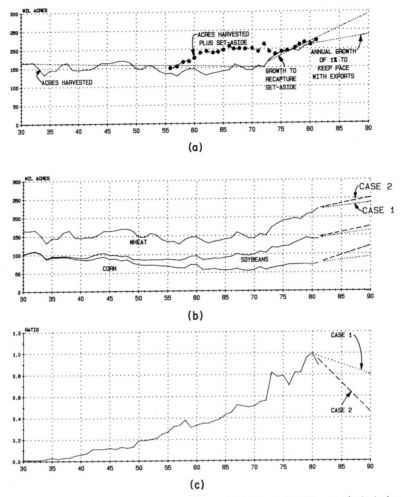

Fig. 8. Area harvested, in use of crop acreage for gasohol (ethanol). (a) U.S. area of principal crops (wheat + corn + soybeans) without major gasohol programs. (b) U.S. area of principal crops (wheat + corn + soybeans) with major gasohol programs. (c) Soybean-to-corn acres ratio.

Of more concern than the absolute size of the increase in Case 1 or Case 2 is the change in the ratio of soybean-to-corn acres. Case 2, for instance, would return this ratio to 0.45, similar to the situation in the 1950s and early 1960s. This would reduce the opportunity of soybean-to-corn rotation, with its attendant benefits to soil and to flexibility at planting time. It is well-known that soybeans, being legumes, fix nitrogen from the atmosphere on their roots and thus require little commercial fertilizer, about 10% of that applied to corn. The nitrogen content of soybean residue, furthermore, may provide a better source of nitrogen for the following corn crop because of the time-release factor of the residue's natural decay in the soil; this leads many, but not all, farmers to claim higher corn yields in a rotation sequence.

Flexibility at planting time is crucial in years of wet weather in the spring, when farmers cannot plant corn at the optimium time for maximum yields and they switch to soybeans. This happened most recently in the eastern cornbelt in 1981 and the western cornbelt in 1982. Soybeans and corn also have slightly different "critical moisture periods" during the summer, so the present division in acreage offers some insurance that not both crops will fail due to the same irregularity of weather. The difference in time of planting and harvest also allows the farmer to spread labor and equipment over more total acres.

XI. CORN–SOYBEAN PRICE IMPACT OF A MAJOR GASOHOL PROGRAM

The ratio of soybean acres to corn acres grew slowly but steadily through the 1960s, but coincident with the "Russian market" of 1973 the ratio of soybean acres to corn acres jumped dramatically; it did not again return to prior levels through the 1970s and the early 1980s. As can be seen in Fig. 9, this change took place in response to record soybean prices, which took the soybean-to-corn price ratio up to 4.04 (from levels around 2.1 in the 1960s). The 1973 price followed U.S. soybean production declines, relative to corn, also illustrated in Fig. 9.

Lapses in the ratio of soybean production to corn production (note that the scale of this ratio in Fig. 9 is inverted) are usually tied to peaks in the ratio of prices, note especially 1973 and 1977. Although the ratio of acres jumps with prices and production in 1973, it is more difficult to analyze the acreage ratio thereafter. Certainly there are factors beyond those shown in the graph, including the U.S. government feed grain set-aside programs in 1978 and 1979. Farmers could turn to soybeans without any restrictions and did so, even though the price ratio was unfavorable.

The bottom portion of Fig. 9 shows what may be called the "structural change" in U.S. agriculture. This occurred in 1973 as world demand, especially from the USSR, boomed. The message of the market (price) was to produce more of everything but especially more soybeans, relative to corn and other grains. The mean ratio of soybean-to-corn price went from 2.1 in the 1960s to 2.5 in the 1970s, sending the acreage ratio from 0.44 to 0.84. What then might happen to price, or what would price (the job of the market) have to do in order for our Case 2 to become a reality? Case 2 called for 10 billion gallons of ethanol from corn, which might be gotten through 40 million acres of additional corn, 25 million acres less soybeans, or a soybean-to-corn acres ratio of 0.45. This new ratio, say in 1990, is about equal to the mean of the 1960s, so we should be able to infer that the price ratio, at a minimum, would need to return to the levels of the 1960s, say 2.1.

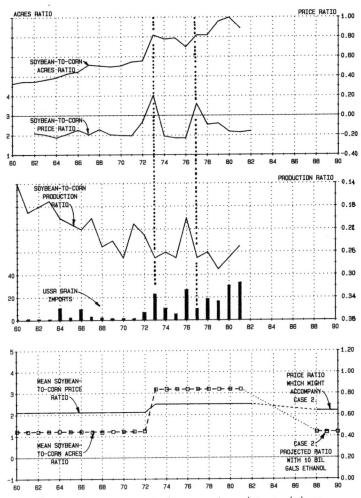

Fig. 9. Soybean-to-corn ratios for acres, price and structural changes.

But if the world's diet continues on the present course, soybeans ought to have at least the same value in 1990 as they do now, discounting inflation. If soybeans are presently $7.50/bushel when corn is $3.00/bushel (a ratio of 2.5), corn will be $3.60/bushel with a new ratio of 2.1. In other words, the minimum price increase for corn due to a major gasohol program, in this line of reasoning, would be about 20%. Actually, to turn around the forces let loose in the 1970s by the export market and to compensate for the agronomic disadvantages discussed previously, the market might have to do twice this much, say 20–40%.

The above argument is not meant to be numerically precise. The common sense version of it runs as follows: the world market has put relative prices on both corn and soybeans, mainly on the basis of their nutritional performance in livestock rations. If a new factor enters in the market, say a major gasohol program using corn, such a factor will have to bid corn away from the existing uses. The additional bid required to get major quantities of corn will likely be significant. This additional bid is independent of fluctuations for other, previous factors that were discussed in the topic on relation of gasoline price to corn price. In other words, changes in the weather or in international affairs (say, for instance, the entry of China into export trade on a scale similar to the USSR) would add or subtract from corn price quite separately from the "structural surcharge" discussed on this page, which, whether 20% or 40%, promises to be significant and to prolong the time before the corn-to-gasoline price ratio remains in the zone of commerical interest without government subsidy.

XII. INFERENCES ABOUT FERTILIZER, PESTICIDES, AND EROSION

Research on erosion has recently been entering a boom of its own, as have been interpretation of the research warning of imminent peril. Lester Brown has written for years on the evil of erosion. Lauren Soth (1981) recently published an article that associated erosion with the pressure put on the land by export demand. At the same time, Theodore Schultz has debunked these analyses. Because erosion is so widespread and yet so gradual, it is inherently difficult to measure. Also, crop yields continue to increase, which makes immediate concern all the more difficult.

An alternate avenue of evidence, although most certainly inferential rather than direct, comes from the U.S. Department of Agricluture's annual statistics (1981) on farm productivity. The top portion of Fig. 10 shows rising farm output since 1940, along with fairly stable farm input (adjusted to 1967 prices), which yields the familiar and comforting line of upward bound farm productivity. This is the way a well-tended and well-maintained "factory" should behave, that is, ever more output for the same input.

The key to the rise in total farm productivity has been the continuous fall in farm labor, which in 1967 and 21% of farm input. Other factors were as shown in Table VI.

By 1980, the cost of agricultural (ag) chemicals (fertilizer, lime, and pesticides) has grown to $4.5 billion in 1967 dollars and from 7 to 11% of total input costs, though the method used by U.S. Department of Agriculture of adjusting productivity indices to 1967 price–quantity ratios does not highlight this 60% jump in ag chemicals. If the real cost of ag chemicals is rising faster than the real output of the land, it can reasonably be argued that the land is deteriorating or that decreases in labor input are being enjoyed at the expense of ignoring needed conservation efforts.

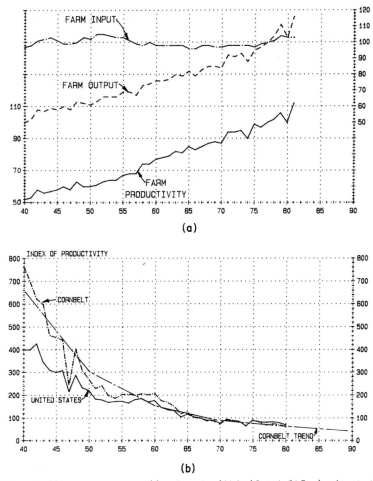

Fig. 10. (a) Total farm output versus total farm input (total United States). (b) Feed grain output versus agricultural chemical input (total United States versus cornbelt).

TABLE VI
Total Farm Productivity

Labor	$8.0 billion (1967)	21%
Real estate	8.9	23
Mechanical power	10.7	28
Agricultural chemicals	2.6	7
Feed, seed, livestock	2.7	7
Taxes, interest	4.1	11
Miscellaneous	1.2	3
Total	38.2 billion	100%

The data kept by the U.S. Department of Agriculture result in the curves shown at the bottom of Fig. 10, feedgrain output versus ag chemical input, for the total United States and the cornbelt. It should be noted that while "feedgrain output" is a distinct category in U.S. Department of Agriculture data, "ag chem input" is for all sectors of farming, not just for feedgrains. It is well known, however, that the majority of ag chemicals are used for feedgrains, so the extrapolation presented here should be fairly safe. The trend is clearly downward. The cornbelt can be seen to be descending slightly more than the total United States recently, possibly due to the fact of new lands being devoted to corn outside of the cornbelt, e.g., Michigan, eastern Kentucky, and the Pacific northwest. Also, irrigation in Nebraska is not counted as an "ag chem" expense.

The period of the 1970s is rather flat in farm input, possibly coincident with the increased rotation to soybeans (whose nitrogen fixation from the atmosphere is regarded as "free" fertilizer, in these statistics). A simple power curve, however, fits the data well, from 1940 through 1980. Extending this trend to 1990 shows a drop in the index from 61 to 40. To return 1990 productivity to 1980 levels would thus be seen to require 50% more ag chem inputs, more than the present trend in ag chemicals, which has been 2.5% per year. So if this inferential evidence is to be admitted, it will be difficult to argue for a major gasohol program from corn without also admitting exacerbation of the ag chem productivity problem and the relationship to soil erosion.

XIII. POTENTIAL AND PROBLEMS OF ENERGY FROM CROP RESIDUES AND OTHER BIOMASS SOURCES

The "average American" who drives across wheat, corn, or soybean country after harvest is likely to think, observing the straw and stubble, "Look at all that unused material, going to waste!" Is somebody missing a "free lunch" with regard to these residues?

In the past decade, various researchers have attempted to quantify the potential of crop residues and similar biomass, and Table VII shows results from two of the most recent efforts. Since we have been mainly concerned with food versus gasoline, the energy potential is stated in terms of maximum potential liquid; other quantities of energy are available from the same biomass, if the goal is gas or direct combustion. The potential energy in Table VII is also stated as "net," which means that allowances for collection, transportation, and conversion (each an energy-consuming step) have been made. The total impact of all the sources listed is 2.71 quads, which is 17% of U.S. gasoline use, an impressive amount. But there is a limitation.

The relative importance of the sources is noted in Table VII. Wood residue is

TABLE VII
Current Biomass Sources and Maximum Potential Net Liquid Energy[a]

	Total biomass (dry MMT)	Available for energy conversion (dry MMT)	Maximum potential net liquid (Q)
Wood	715	285	.91
Forage	750	130	.75
Crop residues	430	75	.64
Corn	160	40	.36
Wheat	85	20	.15
Oats	20	7	.05
Rice	5	5	.04
Barley	15	4	.03
Soybeans	70	—	—
Other	70	—	—
Societal wastes	265	115	.29
Grains	355	20	.12
Animal wastes	175	50	—[b]
Other	25	10	—[b]
Total	2,175	690	2.71
U.S. total energy use			78.0
U.S. gasoline use			16.0

[a]Data from Department of Energy (1981) and Pimentel (1981).
[b]Energy form would be gas.

the largest source and is generally separate from food. Societal wastes (such as sewage, municipal solid wastes, industrial wastes) are also separate from food. Animal wastes and other biomass sources (bagasse, aquatic plants, etc.) have no contribution to liquid fuel. Forage, crop residues, and grains remain. Together they have a potential of 1.39 quads or 9% of gasoline supply. The food conflict with respect to energy conversion of forage is direct, since the great majority of forage is presently fed to livestock. If the forage is used for fuel, vastly greater quantities of grain would be needed to maintain livestock output at the same rate; yet acreage for this additional grain would have to come from the very range and pastureland under question.

Two biomass sources are available, these are grain and crop residues, with the former having already been considered at length. With crop residues we are faced with two definitions of "net" energy, which highlight the potential conflict between food and energy. The 0.64 quads shown in Table VII for the potential liquid energy is "net" in the sense of allowing for collection, transportation, and conversion. Pimentel *et al.* (1981) have shown that if "net" energy is calculated after also allowing for energy to replace nutrients in the residue and to offset added annual soil loss from removing the residue, the potential for crop residues drops from 4% of gasoline use to slightly less than 1%. The point is simply that crop residues have important, energetic functions in the food production chain, which might be easy to ignore on the surface. The temptation to scoop up corn silage "wasting" in the field is reduced when not only the costs of drying it, hauling it, and processing it are comtemplated but also the costs of buying more fertilizer the following spring and realizing less yield from less organic soil.

XIV. MAIN JOB OF THE FARMER: CROP—NOT CROP RESIDUE

The predominance of corn, particularly with respect to crop residues is given in Table VII. Of the estimated 75 MMT available for energy conversion, 40 MMT is from corn, of which most is from the cobs: U.S. corn production = 7 billion bushels; U.S. cob production = 7 billion bushels × 10 lb/bushel = 70 billion lb = 32 MMT. Presently, only about 2% or 600,000 tons of cobs move from farms for uses beyond soil maintenance. Mushroom composting, furfural processing, and industrial grit production are the leading uses of cobs. Problems in gathering the supply illustrate the conflicts between the farmer's main job (food) and what he certainly must regard as a far secondary job, energy or industrial applications of residues.

The physiological or natural role of the cob in corn production is to hold the grain and to serve as a "moisture sink" after harvest. Through the first half of this century, corn was harvested by ear, the ears placed in open-mesh cribs, and natural circulation allowed to dry the corn grain before shelling from the cob. Corn on the cob, however, occupies twice the volume as the same weight of shelled corn, and corn on the cob ("ear corn") is also much more difficult to handle than smooth-flowing shelled corn. After World War II, the harvesting process for corn began to change with the introduction of picker–shellers and combines. The energy price of this change, over 95% complete in 1980, is shown in Table VIII. The new method is three times more energy intensive, costing the U.S. corn harvest about 7 billion bushels × 56 lb/bushel × 224 BTU/lb = 0.08 quad. This is roughly one-fifth of the net energy gain shown in Table VII for corn residues altogether.

The author is associated with an industrial corn cob refining operation in Ohio and Indiana, whose problems of obtaining cobs must be illustrative of the problems of gathering any or all crop residues. Private data over the past decade for this operation (which uses nearly 100,000 tons of cobs per year) show the following:

1. Receipts of ear corn (the source of cobs) vary inversely with corn price,

TABLE VIII
Energy per Pound Required to Harvest and Store Corn

	Shelled corn method	Ear corn method
Combine	50 BTU/lb	—
Haul to bin (1 mile)[a]	3 BTU/lb	—
Dry[b]	250 BTU/lb	—
Store in one bin (1 year)[c]	27 BTU/lb	—
Pick[d]	—	42 BTU/lb
Double haul to cribs (1 mile)[a]	—	6 BTU/lb
Double store in two cribs (1 year)	—	54 BTU/lb
Shell[e]	—	4 BTU/lb
Total	330 BTU/lb	106 BTU/lb
Difference: 224 BTU/lb		

[a] Average small truck carries 7920 lb and requires 19,000 BTU to move this load 1 mile, yielding 2.4 BTU/mile rounded up to cover farm wagons and fields. (From U.S. Department of Commerce, 1975.)

[b] A conservative estimate of drying energy (from numerous sources and our experience) is 14,000 BTU per bushel (drying from 25% moisture to 15.5%), which is 250 BTU/lb.

[c] Calculated from energy cost to produce steel, depreciated over 20 years. (From Pimentel, 1981.)

[d] Data from U.S. Department of Agriculture (1977).

[e] Experience at our mill indicates about 2 BTU/lb, adjusted upward for smaller scale, less efficient shellers.

directly with corn production, and inversely with harvest completion beyond October 1.

2. Ear corn premiums (the payments for cobs) vary directly with corn price, inversely with production, and inversely with on-farm corn stocks.

Simply put, in an abundant harvest with good weather, cob supply is likely to be good, unless corn price (as from heavy export demand) is high, in which case the farmer is more interested in his "main job." Or in a more simple analogy: asking a busy farmer to bring you crop residue as well as the crop is like asking a busy newspaper executive to run a paper route in the evening. There is undoubtedly money to be made in either case but not enough to cover the distraction or nuisance from the main job. There should be no surprise that cob acquisition costs have thus far been too high to permit cobs to compete with such standard energy sources as coal.

XV. CONCLUSION

The recent history of food and fuel shows that converting relatively small amounts of food to fuel, although not yet profitable, would do little harm, but that converting large amounts would lead to problems and conflicts.

From the standpoint of the "average American" (Table I), the argument is as follows. Small amounts of gasohol (say, Case 1, $2\frac{1}{2}$ billion gallons of ethanol from 1 billion bushels of corn) would not be likely to raise the real price of food. The same quantity of corn added to export during the 1970s had no real impact on food prices. The present levels of food assistance to poor countries, amounting to about 5% of U.S. exports, would be little affected. Current developed country trading partners may be dismayed, however, to see so much corn (in terms of world trade) going for so little impact on U.S. fuel needs. The "energy balance" question largely disappears when coal is used in gasohol plants, as corn can be seen as the agent for converting coal to high-quality liquid fuel.

The situation changes, however, when we consider major amounts of gasohol (Case 2: 10 billion gallons of ethanol from 4 billion bushels of corn). The first problem would be disposal of more DDGS than the feed ingredient markets, nationally or internationally. The second problem would be a shift in the U.S. soybean-to-corn acres ratio, which could be seen taking place only in response to greatly increased corn price, both in absolute terms and in relation to soybeans. This conflict not only works against "cheap food" but also against the agronomic good inherent to soybean-corn rotation; also significantly more fertilizer and other agricultural chemicals would be required. Little change may be foreseen, incidentally, in farm structure in either Case 1 or Case 2 (but particularly in Case 2) where increased prices would tend to lengthen the time that small, marginal farms could stay in business before falling prey to larger, more efficient producers.

The key to the amount of alcohol produced, in a generally free market sense, will be the relationship between gasoline price and corn price, each of which is subject to sometimes separate, sometimes related aspects of international politics. Export demand for corn in the coming decades is much more likely to strengthen than weaken. This follows from the historically well-documented increase in meat demand among improving economies, as well as from steadily increasing population pressure and from the fact that 90% of Russia's crop-growing areas are north of the latitude of Minneapolis (45°), lowering the possibilities of yields like those of the U.S. cornbelt; over one-half of China's growing regions lie south of 35° latitude, making them unsuitable for today's most high yielding proteinaceous crops.

Corn price, unlike gasoline, is heavily dependent on annual weather. Abundant production in the U.S. depends on the right combination of precipitation and temperature, especially in the last 2 weeks of July and first 2 weeks of August. This operation provided by climate is energetically intensive; probably two or three orders of magnitude greater energy is provided by nature to the corn crop than man can contemplate by his own means. The most relevant question of all, in the search for food–fuel conflicts, is simply, "How long will the present favorable climate last?"

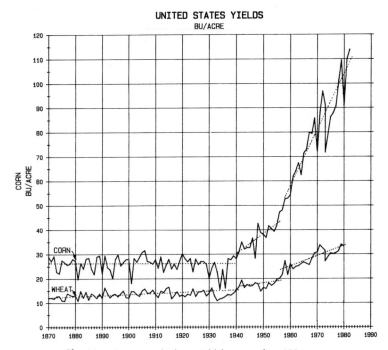

UNITED STATES YIELDS
BU/ACRE

Fig. 11. U.S. corn and wheat yield for more than 100 years.

The U.S. corn and wheat yields for the past 100 years are shown in Fig. 11. There have been decades of relative "smoothness" or reliability, for instance the 1910s, 1920s, 1950s, and 1960s, and decades of great variability, such as the 1900s, 1930s, and recently the 1970s. In 1980, corn yield dipped 15 bushels from the trend, a change which meant a loss of production of perhaps 1 billion bushels or about half the U.S. corn exported that year or about the amount needed for gasohol for Case 1. Yet in 1981 and 1982 the yield leaped above trend by the same amount. This 100-year period of recorded yield history is exceedingly short on the geological scale, where ice ages and colder climates are more normal than that which we have now. If a corn-based ethanol program were initiated at the same time as a downturn in favorable climate, the conflicts so far discussed would seem trivial. Although evidence to make judgment about changing climate is still lacking, the gasohol investor would be prudent, indeed, to study weather and climate relationships.

Most of the conclusions for conversion of corn to gasohol may be applied to the conversion of crop residues, because the main job of the farmer is food. Other jobs, such as collecting, drying, and transporting residue interfere with the main job at key times, which means the residues will not indeed be a "free" resource; in fact, they may cost about the same as corn itself.

REFERENCES

Department of Energy. Biomass Energy: Report of the Energy Research Advisory Board Panel on
   Biomass. Washington, D.C.
Feed Industry Redbook (1981). Communications Marketing, Inc., Edina, Minnesota.
Isgrigg, W. (1980). Gasohol: Its impact on the feed industry. *Feed Manage.* **31**(11), 20–24.
Pimentel, D. (1981). Biomass energy from crop and forest residues. *Science* **212**, 1110–1115.
Soth, L. (1981). The grain export boom—should it be tamed? *Foreign Affairs* **59**(9), 895–912.
U.S. Department of Agriculture (1977). A guide to energy savings for the field crop producers. ERS,
   PB–270 071. U.S. Dept. of Agriculture, Washington, D.C.
U.S. Department of Agriculture (1980a). Agricultural Statistics. U.S. Dept. of Agriculture, Wash-
   ington, D.C.
U.S. Department of Agriculture (1980b). Gasohol: prospects and implications. ESCS No. 458. U.S.
   Dept. of Agriculture, Washington, D.C.
U.S. Department of Agriculture (1981). Economics indicators of the farm sector. U.S. Dept. of
   Agriculture, Washington, D.C.
U.S. Department of Commerce (1975). Statistical Abstracts. U.S. Dept. of Commerce, Wash-
   ington, D.C.

Chapter 10

Potentials in Producing Alcohol from Corn Grain and Residue in Relation to Prices, Land Use, and Conservation

EARL O. HEADY AND DOUGLAS A. CHRISTENSEN*

The Center for Agricultural and Rural Development
Iowa State University
Ames, Iowa

I. INTRODUCTION

A large amount of interest in the agricultural sector as an energy user and as a potential producer has prevailed since the formation of the OPEC monopoly and the abrupt price increases for petroleum products. Agriculture alone, of course, represents a minor part of total U.S. energy consumption. Energy use by agriculture is as small as 1% of the total national use, even though the United States has one of the most energy-intensive farming sectors in the world. The great opportunities for energy economizing reside in other sectors, such as automobiles and dwellings. Potentially, of course, agriculture could become a larger *producer* of liquid energy to be *used* in other sectors. Some rather large changes will need to occur in the prices of other energy sources as compared to farm commodity

*Present address: SCS National Technical Center, P.O. Box 6567, Fort Worth, Texas 76115.

FOOD AND ENERGY RESOURCES

prices before this transformation of agricultural products takes place. The crescendo of interest generated for producing alcohol from grain during the Carter Administration has subsided to a large extent. The interest of farmers for corn-based alcohol production also has declined greatly, although many still hope that it can be used as a means to bolster grain prices. Aggregatively, of course, farmers could be better off income-wise with smaller energy supplies and restrained growth in agricultural production. The demand for major U.S. agricultural commodities is inelastic. Hence, for given levels of population and income, a 1% increase (decrease) in agricultural output will cause price to decline (increase) by more than 1%. Thus, agricultural prices will be relatively higher as output increases more slowly against given population and income levels. Naturally, each U.S. farmer would be better off if his fuel prices were lower and commodity prices were at present levels. But the farmer would be even better off if high energy prices restrained farm output and caused even higher prices, even though his fuel and fertilizer prices have increased.

II. FOOD OR FUEL FROM AGRICULTURE

While the prospects over the long pull are favorable for agriculture and the food sector, we do have some very pressing issues facing us. One of these is the extent to which agricultural resources are used to produce food or to produce fuel. The resolution of these issues involves complex values and attitudinal, political, economic, and scientific aspects, which will not all be determined by agriculture. Increasingly, controls over the use of agricultural resources and policies are moving out of the hands of the farm public and into the hands of the consuming sector and general society. This is true mainly because farm families are less than 4% of the national population, while consumers are 100% of it. Too, use of agricultural resources will be partly determined by taxation policy, the distribution of income in our society, and the prices which some segments of the population will pay for the various products and services from our resources. The grain to produce the alcohol required for the average annual usage of an American automobile would feed about 23.5 people for a full year.

A. Government Financial Initiative

The January 1980 goal of the Carter Administration of producing 500 million gallons of ethanol by 1982, the equivalent of about 200 million bushels of corn and utilization of 2.1 million acres of land (depending on transformation rates and location of production), was not necessarily a decision of agriculture. How much fuel will be produced in agriculture in the short run is heavily weighted by politics. In addition to $1 billion already appropriated to enhance gasohol production, President Carter "found" nearly another $500 million for this purpose just before the 1980 election and his officials immediately approved loan guarantees for 15 additional alcohol projects. The Reagan Administration, winning handily without such hurried promises, has de-emphasized fuel production from grain. In the long run, the amount of fuel produced by agriculture will be based mainly on economic factors, on technological developments, and on the consideration for using grain to meet world nutrition needs. The citizens of the United States also may feel humanitarian concern for the 500 million malnourished and 1 billion persons living in absolute poverty over the world. Humanitarian concerns and world accords may be the final determinants of how much fuel will be produced from American agriculture.

Agricultural profitability does not depend on liquid energy production from grain in the long run. World food demand is likely to increase rapidly enough that U.S. agricultural capacity can probably serve mankind best through grain exports.

B. Philosophical Aspects

Some of the economical potentials in shifting agricultural resources from food to fuel production have been discussed. More difficult to analyze and answer are philosophical questions about how far the United States should go in encouraging use of food crops for fuel considering (a) a growing scarcity and limit to world resources and (b) the great inequality of people in rich and poor countries to be able to bid for and to obtain these scarce resources of the world. Europeans stopped building castles many decades ago. Over the last four decades, however, Americans have built millions of them—on wheels. They are owned two to a family, guzzling gas as they roam the streets and highways. Are we going to subsidize the conversion of agricultural land and grain to maintain this fleet of castles while our European counterparts emphasize gas-efficient automobiles with fuel at twice our price or while the 1 billion absolute poor of the world are unable to bid for the world's scarce supplies of both petroleum and grain? These are complex questions to be answered in the future. However, we now turn to some more specific questions related to alcohol production from agriculture.

C. Strategies

Given the uncertainties of the world and its frail decision-making framework, all conceivable strategies and alternatives for producing energy in the future should be evaluated. For security reasons, a limited amount of production potential from agriculture should be maintained, along with the physical facilities for transforming the production into immediately usable forms of energy, even where it is not economic to do so under normal and present circumstances. This means that there may well be a need to maintain production of some direct energy from agriculture so that ongoing experience, facilities, and skills could readily be translated into larger-scale production if or as needed. At present, one cannot be certain of the relative prices that liquid fuels will take in the long run when produced from the various sources such as petroleum, coal, oil shale, enhanced crude oil recovery, grain, and other farm or biomass sources. Fuel derived through agriculture could be cheap in 20 years. The opposite also could be true. The political, institutional, and economic forces that will determine the outcome cannot now be predicted. With accentuated growth in income by undeveloped countries and extended international trade, coupled with lessened world political tension, world demand and real prices for U.S. grain for food could grow so greatly that grain could not compete with other materials as a source of motor fuels. On the other hand, if the Middle East should develop into a block insulated from the world or if the Soviet Union annexes the Middle East and use of its oil as a means of extending its harsh dictatorship of 60 years into another 200 years while lagging world economic development and trade restrains U.S. grain exports, grain could become an economic source for a greater part of the U.S. energy requirements. These extreme possibilities, and many between them, are about equally probable in the next 20 years. Accordingly, mixed strategies are necessary, which would include some (limited) commercial fuel from agriculture as an ongoing activity, even if it must be partially subsidized or protected through tax rebates, import duties, or other means. Not required, however, is that a major portion of the grain produced in excess of domestic consumption require this same protection or that a majority of agricultural resources be so used.

D. Small-Scale Production

Energy can be generated in agriculture at many scales, utilizing numerous sources and technologies. On a small-scale basis, farmers can generate methane gas from animal wastes for diversified uses. These are known processes that farmers could use under appropriate economic conditions. Similarly, the use of crop residues for drying corn, heating buildings, and related heating purposes is a feasible on-site activity that may become rather commonplace in the future. Energy production in these forms and amounts is not competitive with food production. We consider these possibilities somewhat apart, however, from a major national effort that would divert a large portion of our grain and normal cropland to the production of fuel and away from foods.

E. Large-Scale Production

A large amount of the U.S. grain production could be utilized in the generation of fuel without cutting into domestic consumption. Recently, the United

States has been exporting 30% of our corn, 45% of our rice, 58% of our wheat, 40% of our soybeans, and 35% of all other grains. The export totals 123 million tons of grain, the weight equivalent of more than 4 billion bushels of corn. If all of the U.S. grains that were exported in 1980 had been used instead for ethanol, about 11.5 billion gallons could have been produced; that is slightly more than 10% of the annual gasoline consumption. The grain or alcohol would be the equivalent of 164 million barrels of oil, which amounts to about 7.1% of the annual oil imports. Automobiles and transportation consume 52% of the U.S. annual oil consumption. It is not difficult to foresee slight modifications in the makeup of the automobile population or in its use and further design that would reduce oil consumption by 164 million barrels without a great discomfort in life. Or perhaps the design and temperature control of dwellings and other buildings or other modifications in life-style would readily represent the equivalent of 164 million barrels of oil. With petroleum at $40 per barrel equivalent in ethanol, the ethanol produced from all of the U.S. 1980 grain exports would have had a value of about $6.6 billion. However, at $3 per bushel, the value of exported corn alone was about $7.7 billion.

F. All-Out Production

If we would go "all out" in producing energy from agriculture, 300 million acres of corn would be required to produce 10% of the nation's total energy. This is nearly three times the recent acreage of corn and over 75% of the nation's recent cropland usage (Heady, 1981). If we tried to produce 10% of the nation's energy from agriculture, food prices would skyrocket and divert grains back into food uses. What are other opportunities? Some people suggest that wood rather than grain is a more economical source of biomass for energy production. Apparently 76 million acres out of 740 million acres (with only 488 million acres suitable for commercial timber production) of forestland also could produce one-tenth of the nation's gas requirement. To use forestland would have little impact on farm commodity prices but would put considerable pressure on prices for lumber. Price-wise, neither agriculture nor forestry could go to these extremes in even a relatively small alleviation of our energy situation. While only a small dent in total energy use from other sources would occur, a mammoth uplift in farm commodity prices would be caused. To devote 75% of U.S. normal cropland to provide 10% of our energy, or even half that amount, would provide a food price regime that soon would cause us to lessen energy consumption to "bring things in line."

While judgments such as those mentioned can be made, a range of research is needed that would indicate potentials, both physical and economical, to produce liquid and related fuels in agriculture. We need to investigate the extent to which fuel can be produced from conventional crops, such as feed grains and sweet sorghum, and the trade-offs, in both quantities and prices, in producing food and fuel from agriculture. We also need to determine the extent to which fuel can be produced from nonfood crops and materials in agriculture and how these possibilities relate to farm commodity and food prices. We also need to know the impact of possibilities in energy production on the structure of agriculture and the conservation of basic natural resources.

III. NATURE OF THIS ANALYSIS

The nation's major energy problems cannot be solved through agriculture. However, potentials for relieving energy needs must be considered. The possibility of converting agricultural crops to other energy forms, particularly liquid fuel, is certain to be a continuing or recurring issue before American society. Hence, the many facets of using and producing liquid fuels in agriculture must be examined. The potentials in producing fuel in agriculture while conserving soil and water resources at appropriate levels is one of these dimensions that require analysis. Of course, the amount of energy produced also will affect the nation's grain exports. In this chapter, we analyze the possibility of producing various levels of alcohol from agriculture under different export levels while still holding soil erosion to levels that do not endanger land productivity. The study is limited in scope since conversion of only corn grain and residue into ethanol is considered. Only one conversion rate is considered. However, we have completed other studies which consider other conversion rates, energy price alternatives, and commodity price impacts (Christensen *et al.*, 1983; Christensen *et al.*, 1981; Dvoskin and Heady, 1976; Dvoskin *et al.*, 1978; English *et al.*, 1980; Heady, 1981; Nastari *et al.*, 1984; Short *et al.*, 1981; Turhollow *et al.*, 1983). Studies are underway that consider other biomass sources and alternative conversion rates for grain and crop residues (Turhollow *et al.*, 1984a,b).

IV. PROGRAMMING

A. Conservation and Tillage Practices

The study was made using a linear programming model of mainland U.S. agriculture. The model includes 105 producing regions (Fig. 1), with five land classes specified in each to allow an analysis of estimated soil loss under a variety of cropping systems, conservation practices, and tillage practices. Different soil types or land classes are used so that the model can select those from which alcohol might be generated without causing excessive erosion. A transportation submodel is used to allow shipment of agricultural commodities among the 28 market regions (Fig. 2) included in the model. It includes transportation of

Fig. 1. The producing areas with irrigated lands (dotted areas).

alcohol as well as regular agricultural products. The transportation activities cause the production, tillage methods, conservation practices, land and water use, and crop and livestock systems to be interdependent among producing areas. Thus, resource use and farming systems of western Tennessee and Iowa affect those used in the Palouse Region of Washington, Central Illinois, and Eastern Colorado, and vice versa. Both ground and surface water supplies are defined in the producing areas west of the Missouri River. Because the model embodies

Fig. 2. The 28 market regions.

interregional relationships, more water used to irrigate level land in one area can substitute for rain-fed erosive land in another area. The land base in the model is taken from the National Resource Inventory (NRI) by the Soil Conservation Service (SCS) (U.S. Department of Agriculture, 1977). The conversion rates of corn grain and residue into ethanol are from G. Tsao (personal communication). Since our analysis projects yields for the year 2000, a conversion rate of 3 gal of ethanol per bushel of corn and 20 lb of corn residue per gallon of alchol is used. The estimated soil loss for each land group, cropping system, conservation practice, and tillage method are made by the Universal Soil Loss Equation (Wischmeier and Smith, 1965). A yield decline function adjusts productivity in terms of top soil lost by erosion as estimated by Dyke and Hagen and reported in English *et al.* (1982). The mathematical specification of the model is not detailed here since it is given in English *et al.* (1982).

B. By-Products as Feed

In this study, we assume that alcohol production is split evenly between dry mill and wet mill methods. The by-products of the wet mill method can be fed to nonruminants as well as ruminants and thus substitute for soybean oil meal over a wider range. The alcohol by-products are allowed to substitute for soybean oil meal at a weight ratio of 2:1.

C. Land Use

Land, in addition to cropland now in production, is allowed to be brought into crops. The land includes the 37.5 million acres not now cropped identified by the SCS's NRI survey (U.S. Department of Agriculture, 1977). With the land classes numbered from 1 through 5 in terms of erosion hazard, this additional land mainly enters land classes 2 and 3. Land conversion costs are included as appropriate. Most cropland or potential cropland in the United States falls mainly into two groups: land for which the productivity is more or less independent of organic matter and land that rapidly develops plow pans, loses permeability and water-holding capacity readily, and has a rapidly increasing density of organic matter as noted by Shrader (1977). Most of the residue on the latter soils is needed to maintain productivity. In this study, residue removal is allowed only on the first of these two groups in the corn belt and only on irrigated lands of this group in the Great Plains where wind erosion is a hazard. Ten percent of residue on all land is assumed used for feed as estimated by Buchele and Marley (1979). Conservation practices include contouring, terracing, and strip cropping. Tillage methods include fall plow, spring plow, and minimum tillage. Crop residue removal costs are adjusted from those estimates by English *et al.* (1980).

D. Consumer Demands

Population and per capita income were projected to estimate consumer demands by market regions in the year 2000. Demands were fixed for all scenarios analyzed. Exports were set at 112.9 million tons of feed grain, 2.2 billion bushels of wheat, and 4.8 million tons of oilmeal. Crop yields were projected to the year 2000 on the basis of regression time trends.

V. SCENARIOS EXAMINED

A base solution (Base) was computed for the year 2000 for purposes of comparison with other scenarios or solutions. The Base does not include alcohol production from either grain or residue. It does not include any restraints on soil loss. In the Base solution, agriculture is organized most efficiently by producing areas and land classes to minimize the cost of production of agricultural commodities. A competitive equilibrium is supposed wherein each resource gets its market rate of return except land and water, whose returns are determined optimally. Corn, grain sorghum, corn silage, wheat, oats, barley, cotton, and all hays and pasture on public lands are included endogenously in the model for all scenarios or solutions. Production of fruits, nuts, vegetables, tobacco, and minor crops are treated exogenously.

Four solutions were determined that suppose, respectively, the production of 6 billion (G6), 8 billion (G8), 10 billion (G10), and 12 billion (G12) gallons of alcohol from corn grain. In these scenarios, no alcohol is produced from crop residues and no restraints are used for soil loss. In each scenario, crop and alcohol production occurs in producing areas and on land classes that give the most efficient national pattern in terms of costs of production and transportation. Next, four solutions were made, respectively, of 6 billion (R6), 8 billion (R8), 10 billion (R10), and 12 billion (R12) gallons of alcohol made from crop residue. None is made from grain and no restraint is placed on soil erosion. Other conditions and specifications of the model are the same. Next, 10 billion gallons of alcohol are produced, half from corn grain and half from crop residue (GR10), and no restraints are placed on soil loss. Finally, a solution was made in which 10 billion gallons of alcohol is produced from crop residue but soil loss in any region and on any land class cannot be larger than agronomic T-values (RT10), the annual rate of gross soil loss that will allow yields to be maintained.

The alcohol production levels of all of these scenarios can be produced in the year 2000 under the assumptions incorporated in the models. The model determines the amount of land required in each producing region and on each land class to meet national and regional demands at lowest production and transportation costs. The results at the national level and by major U.S. zones are summarized as shown in Fig. 3, rather than by the producing areas and market regions. While there are many results from application of these large-scale models to U.S. agriculture delineated by producing areas, land groups, and market regions, only results that are most pertinent for the analysis are summarized.

A. Alcohol Production from Grain Alone

Table I shows corn production for the year 2000 from endogenous land in the seven major zones depicted in Fig. 3. Corn production must rise above the Base (zero alcohol production) for each amount of alcohol produced. However, the amount of soybeans needed declines with alcohol production as the distillers dried grains (DDG) is substituted for soybean oilmeal in livestock production. As compared to the Base, corn production increases nearly 50% for production of 12 billion gallons of alcohol. At the same time, soybean production decreases by 28% (Table II). As alcohol production increases, corn production rises in each corn-producing zone. Because of its comparative advantage, however, most of the increase comes in the North Central zone, which produces 75% of the additional corn required in the G12 scenario over the Base.

While the North Atlantic zone reduces soybean production by the greatest percentage (37%), the North Central zone reduces soybean production by the largest amount between the Base and the G12. The zone reduces production by 37% or 700 million bushels.

Marginal land used for crop production (classes 3, 4, and 5) increased by 15%

Fig. 3. Seven major zones of the United States.

TABLE I
Corn Production by Zone at Various Levels of Alcohol Production from Grain (million bushels)

Zone	Base	G4	G8	G10	G12
North Atlantic	315	543	552	554	580
South Atlantic	1,404	1,600	1,636	1,750	1,776
North Central	4,547	5,898	6,422	6,879	7,490
Great Plains	1,987	2,184	2,281	2,370	2,364
South Central	195	222	224	225	226
Northwest	0	0	0	0	0
Southeast	2	2	3	5	13
Total	8,450	10,450	11,117	11,784	12,450

between the Base and G12. Total land used increases by about 15 million acres. However, there is a much larger shift of land among producing regions and land classes—and from soybeans to feed grains (mainly corn). Since the major land use shift is from soybeans to corn, producing the high level of alcohol does not increase soil loss by as large an amount as some agriculturists have proposed. While a relatively small amount of more erosive land is added to the total cropland base, three different phenomena simultaneously reduce soil loss. First, corn is grown in place of soybeans. Soybeans are a more erosive crop than corn because they develop a later canopy, have a smaller root system, and leave less residue on the surface. Second, a considerable amount of the added corn production comes from irrigated land that is level and has little erosion. Third, at the higher levels of alcohol production and since they maintain a higher productivity level, a greater amount of spring plowing and reduced tillage become optimal at the higher levels of imputed land rents and commodity prices. For the G12 solution, estimated soil loss on irrigated land was only half that on dryland corn production. Total national soil loss for the endogenous crops was 1.98,

TABLE II
Soybean Production by Zone at Various Levels of Alcohol Production from Grain (million bushels)

Zone	Base	G6	G8	G10	G12
North Atlantic	100	46	46	46	43
South Atlantic	1,004	998	989	972	966
North Central	1,949	1,605	1,479	1,355	1,227
Great Plains	92	91	80	72	62
South Central	33	33	33	33	33
Northwest	0	0	0	0	0
Southwest	0	0	0	0	0
Total	3,218	2,775	2,627	2,480	2,332

1.99, 2.00, 2.00, and 2.01 billion tons per year under the Base, G6, G8, G10, and G12 scenarios, respectively.

While the substitution of distillers dry grain (DDG) for soybean oilmeal provides considerable slack in agricultural producing capacity, the agricultural sector tightens up considerably at the higher levels of alcohol production. As Table III shows, shadow prices (supply prices, or the price level needed to attain the production level) for endogenous crop commodities increased by about 25% between the Base and the G12 solution. (Prices are in 1975 dollars.) However, land shadow prices or rents (the return per acre necessary to draw land into the indicated levels of production of endogenous crops) rise more sharply with level of alcohol production. National average land shadow prices were $67.75, $78.20, $86.23, $93.74, and $101.22, respectively, for the Base, G6, G8, G10, and G12 scenarios. Increases by regions generally paralleled these national averages, except that the increase was somewhat higher in the North Central and Great Plains zones and somewhat lower elsewhere.

B. Alcohol Production from Residue Alone

The five solutions for alcohol produced from crop residues alone with the Base solution are now compared. The levels of alcohol production are the same as those for corn grain alone.

National crop production is affected but little by different levels of alcohol production from corn residue. However, regional production shifts do occur. Alcohol production from corn residue removal occurs only in the North Central zone and parts of the Great Plains and South Central zones due to transportation costs of alcohol, density of residue production over area, and conservation considerations. For example, residue removal is not allowed in areas of severe wind erosion. Under the scenarios with production of alcohol from corn residue, the final demands (amount produced) for the conventional crops endogenous to the model are the same as in the Base.

TABLE III
Crop Commodity Shadow Prices for the Five Scenarios (dollars per unit[a])

Crop	Base	G6	G8	G10	G12
Feed grains	1.86	2.02	2.32	2.21	2.30
Oilmeal	10.14	10.88	11.31	11.75	12.20
Wheat	3.10	3.36	3.55	3.69	3.83
Cotton	204.76	210.07	214.93	217.55	221.92
Hay	57.14	62.38	65.46	68.47	71.66
Silage	17.64	18.89	19.54	20.12	20.93

[a]Units are as follows: feed grain in corn equivalent bushels, wheat in bushels, oilmeal in cwt., cotton in bales of lint, and hay and silage in tons. Dollars are 1975 values.

As the production of alcohol is increased, residue from the North Central, Great Plains, and South Central zones is harvested. At higher alcohol production levels, crop production shifts among zones. Corn production increases in the North Central zone while soybeans and wheat decrease. Soybeans shift, especially into the South Central zone. At the 10 and 12 billion gallons of alcohol production, these shifts are large. (See Table IV for crop production levels for the R10 and R12 scenarios.) As alcohol production is increased on a large scale in the North Central zone, corn production is substituted for soybeans.

The shifts in production among land classes and regions is not enough to allow production of the usual crop and livestock products and also the production of higher levels of alcohol from corn residue. Hence, additional land, 27 million acres for R6 and 29 million acres for R12, is brought into crop production. Also, irrigated land increases as compared to the Base. The increase in irrigated area, as compared to the Base, is 20% for the R12 level of alcohol production.

As alcohol production from corn residue increases, soil loss increases over the Base by 5, 9, 14, and 18%, respectively, under the R6, R8, R10, and R12 solutions (Table V). Most of the additional soil loss occurs in the North Central and Great Plains zones, where the combined loss increases by 31%. Small increases also occur in the South Central and Southwest zones. Soil loss would be greater at the higher alcohol levels except that more land shifts to spring plowing and reduced tillage. However, the shift in tillage methods does not offset the erosiveness of residue removal.

Increases in crop shadow prices are modest for alcohol made from corn residue as compared to that made from corn grain (Table VI). The changes are modest since production of conventional agricultural commodities is the same under the alcohol residual scenarios as under the Base. As long as conventional commodity demand levels in the Base scenario and the various alcohol levels can be produced with existing crop residue and more of other crops is not required, it is logical that shadow price changes would be small. This possibility could also be due to the presence of considerable production flexibility in U.S. agriculture as some land not now in crops can be brought into production and crops can be reallocated among regions and land classes.

Production of alcohol from residue has a rather minimal effect on farming costs, marginal land usage, and commodity shadow prices because greater corn grain production is not generally required. The effects are slight since residue removal can occur on land otherwise already in corn. Also, alcohol from residue does not generate a by-product feed that substitutes for soybeans. Thus, there is not revamping of crop systems and location. Generally, alcohol production from corn residue would have only small effects on markets and prices of all other crops.

TABLE IV
Regional Corn, Soybean, and Wheat Production, Scenario Two[a]

				Major zone				
Crop	North Atlantic	South Atlantic	North Central	Great Plains	South Central	Northwest	Southwest	United States
				Residue 10				
Corn	−58,355	−594,401	+447,133	+176,263	+29,361	NC[b]	NC	NC
Soybeans	+7799	+168,426	−180,644	+3556	+862	NC	NC	NC
Wheat	NC	+18,407	−30,563	+1120	+4110	+4557	+2345	NC
				Residue 12				
Corn	−168,452	−1,383,912	+1,265,464	+251,492	+35,409	NC	NC	NC
Soybeans	+10,191	+403,888	−434,172	+19,231	+862	NC	NC	NC
Wheat	NC	+24,475	−49,286	+2057	+8468	+9858	+4423	NC

[a]Deviation from base in thousands of bushels.
[b]No change.

TABLE V
Regional Gross Soil Loss in the Residue 12 Solution

Land group	Zone							
	North Atlantic	South Atlantic	North Central	Great Plains	South Central	Northwest	Southwest	United States
Aggregate	67 (−8%)[a]	376 (+3%)[a]	743 (+40%)[a]	(million tons) 590 (+20%)[a] (tons per acre)	498 (+10%)[a]	66 (0%)[a]	13 (+15%)[a]	2,352 (+18%)[a]
1	2.09	4.44	2.98	3.96	4.74	1.13	.15	3.46 (+41%)[a]
2	4.16	6.83	4.10	3.12	4.76	1.90	.35	4.51 (+18%)[a]
3	11.03	13.31	13.14	9.92	18.14	3.67	3.30	11.97 (+13%)[a]
4	18.64	11.24	8.94	13.03	7.28	6.07	2.69	10.28 (−5%)[a]
5	70.40	34.22	8.80	35.87	55.36	28.59	1.70	29.33 (−1%)[a]

[a]Percentage change from Base values.

251

TABLE VI
Crop Shadow Prices for Specified Scenarios (dollars per unit)[a]

	Scenarios				
Crop	Base	R6	R8	R10	R12
Feed grains	1.86	1.86	1.86	1.87	1.87
Oilmeal	10.14	10.16	10.31	10.41	10.92
Wheat	3.10	3.13	3.16	3.22	3.53
Cotton	204.76	204.76	205.51	209.34	214.45
Hay	57.14	57.80	58.43	59.25	62.56
Silage	17.64	18.02	18.32	18.69	19.48

[a]1975 dollars. Units are as follows: feed grains in corn equivalent bushels, oilmeal in cwt., wheat in bushels, cotton in bales of lint, and hay and silage in tons.

1. Grain-Residue Production

In the GR10 scenario, the production of 10 billion gallons of alcohol, half from corn grain and half from residue, corn production increases over the Base scenario by 20% and soybean production declines by 11%. The GR10 solution requires an additional 33.8 million acres of land to the cropland base. The shadow prices of commodities rise only modestly under this combination.

The proportion of alcohol produced from grain does not add to erosion because grain (corn) largely replaces soybeans and reduced tillage cultivation is used in this alternative compared to the Base. However, the proportion of alcohol produced from residue increases soil erosion. As expected, the GR10 result falls between the G10 and R10 scenarios in amount of soil loss per acre on each of the five land classes.

The residue component of the GR10 scenario has little impact on the costs of farming and on changes in cropping systems. Hence, the increase in crop shadow prices for this alternative falls between those for alcohol produced from grain and those for alcohol produced from residue.

2. Soil-Loss Restraint

In the T10 scenario, 10 billion gallons of alcohol are produced from corn residue under the restraint that the gross annual soil loss on any land group in any producing region cannot be greater than its T-value as expressed in the Universal Soil Loss Equation. Under this restraint, national annual soil loss would be less than half that in the Base scenario, with no alcohol production. The soil loss is only about one-third as much as in the R10 scenario (10 billion gallons of alcohol from corn residue without a soil-loss restraint). The results for the T10 scenario suggest that the nation could produce 10 billion gallons of alcohol from corn residue without increasing soil loss (or, in fact, while decreasing it) under a program to get an appropriate number of soil conservation practices put in use.

As compared to the Base, soil loss under T10 declines in each zone except the Southwest, where soil loss increases about 13%. This increase results from a greater acreage of row crops in the Southwest. Soil loss decreases, in the T10 scenario as compared to the Base, in the South Atlantic and Great Plains; this is due both to use of more erosion control practices and to a shift of some corn acreage into the North Central zone, where corn production has a comparative advantage. Due to this shift, the North Central zone has a greater percentage of the nation's total soil loss under the T10 as compared to the Base scenario. Also, a large amount of corn is shifted to the North Central zone to be grown on land that has a minimal erosion hazard. In total, the T10 scenario includes a much larger amount of erosion control farming methods than do any of the other scenarios, which is illustrated in Table VII in the comparison between T10 and R10.

However, to produce 10 billion gallons of alcohol from corn residue while still conserving the soil comes at a high cost in shadow price levels. As Table VIII shows, prices for T10 are higher than for any other scenario and roughly twice those for the Base, which does not include any alcohol production. While a solution was not run with 10 billion gallons of alcohol from grain while soil loss was restrained to T levels to compare with T10, the increase in shadow prices over other scenarios would be even greater than for the T10 solution. (Even the

TABLE VII
Land Use by Conservation and Tillage Practice, U.S. Totals for Scenarios T10 and R10[a]

Conservation practice	Tillage practice	T10	R10
Straight row	Fall plow	7822	13,388
	Spring plow	130,424	251,104
	Minimum tillage	95,714	85,784
Contouring	Fall plow	1829	0
	Spring plow	67,752	13,242
	Minimum tillage	28,241	0
Strip cropping	Fall plow	0	0
	Spring plow	7823	236
	Minimum tillage	7335	626
Terracing	Fall plow	161	0
	Spring plow	10,641	3055
	Minimum tillage	4030	215
Total		361,772	367,650

[a] In thousands of acres.

TABLE VIII

Crop Shadow Prices for T10 in Comparison with G10, R10, and the Base Scenarios (1975 dollars per unit)

Crop[a]	T10	G10	R10	Base
Feed grains	3.25	2.21	1.87	1.86
Oilmeal	20.17	11.75	10.41	10.14
Wheat	6.80	3.69	3.22	3.10
Cotton	267.00	217.55	209.51	204.76
Hay	103.74	68.47	58.43	57.14
Silage	31.04	20.19	18.32	17.64

[a] Units are as follows: feed grains in bushels of corn equivalent, oilmeal in cwt., wheat in bushels, cotton in bales of lint, and hay and silage in tons.

G10 scenario had considerably higher prices than other scenarios.) This would be true because a 10 billion gallon production from grain with soil loss held to T levels would draw from the grain supply, as well as "tighten up" agriculture by causing interregional shifts in crop production, limiting production on some land groups, and forcing use of some more expensive conservation practices. The increase in prices for T10, as compared to the base and other scenarios, comes from the latter set of effects, since the T10 solution draws from the corn residue supply rather than from the grain supply.

VI. OTHER RESEARCH

Our research has examined the potential of U.S. agriculture to produce ethanol from corn grain or corn residue in relation to soil erosion and conservation. The analysis was made with a tool of operations research, linear programming, because time series data are not available to allow statistical prediction of potential alcohol production and soil erosion from agriculture. The analysis suggests that the nation's agriculture has the capacity to produce a rather large amount of alcohol from either corn grain or corn residue. Production from residue would have minimal impact on the ability to produce and export food and on farm commodity prices. Hence, production of alcohol from residue would be least competitive with the interest of consumers in the United States and other countries.

Other crops also might be used as the biomass source for alcohol production. Potentials include kenaf, woody grasses, several kinds of trees, sweet sorghum, and sugarcane. Some of these could be grown where they would compete with food crops for land. Others could be grown on land that is marginal or not now used for food crops. Some would promote soil erosion while others would not. There is a need to incorporate all potential crops that can serve as a biomass source for alcohol production. A better understanding would result in the potential of fuel production in agriculture and the extent that it is competitive with food production and resource conservation. We have already examined potentials in kenaf and woody grass production (Turhollow *et al.*, 1984b). However, a larger number of alternatives need to be examined simultaneously. Since observations of the past do not exist with respect to production of these "new" crops for energy production, other empirical methods of analysis are difficult. Some have been applied in this study to evaluate the price impacts of energy production in agriculture. However, others need to be evaluated for the future.

REFERENCES

Buchele, W. F., and Marley, S. G. (1979). Energy production from crop residue. *Iowa Agric. Home Econ. Exp. Stn.*, No. J-9248.

Christensen, D. C., Schatzer, R. J., Heady, E. O., and English, B. C. (1981). The effects of increased energy prices on U.S. agriculture: an econometric approach. CARD Report No. 104, Center for Agricultural and Rural Development, Iowa State University, Ames, Iowa.

Christensen, D. A., Turhollow, A. F., English, B. C., and Heady, E. O. (1983). Soil loss associated with alcohol production from corn grain and corn residue. CARD Report No. 115. Center for Agricultural and Rural Development, Iowa State University, Ames, Iowa.

Dvoskin, D., and Heady, E. O. (1976). U.S. agricultural production under limited energy supplies, high energy prices and expanding exports. CARD Report No. 69. Center for Agricultural and Rural Development, Iowa State University, Ames, Iowa.

Dvoskin, D., Heady, E. O., and English, B. C. (1978). Energy use in U.S. agriculture: an evaluation of national and regional impacts from alternative energy policies. CARD Report No. 78. Center for Agricultural and Rural Development, Iowa State University, Ames, Iowa.

English, B. C., Short, C. C., and Heady, E. O. (1980). Economic feasibility of using crop residues to generate electricity in Iowa. CARD Report No. 88. Center for Agricultural and Rural Development, Iowa State University, Ames, Iowa.

English, B. C., Alt, K., and Heady, E. O. (1982). A documentation of the resources conservation act's assessment model of regional agricultural production, land and water use and soil conservation. CARD Report No. 107T. Center for Agricultural and Rural Development, Iowa State University, Ames, Iowa.

Heady, E. O. (1981). Energy: Use of agricultural resources for food and fuel. Gamma Sigma Delta Lecture. Iowa State University, Ames, Iowa.

Nastari, P., Christensen, D. C., and Heady, E. O. (1984). Economics of on-farm production of alcohol from corn. Forthcoming CARD report. Center for Agricultural and Rural Development, Iowa State University, Ames, Iowa.

Short, C. S., Turhollow, A. F., Heady, E. O., and Lee, K. C. (1981). Regional impacts of groundwater mining from the Ogallala Aquifer with increasing energy prices in 1990 and 2000. CARD Report No. 98. Center for Agricultural and Rural Development, Iowa State University, Ames, Iowa.

Shrader, W. D. (1977). Proceedings of the Midwest Research Institute Conference on Biomass. U.S. Department of Energy, Kansas City, Kansas.

Turhollow, A. F., Jr., Short, C. C., and Heady, E. O. (1983). Potential impacts of future energy price increases on U.S. agricultural production. CARD Report No. 116. Center for Agricultural and Rural Development, Iowa State University, Ames, Iowa.

Turhollow, A. F., Jr., Christensen, D. A., and Heady, E. O. (1984a). The potential impacts of large-scale fuel alcohol production from corn grain sorghum, and crop residues under varying technologies and crop export levels. Forthcoming CARD report. Center for Agricultural and Rural Development, Iowa State University, Ames, Iowa.

Turhollow, A. F., Jr., Shen, S., Oamak, G. and Heady, E. O. (1984b). The potential for biomass production from wood, grasses, herbaceous grasses, and kenaf. Forthcoming CARD report. Center for Agricultural and Rural Development, Iowa State University, Ames, Iowa.

U.S. Department of Agriculture (1977). Potential cropland study. Soil Conservation Service, U.S. Govt. Printing Office, Washington, D.C.

Wischmeier, W. H., and Smith, D. D. (1965). Predicting rainfall erosion from cropland east of the Rocky Mountains. Agricultural Handbook No. 282. Washington D.C.

Index

FOOD SCIENCE AND TECHNOLOGY

A SERIES OF MONOGRAPHS

Maynard A. Amerine, Rose Marie Pangborn, and Edward B. Roessler, PRINCIPLES OF SENSORY EVALUATION OF FOOD. 1965.

S. M. Herschdoerfer, QUALITY CONTROL IN THE FOOD INDUSTRY. Volume I — 1967. Volume II — 1968. Volume III — 1972.

Hans Riemann, FOOD-BORNE INFECTIONS AND INTOXICATIONS. 1969.

Irvin E. Leiner, TOXIC CONSTITUENTS OF PLANT FOODSTUFFS. 1969.

Martin Glicksman, GUM TECHNOLOGY IN THE FOOD INDUSTRY. 1970.

L. A. Goldblatt, AFLATOXIN. 1970.

Maynard A. Joslyn, METHODS IN FOOD ANALYSIS, second edition. 1970.

A. C. Hulme (ed.), THE BIOCHEMISTRY OF FRUITS AND THEIR PRODUCTS. Volume 1 — 1970. Volume 2 — 1971.

G. Ohloff and A. F. Thomas, GUSTATION AND OLFACTION. 1971.

C. R. Stumbo, THERMOBACTERIOLOGY IN FOOD PROCESSING, second edition. 1973.

Irvin E. Liener (ed.), TOXIC CONSTITUENTS OF ANIMAL FOODSTUFFS. 1974.

Aaron M. Altschul (ed.), NEW PROTEIN FOODS: Volume 1, TECHNOLOGY, PART A — 1974. Volume 2, TECHNOLOGY, PART B — 1976. Volume 3, ANIMAL PROTEIN SUPPLIES, PART A — 1978. Volume 4, ANIMAL PROTEIN SUPPLIES, PART B — 1981.

S. A. Goldblith, L. Rey, and W. W. Rothmayr, FREEZE DRYING AND ADVANCED FOOD TECHNOLOGY. 1975.

R. B. Duckworth (ed.), WATER RELATIONS OF FOOD. 1975.

Gerald Reed (ed.), ENZYMES IN FOOD PROCESSING, second edition. 1975.

A. G. Ward and A. Courts (eds.), THE SCIENCE AND TECHNOLOGY OF GELATIN. 1976.

John A. Troller and J. H. B. Christian, WATER ACTIVITY AND FOOD. 1978.

A. E. Bender, FOOD PROCESSING AND NUTRITION. 1978.

D. R. Osborne and P. Voogt, THE ANALYSIS OF NUTRIENTS IN FOODS. 1978.

Marcel Loncin and R. L. Merson, FOOD ENGINEERING: PRINCIPLES AND SELECTED APPLICATIONS. 1979.

Hans Riemann and Frank L. Bryan (eds.), FOOD-BORNE INFECTIONS AND INTOXICATIONS, second edition. 1979.

N. A. Michael Eskin, PLANT PIGMENTS, FLAVORS AND TEXTURES: THE CHEMISTRY AND BIOCHEMISTRY OF SELECTED COMPOUNDS. 1979.

J. G. Vaughan (ed.), FOOD MICROSCOPY. 1979.

J. R. A. Pollock (ed.), BREWING SCIENCE, Volume 1 — 1979. Volume 2 — 1980.

Irvin E. Liener (ed.), TOXIC CONSTITUENTS OF PLANT FOODSTUFFS, second edition. 1980.

J. Christopher Bauernfeind (ed.), CAROTENOIDS AS COLORANTS AND VITAMIN A PRECURSORS: TECHNOLOGICAL AND NUTRITIONAL APPLICATIONS. 1981.

Pericles Markakis (ed.), ANTHOCYANINS AS FOOD COLORS. 1982.

Vernal S. Packard, HUMAN MILK AND INFANT FORMULA. 1982.

George F. Stewart and Maynard A. Amerine, INTRODUCTION TO FOOD SCIENCE AND TECHNOLOGY, SECOND EDITION. 1982.

FOOD SCIENCE AND TECHNOLOGY

A SERIES OF MONOGRAPHS